INDIAN RESILIENCE AND REBUILDING

The Modern American West
David M. Wrobel and Andrew G. Kirk, Editors

Carl Abbott
The Metropolitan Frontier: Cities in the Modern American West

Richard W. Etulain
*Re-imagining the Modern American West: A Century of Fiction,
History, and Art*

Gerald D. Nash
*The Federal Landscape: An Economic History of the
Twentieth-Century West*

Ferenc Morton Szasz
Religion in the Modern American West

Oscar J. Martínez
Mexican-Origin People in the United States: A Topical History

Duane A. Smith
*Rocky Mountain Heartland: Colorado, Montana,
and Wyoming in the Twentieth Century*

William G. Robbins and Katrine Barber
Nature's Northwest: The North Pacific Slope in the Twentieth Century

R. Douglas Hurt
The Big Empty: The Great Plains in the Twentieth Century

Robert L. Dorman
Hell of a Vision: Regionalism and the Modern American West

Indian Resilience and Rebuilding

Indigenous Nations in the Modern American West

DONALD L. FIXICO

THE UNIVERSITY OF
ARIZONA PRESS
TUCSON

To my brother Gerald (1957–2011),
always a warrior at heart

The University of Arizona Press
© 2013 The Arizona Board of Regents
All rights reserved

www.uapress.arizona.edu

Library of Congress Cataloging-in-Publication Data
Fixico, Donald Lee, 1951–
   Indian resilience and rebuilding : indigenous nations in the modern American west /
Donald L. Fixico.
      pages cm — (Modern American West)
   Includes bibliographical references and index.
   ISBN 978-0-8165-1899-9 (cloth : alk. paper) — ISBN 978-0-8165-3064-9 (pbk. : alk. paper)
   1. Indians of North America—Historiography.   2. Indians of North America—
Government relations.   3. Indians of North America—Politics and govern-
ment.   4. Self-determination, National—United States.   5. United
States—Historiography.   I. Title.
   E78.8.F58 2013
   323.1197—dc23
                                                                        2013011210

Publication of this book is made possible in part by the proceeds of a permanent
endowment created with the assistance of a Challenge Grant from the National
Endowment for the Humanities, a federal agency.

18 17 16 15 14 13   6 5 4 3 2 1

Contents

Illustrations

Figures

Maps

Acknowledgments

This book is a part of the Modern American West series edited by Richard Etulain (now retired) and David Wrobel. I have known both as friends for many years. Finally, I am happy to say thank you, Dick and David, for your patience while I produced this book, and I hope that it meets the expectations of the series. Patti Hartman at the University of Arizona Press, whom I have known for many years, has since retired, and we have had many conversations over the years. I am grateful to her for starting the series and to Kristen Buckles, who has inherited this book project. Thank you, Kristen, for supervising this book into print. I am also grateful to Kathryn Conrad, Allyson Carter, Joshua Harrison, Miriam Warren, Lela Scott MacNeil, Abby Mogollon, Leigh McDonald, and others at the press who I have communicated with to improve this book better. I want to thank Michael Haggett, production editor at Westchester Publishing Services and copyeditor Trish Watson for making my written thoughts more clear. I am indebted to external readers Kathleen P. Chamberlain and Paul C. Rosier for their insightful comments for making this a better book. Thank you Linda Gregoris for the indexing.

In a personal way I have lived half of the twentieth century, and I feel that my own family and relatives are a part of this book. I have lived in the modern American West for most all of my life. I am a full-blood, with each grandparent coming from a different tribe—Shawnee, Sac and Fox, Muscogee Creek, and Seminole. My autobiographical instinct is a part of the feelings of being Indian in these pages.

I am grateful for the staff at Archives II at College Park, Maryland, for their help during my research trips to examine the holdings of the Richard Nixon Presidential Materials Project papers. In examining documents and accounts of Indian affairs in the 1970s, I am grateful for the help of the staff in the Special Collections of the I.D. Weeks Library at the University of South Dakota, Vermillion. I appreciate the help received from Diane Covill and Mary Eitreim of the Special Collections, and from my colleagues and friends Dr. Herbert Hoover of the History Department and Mr. Imre Meszaros, director of the library, and my good friend the late Dr. Leonard Bruguier, former director of the American Indian Institute.

I am also grateful for the assistance and advice on researching from Catherine Sewell, Greg Cumming, and Michael Duggan of the Ronald Reagan Presidential Library at Simi Valley, California, and Susan Naulty of the Richard Nixon Presidential Materials Project. I am appreciative of the assistance from Gary Lundell of the Manuscripts and Archives Division of the Allen Library at the University of Washington, Seattle. I am grateful for the assistance from Karen J. Underhill of the Special Collections and Archives of the Cline Library at Northern Arizona University in Flagstaff. I am grateful to her staff members, Bill Mullane, Bob Coody, Jolene Manus, Stacey Collins, and Deb Dohm. I am grateful for the assistance at the George Bush Presidential Library at College Station, Texas, from Robert Holweiss, Melissa Walker, and John Laster and at the William Clinton Presidential Library in Little Rock, Arkansas, from Dana Simmons and Adam Bergfeld.

I want to thank several people for their assistance with photographs for this book: Curator John R. Lovett, Western History Collections at the University of Oklahoma; Eunice Kahn, Navajo Nation Museum; Claire-Lise Benaud; Center for Southwest Research/Special Collection at the University of New Mexico; R. Sean Evans, Cline Library Special Collections and Archives at Northern Arizona University; Betty Murphy, Heard Museum as well as Neil E. Millican, Library Specialist in the ASU Archives and Special Collections and Robert Spindler, University Archivist and Head of Archives and Special Collections at ASU. I am also grateful to Michelle Martin who introduced me to the art of taking better photographs for this book and I want to thank Thomas Jonas for making such great maps for this project.

On a personal level, I am grateful for the advice and mentoring of Father Francis Paul Prucha, Reginald Horsman, and H. Wayne Morgan for their influence in forming me as a historian in my early years. At present, I would like to express gratitude to my current graduate students who have listened to my seminar thoughts about Indian resilience and rebuilding: Monika Bilka, John Goodwin, Grace Hunt-Watkins, Chelsea Mead, Meaghan Heisinger, Farina King, Billy Kiser, Karl Snyder, and Katie Sweet.

I am grateful for the support of President Michael Crow, Provost and Executive Vice President Betty Phillips, Executive Dean Robert Page, Dean George Justice SHPRS Director Matt Garcia, and History Faculty Head Phil VanderMeer, and Kyle Longley who succeeded Phil. I want to say thank you to my colleagues in my department for making it a great one and to Norma, Roxane, Michael, and Susan as well as Stephanie, Liz and Beatriz for making the daily life in our School of Historical, Philosophical and Religious Studies a pleasant one. I want to thank Clara Keyt, my research assistant at Arizona State University, for helping me with this book, and I am especially grateful to my research assistants Brianna Theobald and John Goodwin, who helped in the latter stage of this project to get it done. I am eternally grateful for my parents, John and Virginia Fixico, as well as my siblings. At home I am always thankful for the support from my son, Keytha. He has been patient while I worked on this book that reduced our quality time together This book involves so much of my memories of my grandparents, Grandma Rachel Dirt Wakolee, Shawnee; Grandpa Glade Wakolee, Sac and Fox; Grandma Lena Spencer Fixico, Muscogee Creek; and Grandpa Jonas Fixico, Seminole. They are all gone and have been for a while, having lived most of the twentieth century, and I have learned much from them. I miss them dearly. It is with hope that this volume will help others to understand American Indians, "seeing" things as they do and learning about them from an inner perspective while rebuilding their nations.

INDIAN RESILIENCE AND REBUILDING

Rebuilding Nations and the Indian Problem

Why Does It Matter?

For people unfamiliar with the West, traveling there is an experience, and you will always remember your first time. If you live there, you have learned to adjust to it like indigenous people. The West is a vast region of seventeen states, including Alaska and Hawaii, with barren desert areas in the Southwest. The barrenness is disassociated from the eastern deep-green Black Hills, for example, making the West a contradiction of this and that. In its own way, the desert colors resonate with their own beauty. As George Lee, a Navajo, described his homeland of the Four Corners area, "My spiritual eyes are taught while gazing upon the vastness of the endless desert vision. So unending is the vista that the supple curve of Mother Earth's horizon heals the hungering heart. Always, as far as memory goes, this land has been one of everlasting enchantment."[1] Native love for the earth runs deep, permeating the souls of the indigenous. Indians are of the natural world.

Four main deserts exist in the United States, and all of them are in the West—Sonoran, Mohave, Chihuahuan, and Great Basin, including 20 smaller ones within the four larger ones. Attached to the Southwest is the Basin area, the West Coast, Pacific Northwest, and Columbia Plateau. The Northern, Central, and Southern Plains span like a mighty north-south corridor bordered by prairie lands that touch the great Mississippi River. This broad area of nearly 502,000 square miles has been called the "Big Empty" by Douglas Hurt.[2] This is the vast West, home to many—humans, flora, and fauna—and demanding of all. The seemingly near emptiness becomes endless space, and perceptions of distance are lost in

3

the vast West. Distortion occurs, and one has to understand nature's way in order to obtain the water that is necessary for living.[3] The human body consists of 65–75 percent water, requiring eight eight-ounce glasses, or four liters, every twenty-four hours.

Green is alien in the desert, except for knots of pine forests climbing and resting on mountainsides, like in the Black Hills, and other tree types in various parts of the Southwest, California, and the Pacific Northwest. Noted Laguna writer Leslie Silko described the Southwest through the eyes of one of her characters in her renowned novel *Ceremony*: "'This is where we come from. This sand, this stone, these trees, the vines, all the wildflowers. This earth keeps us going.' He took off his hat and wiped his forehead on his shirt. 'These dry years you hear some people complaining, you know, about the dust and the wind, and how dry it is. But the wind and the dust, they are part of life too, like the sun and the sky. You don't swear at them. It's people, see. They're the ones. The old people used to say that droughts happen when people forget, when people misbehave.'"[4] The earth becomes a teacher, a harsh one that instructs human beings and other life in lessons of survival. One might call this a difficult love, a love for such a land.

In this earth's bosom, the elements allow no escape. One only learns to cope with periodic rains that risk the danger of flash floods, winter's plunging cold temperatures at night, and the almost unbearable heat of the warmest summer days. In the West, the plains spiral up to 100 degrees Fahrenheit during the summer and the air is dry, waiting for a cool rainstorm on the horizon. In the Desert Southwest, summer temperatures can soar up to 115 degrees or more of pure heat. The ovenlike sun is ubiquitously tormenting and intensely penetrating. Other parts of the West are equally demanding in their own way, and people learn how to adapt, which is a main reason for this book.

In 1881 the legendary Lakota leader Sitting Bull sat on the ground with fur trader Gus Hedderich. The great war leader squinted his eyes while meticulously studying the trader's weathered face and the steady rhythmic movement of his leathered-skinned hand. Then, Sitting Bull drew his name, a picture of a buffalo sitting. The trader drew a sitting buffalo and then wrote "Sitting Bull" under the picture. In the next several minutes, the trader patiently taught Sitting Bull how to write his name in English. In that pivotal moment, Sitting Bull practiced penning his name over and over. Later he would sell his autograph for $1.50 and $2.00 while he briefly traveled as a part of Buffalo Bill's Wild West Show.[5] The act of learning to write his name exemplified the Indian cross-cultural adaptation of white-world cultural tools. Learning to read and write would help the famed leader and many Native people reinvent themselves and initiate another cycle of rebuilding their nations, this time in a capitalistic era called the twentieth century.

Rebuilding means sorting out tasks and solving problems. In the late nineteenth century, the so-called Indian Problem arose as good-hearted reformers—Friends of the Indian—wanted the government to alleviate the impoverished living conditions on reservations. As oppressed people, Indians faced an uphill challenge of reinventing themselves or dying. Any problem begins with a question that someone asks because they think that something is wrong. What has been historically stated as the "Indian problem" will be responded to in the context of an indigenous paradigm throughout this book. Since the majority of Indian written history is by non-Indians, a Western paradigm is constantly invoked of writing "about" Native people rather than analyzing from "inside" indigenous worldviews. Working and analyzing from within an indigenous paradigm set the analytical parameters for this discourse. This contextualization approach also posits that an indigenous worldview is further divided in multiple worldviews of Cherokee, Comanche, Navajo, and so forth.

As fundamental as this is, the Indian problem was an issue of concern when Elwell Otis first raised it as the "Indian Question" in his book published in 1878 about the dilapidated reservation conditions.[6] He served in the Plains Indian wars at the rank of brigadier general in the regular army. George Manypenny, who served as Indian commissioner from 1853 to 1857, responded to Otis's book with his *Our Indian Wards* in 1880, as his work focused mainly on the opening of Kansas and Nebraska to white settlement.[7] In this concern of reformers wanting Indian conditions addressed by the government, Helen Hunt Jackson's 1881 classic *A Century of Dishonor* brought national attention to the destroyed Indian livelihood in the seven cases that she describes.[8] This Indian reform movement continually focused on the plight of Native people. Finally, former Indian commissioner Frances Leupp wrote *The Indian and His Problem* in 1910, an overview perspective with suggestions for future commissioners that addresses the various issues that Indians faced at the turn of the twentieth century. Leupp let it be known that answers for a better way of life were desperately needed on reservations.[9]

The following pages address the Indian problem, but as part of a greater story of nation rebuilding, and Indians reinventing themselves as an elemental part of the process. The mainstream majority might ask why it matters whether the Indian tribes of the West have worked hard to try to restore their communities and tribal governments. Are they not supposed to? Or, who cares? To Indian people, it does matter that Indians are addressing the problem.

These colonized people who seemed on the verge of extinction in 1890 have turned around 180 degrees. They have become major players in some regions in the midst of the weakened economy of the United States in the early twenty-first century. Is it not in money that Americans measure success? Not all Americans would say this. However, how much one earns annually and how much wealth one accumulates are the believed standards in America, where many people believe that every person's dream is to become rich, powerful, and perhaps famous, and that this yields happiness. Within their own parts of the continental U.S. West, some indigenous communities have become or are well on the way to becoming rich and powerful. It is difficult to make a general assessment of all the hundred or so Indian tribes in the modern West, but it is arguably more important to understand the impressive progress and the driving forces that have made this possible for the majority of the Indians nations in more or less one hundred years.

In applying ethnohistorical analysis and political economy theory, I use a multilayered approach to argue that Native people reinvented themselves in order to rebuild their nations. In the process, they cross-culturally borrowed and adapted four essential tools: education, navigation within cultural systems, modern Indian leadership, and indigenized political economy. Working under the rubric that "adaptation" is a keystone to this study, it makes most sense to envision two thematic threads of *resilience* and *rebuilding*, which divide the chapters into two parts. Native people resiliently survived the first half of the twentieth century while retaining their tribal identities. Once in conversing with Dennis Banks, cofounder of the American Indian Movement (AIM), he said that the right timing enabled AIM to be born and to be effective. In the second part of this book, "Rebuilding," we see that Indians also used their imagination and resourcefulness to apply the tools they had acquired to work toward self-determination with their inherent sovereignty.

These tools proved to be forced education from boarding schools that Indians began to use against mainstream hegemony. Native people learned to navigate within the mainstream cultural system during relocated urbanization, thus becoming bicultural. A modernized Native leadership had to be forged in the activist era that was articulate, visionary, intelligent, and proactive. Lastly, a modern political economy was adapted and indigenized that addressed the history of past U.S.-Indian relations, economic understanding of American capitalism, learning the law to empower tribal nations, the political science of negotiations with governments at all levels and with other non-Indian entities, and the sociology of understanding all relations in a postmodern Indian era. *Political economy* is a Western term that economists and many scholars use in describing the progress of a community or nation. An Indianized version of political economy is tribal political economy: how Native communities have adopted parts of white capitalism like wealth accumulation and wage labor to rebuild tribal communities.

The twentieth century has been the most progressive century in the history of humankind, and it has been one of the most destructive eras of imperialist oppression and blatant exploitation of peoples, including Hitler's Nazism, Soviet communism, Middle Eastern dictatorships, South African apartheid, Chinese communism, and the rise of North Korea. In each case, the victims, especially the indigenous, have suffered horrifically, but how have they sustained themselves? In 2010 roughly 370 million indigenous people (less than 6 percent of the world's population) constituted 5,000 kinds of Native peoples in 72 countries. Their courses are predictable in the postmodern history of sharp population declines, complete mainstream absorption, language loss, and ethnic cleansing from the late nineteenth century to the present.

Yet in America, in the modern West, something drastic has happened: the vanishing race of the late nineteenth century chose not to disappear. The end of the trail did not happen as sculptor James Earle Frazer depicted it in his creation called *The End of the Trail*. Like so much gilding in America, where people choose to believe myths and illusions instead of the truth or facts, Indians have been rebuilding. They are nations within a nation, although some may argue against this statement. Nation building involves constructing a national identity by employing the power of a state-like government. This is the case of American Indian tribal nations whose postmodern tribal governments look very much like those of the U.S. government and its constituent state governments.

The point of this book is that Indian nations have had to rebuild their communities and governments following the near nadir of the population decline in the late nineteenth century. As science and academic disciplines found and established their identities in the fin de siècle, much of this confirmation was in the suppression of indigenous people in North America, South America, and other parts of the world. British anthropologist and founder of social anthropology Sir Edward Tylor wrote *Primitive Culture* in 1871, in which he explained the theory of survival, positing that some previous customs, like useless baggage, are not retained by a community as it adapts and develops.[10] Six years later, American anthropologist and social theorist Lewis Henry Morgan published *Ancient Society*, in which he argued that his theory of social change—charting a movement from savagery to barbarism to civilization—was essential for a society.[11]

A poignant observation here is that Native people have been constantly rebuilding their nations following removal to the West or to reservations, again following the American Civil War, and after the reservation era of the late nineteenth century. Rebuilding nations and readapting are part of the indigenous nature of American Indians; they have been doing this even before the arrival of Columbus. I theorize that, in this Circle of Life, Native communities practiced a moral economy of sharing goods and wealth so that no one was left out and all had sufficient food and shelter. This situation develops into a modern political economy where power, rank, and class distinction become a part of society. Then, the Circle of Life repeats itself in the indigenous paradigm as long as the Native community retains a communal orientation at its heart, thus establishing a tribal political economy.

Furthermore, I argue that three fundamental concepts help one to understand the rebuilding process of Native nations since 1900: Native logic, finding voice, and historic cycles:

1. Native logic is different from the Western paradigm of thought and is predicated on the notion that Indians are circular in their philosophy and are very visually oriented in their actions and decision making.
2. Finding voice is the process by which Native people try to make their Indian perspective understood in the modern history of Indian-white relations. Much of the time, the mainstream, especially the federal government, ignores and neglects what Indians have to say. While Native people hear themselves, it has often been said that white bureaucrats have no ears.
3. Historic cycles are the concept that one can understand many things in the earth's at-large community as one of circles and cycles, repeating patterns and trends. Opposite from a linear view, historic cycles are the theorem that things such as events and experience repeat themselves in a very similar manner or the same way. As an example, Native nations have continued to rebuild themselves in historic cycles.

"Indian Country" is metaphorical to most people, but it is used here as a concept to construct a collective Indian perspective in the West for general reference throughout the following pages. Being in the West, Indian Country is a place west of the Mississippi to the Pacific Ocean, north to Canada, and south to Mexico. With this in mind, this book attempts to provide an overview of Indian Country as Native nations progressed mightily in the modern American West from the late nineteenth century to the present.

In essence, this study attempts to achieve two goals. First, the Indian experience of rebuilding their nations in the West is the focus. Second, bearing in mind that Native people "see" things differently from the mainstream, being close to their tribal traditions implies that Indians continued to do things their way. I argue that the indigenous people (my people), from a vanishing population of fewer than 238,000 people at the end of the nineteenth century to 2.1 million people belonging to 566 federally recognized tribes with 326 federal reserved land areas by 2010, endured suffering as prisoners of war on reservations, survived white exploitation, and resiliently responded. Within one hundred years, the tribes began to rebuild their nations and had succeeded in the early stage of achieving Indian self-determination by the late twentieth century. This story, however, is about Indian nations in the modern West. The following chapters analyze how this feat was achieved for the majority of western Native nations.

Some critics may say that not all Indian nations have been rebuilt; look at all of the reservations as a whole. This is seeing the water glass as half empty. I suggest we look again and see that many of the Native communities have rebuilt, and others are well on their way: Pequot in Connecticut, Seminole in Florida, Oneida in Wisconsin, and Choctaw in Mississippi. In the West, Chickasaw and Muscogee Creek in Oklahoma, Warm Springs in Oregon, Salt River Pima in Arizona, Navajo in Arizona, and others have rebuilt or are well on their way. But instead of a water glass, imagine a gourd dipper half full—this is Indian thinking in an indigenous paradigm. To begin thinking this way, forget all previous stereotypes of Indian poverty on reservations. Look anew at what has been accomplished by Indians. Notice the trend of growth and development within the latest generation in the modern Indian West.

Nation building is obviously different from rebuilding nations, although similar characteristics would be an important part of the latter. In this study, key components involve leadership, cultural systems, resource management, education, and the flexibility of adaptation. This study also proposes that Native communities and their leaders acquired these tools and used them sufficiently to adjust and reinvent themselves at the risk of becoming less Indian. In the end, retaining Native identity was of the utmost importance as they rebuilt the political economies of their reinvented nations.

Since Dee Brown's classic *Bury My Heart at Wounded Knee* in 1970, an increasing number of publications have presented Native accounts of Indian history.[12] Brown called for reading his introduction while facing east to understand the Indian position of the white man's frontier development encroaching on their lands. Thirty years later, Daniel Richter's *Facing East from Indian Country* essentially proposed a similar perspective and kept Indians at the center stage of history.[13] In this new Indian history of placing Native people at center stage, this volume intends to go beyond and presents history from Native historical realities. In this light, the task here is to provide insightful dialogue within the text of the following chapters that concentrate on the Indian experience in response to the white man's West. But it is much more than experiencing and reacting to Indian-white relations. Rather, "seeing" is imperative for understanding from a Native point of view, as I addressed earlier in another book, *The American Indian Mind in a Linear World* that appeared in 2003.[14]

Essentially, "seeing" comes from cultural foundations steeped in Native values and varies from tribe to tribe. "Seeing," according to Severt Young Bear, Black Elk, Luther Standing Bear, Charles Eastman, and others who have expressed this perception adequately, is expressed within a Native logic while realizing the impact of entities interacting and while considering the good and the bad are a part of the discourse. Furthermore, it is the realization within an Indian reality as defined by community orientation that brings together the physical reality and metaphysical reality as one dimension. Hence, Indian Country is the Indian experience within a Native realm that intersects frequently with the white world, that is, the modern West, in this volume. In imagining the equation of "Indian plus white equals history of interaction," the left side or Indian part of the equation is the basis of this book. However, most non-Indian instructors are teaching from the right side of this equation of Indian-white relations: teaching "about" Indians from a mainstream point of view.

Over centuries of contact, Native people have been forced (sometimes willingly) to adapt to many mainstream cultural ways, while they have reinvented an "Indian" identity. This generic Indian identity consists of a cultural transition from tribal cultures deriving from many diverse Indian nations toward a collective Indianness. A Native perspective has evolved from various well-known and lesser known American Indians as a single Indian voice for helping to substantiate "seeing" and to underscore that there is a Native reality and ethos. These numerous views are based on many tribes' values and even more tribal perspectives that include both Native men and women.

Mostly Indian autobiographies and oral history interviews are helpful as research sources in constructing a collective Native perspective. Fortunately, while writing this book, printed autobiographies containing personal insights have appeared in significant numbers. In addition, biographies about Indian individuals in this century have been helpful. My research over the years also involved collecting and examining speeches and commentaries from newspapers, tribal newspapers, and historical documents.

Writing about the American West has been the popular subject of many authors and early scholars. Walter Prescott Webb, Herbert Bolton, Frederick Jackson Turner, and a multitude of others have studied the West, but they did not centralize Native people as equal partners in shaping history. In fact, few works have done this. For example, Donald Parman produced an impressive synthesis in *Indians and the American West in the Twentieth Century*, a policy history combined with a history of Indian-U.S. government events.[15] In addition, Peter Iverson wrote a popularly used volume, *"We Are Still Here": Native Americans in the Twentieth Century*, which is a social and community history of Indian people.[16] More than a generation ago, James Olson and Raymond Wilson's synthesized work, *Native Americans in the Twentieth Century*, provided an overview of what happened to Indians in this century, and now we are in the twenty-first century.[17]

I present here a narrative description, a type of political and cultural explanation of the "Indian way of doing things" in the twentieth century and afterward. This book champions a main theme of demonstrating how Indians have chosen their own means in responding to external federal policy, social changes, federal laws, and court decisions. On the surface they appear to make progress toward assimilation while identifying as "Indians," but an undercurrent of doing things in an Indian fashion has led to Indian self-determination since the 1970s. This became more apparent with the explosion of Red Power in the 1960s. In tandem, the book presents an Indian perspective and describes how Native people have gone about their business while responding to the dominant society rather than complete assimilation into white society. This was important for rebuilding Indian nations.

Throughout this book I have chosen to use the terms Indian *Native, indigenous,* and sometimes *American Indian.* Most older Indians say they are Indian, or American Indian, but not Native American. Even more, they identify themselves according to their tribe or tribes. But things are changing, and the younger Indian generation, without thinking about these terms, mimics what the mainstream calls us and use the term *Native American.* And I have referred to tribes as nations in this study.

While nation building and state building are often used interchangeably in the United States, experts define a difference between the two. In political science theory, "nation building" advocates establishing a national identity, while "state building" refers to the institutions of the state. In the following pages, nation building and nationhood seem the most appropriate terms for demonstrating the reconstruction of the tribal nations. In an indigenous world, rebuilding the fire would be more appropriate, as sometimes fires symbolized nations such as the Three Brothers of the Great Lakes, or Three Fires (Ojibwa, Ottawa, and Potawatomi). Fire nations might seem an appropriate wording for modern Indian nations in the twenty-first century.

The literature of non-Indian nation building is plentiful among more recent works, such as Joel S. Migdal's *State in Society: Studying How States and Societies Transform and Constitute One Another* (2001).[18] This includes David Chandler's *Empire in Denial: The Politics of State-building* (2006).[19] A year later, Dominik Zaum published *The Sovereignty Paradox: The Norms and Politics of International Statebuilding.*[20] Then followed Nathan Hodge's *Armed Humanitarians: The Rise of Nation Builders* in 2011.[21]

For this book to explain the last hundred years of Native progress, I have borrowed from political economy theory that dates back to 1615. Since then, modern political economy theory has developed through the writings of Karl Marx, John Stuart Mill, Adam Smith, and other thinkers. Modern political economy theory is based on five areas of analysis: history, economics, law, political science, and sociology. In the indigenous paradigm, David Wilkins (Lumbee), in his work *American Indian Politics and the American Political System,* argues for a tribal political economy.[22] Wilkins demonstrates that tribal governments and their communities have survived the American political system and formed their own economies with success. Dean Smith (Mohawk), in *Modern Tribal Development: Paths to Self-sufficiency and Cultural Integrity in Indian Country* proposed a model for economic development that emphasizes Native cultural integrity in not sparing essential traditional values.[23] In conceptualizing this

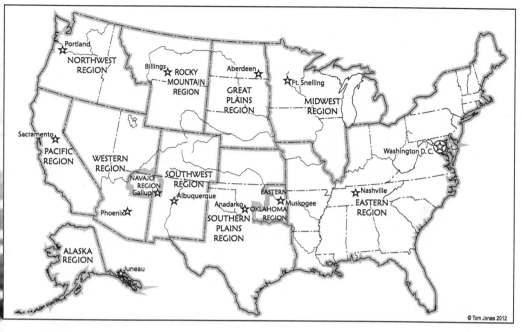

Map 1. Bureau of Indian Affairs regions and area offices.

book, I have been influenced by the work of Gayatri Chakravorty Spivak, including her brief volume *Nationalism and the Imagination* that appeared in 2010.[24] In my study, the subaltern speaks, and has always, although ignored by the American mainstream, and how economic success has made the Indian voice heard by many non-Indians has caught the attention of many people in other parts of the world.

While the problem of poverty has not escaped reservation communities, I would suggest that readers consider all of the progress that Native people have made from the late nineteenth century to the present. While the Indian problem has been resolved on some reservations, Native people are continually addressing the issues with newly acquired tools as they are rebuilding their nations.

Without doubt, the rise of American Indian tribal nations in the postmodern era has not been easy, and many Native communities continue to be burdened by high levels of poverty. Poverty has become a part of Native culture in the twentieth century. Much good has happened due to Indian progress, and everyone should strive to be optimistic in seeing the water gourd as half full.

PART ONE

Resilience

The White Man's Burden

Take up the White man's burden—
Send forth the best ye breed—
Go find your sons to exile
To serve your captives' need;
To wait in heavy harness,
On fluttered folk and wild—
Your new-caught, sullen peoples,
Half-devil and half-child.
                    Rudyard Kipling

Resilience is required of anyone who wishes to survive. Whether bonds of prison or bonds in our own mind, resilience offers hope to a dismal future, even if the end is near. In the last year of the nineteenth century, with the fall of Indian nations, Rudyard Kipling offered the above poem to Queen Victoria signaling American foreign policy in the Philippines following the brief Spanish-American War. These critical words exemplify the colonized suppression that American Indians have had to overcome. Resilience is the ability to recover from a dire situation, and this is an essential step toward rebuilding. Even more, Native people have had to overcome the perception of a defeated people and second-class treatment, in addition to proving to the government and others that they have succeeded in the white man's world of American capitalism.

CHAPTER ONE

Reservation Life and Land Allotments

Adaptation to New Homelands

Now I hear the Government is cutting up my land giving it away to other people. . . . It can't be so for it is not the treaty. These people who are they? They have no right to this land. It never was given to them. It was given to me and my people and we paid for it with our land back in Alabama. The black and white people have no right to it. Then how can it be that the Government is doing this. . . . It wouldn't be justice. I am informed and believe it to be true that some citizens of the United States have title to land that was given to my fathers and my people by the government. If it was given to me, what right has the United States to take it from me without first asking my consent?

CHITTO HARJO, MUSCOGEE CREEK, 1906

The eastern thick darkness paled slowly as deep purple gave way to dawn's red and orange on the horizon. Standing tall, looking distraught, Chitto Harjo prayed to the East for his people as his lamenting words rose from a heavy heart. His deep brown eyes focused on the red sky in the direction of his former homeland hundreds of miles away. Slowly shaking his head with sadness, he looked over the new homeland of his Muscogee Creek people as he stood near the Arkansas River of Tulsa town. The full-blood felt the painful memories of losing loved ones during the long walk to the West. The white man's promises on paper meant nothing. Leaders of his people had signed a treaty in 1832 that called for exchanging their land in the East for land in the West called Indian Territory.[1] Now, the white men wanted to divide the Creeks' land and distribute pieces to each Muscogee. His mind voiced the words, "How could they do this? It is not right." He bent down, clutched a handful of earth in his brown hand, turned it over, and thought about how this earth was the crux of all this disparity.

17

Life on the reservation challenged the indigenous spiritual souls. Day after day, Native people grappled with intrusive changes in their new sedentary lives. Old ways met new ways. The federal government usurped their inherent sovereign right to be free through imposed boundaries described on pieces of paper—the white man's treaties. Throughout Indian Country the federal government established nearly two hundred reservations over the course of the nineteenth century, and bureaucrats believed that they now had an "Indian problem" on their hands. The dwindled Indian population became wards of the United States, and the federal government had fiduciary care of their properties. Yet politicians thought that Indians still had too much land and called them a dying race.[2]

During the reservation era in the late nineteenth century, Native people found themselves challenged by the elemental reasons for life—survival, hope, and endurance. While these years proved to be the most challenging for Indians, bureaucrats and other Americans underestimated the resilience of Native people to survive and persist in their sovereign ways. Indian people endured conditions of imprisonment, and they survived an accursed land allotment policy that bureaucrats deliberately designed to individualize them and strip their reservations of more land.

One would have thought that removing Indians to the West was enough punishment. This callous treatment carried over from early Indian policy east of the Mississippi, transplanting more than three dozen eastern tribes to the West. Of all the 374 ratified treaties, 229 agreements involved ceding land, and 99 addressed establishing reservations.[3] White settler expansion in the spirit of Manifest Destiny mandated new destinations for Indians, who seemingly no longer controlled their own lives. Federal paternalism emerged from the Bureau of Indian Affairs and Congress as these two parts of the government advised the U.S. president on what to do about the indigenous that stood in the way of white progress. Indians knew this man as the Great White Father in Washington, who had taken their lands in exchange for taking care of them. In the eyes of the Indians, the president represented a powerful figure, somewhat like the Great Power that they traditionally depended upon for their livelihood.

The idea of established Indian reservations did not occur following the Plains Indian wars in the late nineteenth century, as one might think. Much earlier, in the 1600s, British colonial officials conceived the idea of the first Indian reservation. As the colonies expanded, officials struck agreements with tribal leaders that established boundaries separating Native peoples from colonists. The first agreement restricting Indians to a reserved area dates back to at least 1640. At the time, Mohican chief Uncas

Figure 1.1. Muscogee Creek leader of the Crazy Snake Rebellion against allotting Creek tribal lands. Courtesy of Western History Collections, University of Oklahoma.

signed a treaty and surrendered a large part of his tribal lands in present-day Connecticut to the British. In return, he retained a reservation for the Mohican people.[4] In 1758, colonial officials of New Jersey created the Delaware Indian reservation at Indian Mills in present-day Burlington County.

Later, British officials negotiated a major boundary called the Proclamation Line of 1763 that set the crest of the Appalachian Mountains as the divide, with the colonists on the east side and Indian nations on the west side. The idea of this natural boundary lasted only a few years, as the British could not contain the westward expansion of its colonists. Following the American Revolution, the nature of British colonial–Indian relations transferred to the newly formed United States. Early officials created the first reservations via treaties. Other methods followed.

Throughout the nineteenth century, the U.S. government employed three methods to establish reservations: executive order of the president, congressional legislation, and treaty (the most common method). The reserved lands range in size from thirty-one small rancherías in California to the enormous 15-million-acre Navajo reservation located in the northeast corner of Arizona, which extends into Utah and creates both a checkerboard pattern and a solid block in northwest New Mexico. In total area, this enormous reservation is approximately the size of West Virginia. A fourth kind of reservation involved state governments making reservations within their boundaries, but these lands do not possess the same legal status as federal Indian-reserved lands. The idea for reservations conveyed the notion that any Indian threat would be subdued and that peaceful Natives lived on these lands.[5]

The surrender of the last two dangerous Indian legends, Sitting Bull of the Hunkpapa Lakota in 1881 and Geronimo of the Chiricahua Apache in 1886, signified a major step toward final peace in the West. One of the most quoted Native individuals, Sitting Bull, acknowledged the end of his life as he had known it in his earlier years, but he wanted to know the government's plan for his people. He realized the old ways were ending and stated to Major David Brotherton, the commanding officer at Fort Buford, "I surrender this rifle to you through my young man, whom I desire to teach in this manner now that he has become a friend of the Americans. . . . Whatever you have to give or whatever you have to say, I would like to receive or hear now, for I don't wish to be kept in darkness longer."[6]

Confined to certain areas, Indians became prisoners on their own lands. By the last decade of the nineteenth century, the total Native population had declined to a mere 238,000 people. Such a rapid demise convinced some people that the Indians would disappear from the face of the earth. Over 1,600 wars, battles, and skirmishes, as well as a dozen deadly diseases (smallpox, influenza, measles, scarlet fever, tuberculosis, cholera, whooping cough, typhus, diphtheria, chicken pox, and typhoid), had sent the Indian population into a downward spiral.[7]

The vanishing Indian seemed starkly evident in the story of Ishi, the last of his Yahi people in California. During the 1850s, ranchers and miners deliberately hunted Indians, killing them for sport. Eventually, the Yahi declined to four remaining individuals. Ishi and the other three did not even dare to light a fire for fear of ranchers and miners seeing it. The foursome traveled over rocks and walked in streams when possible to avoid leaving a trail. Within a short time, three of the Yahi died, leaving Ishi as the only one left behind. Loneliness engulfed him as he faced a grim decision: should he continue hiding and running for his life or surrender to the mercy of whoever might find him? Still unsure, hunger made the decision and drove him to find warmth and hopefully something to eat in a settler's slaughterhouse in northern California near Oroville in August 1911. The butcher who found Ishi telephoned local sheriff John Brooks Webber that he had found a wild Indian. The sheriff brought a couple of cultural authorities with him to study Ishi. Two anthropologists, Alfred Kroeber and Thomas Waterman, arrived. At first they believed that they had discovered the last wild savage on the continent. Waterman had studied the local Native languages and hoped to communicate with Ishi. As he exhausted his list of words from various Native dialects, Ishi remained silent, not willing to trust the white men for fear of being poisoned or killed. Losing hope, Waterman tried his list of words in the Yana language, the same that Yahi spoke. Waterman stumbled in his pronunciation of several Yana words. This caught Ishi's attention. He looked into the caring eyes of Waterman and asked him in Yana, "Are you Yahi?" Desperate to help, Waterman replied that he was Yahi. In the following days, a trustful bond developed between Waterman and Ishi.[8]

The rest of Ishi's story is well-known as he adopted ways of the white man, his oppressor. In this adaptive process, Ishi realized that he had to learn about white society, just as Sitting Bull and other Natives had decided over the previous decades. Furthermore, Indians began to adopt selected values of white society. Simultaneously, Indians retained many of their core tribal values. This flexible characteristic is what makes them "Indian"—the ability to borrow selectively from other cultures.

Native traditional values are inherent to most Indian people who practice tribal beliefs. For example, communalism is a sine qua non predicated on the belief that group emphasis is more important than individuality. Historian Edward P. Thompson introduced the idea of sharing resources in the moral economy of a noncapitalistic society.[9] Native people are connected to a group based on the idea that belonging to a community is crucial for security reasons and sufficient food supply, which demonstrates a moral economy. But this also means being joined with the earth and the natural world. Sitting Bull described himself being as a part of the Black Hills. He said, "Look at me and look at the earth. Which is the oldest do you think? The earth, and I was born on it."[10] In a similar way, Flathead elder Ambrose said, "The Bitterroot [Mountains] is our old home. Here are the graves of our fathers, [who are] buried here."[11]

Lastly, traditional Indian people believe in a metaphysical reality that combines with physical reality. They live with both realities as one; visions, spirits, and the abstract are as real to them as are the trees, rivers, and mountains. The Native sovereign spirit was evocatively steeped in cultural ways. Like any people who have known freedom, Indians felt that their ancient sovereign way of life had been stripped from them. Like prisoners of war, the major tribes posing a threat were defeated by the U.S. military, which destroyed their economy and displaced them to restricted lands.

As scholars of nature, Indians possessed seminal knowledge of their natural environments. Their herbalists, medicine makers, and elders had studied the flora and fauna in their natural universe. By observing the earth assiduously, they learned from it. Native people also knew the landscape thoroughly as erudite sages of the flora and fauna. Their livelihood depended upon this earth knowledge as they hunted and/or cultivated food in their regions. Furthermore, they made an estimated 170 medicines from their knowledge of plants and herbs.[12] The environment offered a natural pharmacopoeia, and this indigenous library included both the living and nonliving things in their physical environment.

Some tribes received reservation assignments in their home regions, leaving their living conditions almost unchanged. Oliver Eastman (Sioux Wahpeton) nostalgically described his grandparents' lives: "The original Wahpetons were along the Minnesota River down to Spirit Lake and anywhere in there where the camping is good. And they prepared their food, and during the summer they picked cranberries, choke-cherries, and they'd make sugar, and of course, they hunted the buffalo, [and] dried the meat. So they had always prepared themselves for winter, there was no starvation."[13] As a part of the natural world, Native people knew all of its sources of food and times to collect it, such as during certain seasons.

Remaining umbilical to the earth has been the Indian way. Yet Indians lost this link at times. The reservation system disconnected many tribes from their sacred sites. It is not possible to say how many were separated from such important places, but tribes like the Mescalero Apache were displaced from Mt. Capitan in New Mexico, the Blackfeet in Montana were displaced from Mt. Ninaistakia, and the Southern Cheyenne were extirpated from the Black Hills. Other tribes were exiled from homelands as well, and they had to adjust to their new foreign home spaces.

The white man's reality of living in separate families and stressing individuality proved to be very different from almost all Native peoples on reservations, creating a polarized effect. Indians found themselves having to adjust to their oppressors' ways, and this included observing and learning white societal values. They became the subaltern in their homelands, with Indian agents and superintendents in control.[14] Under federal control, tribal communities began to rebuild in spite of being dependent on the government and its officials. Within reservation communities, an order of infrastructure developed during the early decades of the twentieth century. Delbert Broker, an Ojibwa, described his tribe's reservation in general and how it systematically provided order: "I look at the reservation as a complete and total society, recognizing that reservations are a complete society. This included five basic institutions such as religion, education, economics, family, and government."[15]

The virtue of generosity remained integral among many indigenous moral economies, where gain and wealth were distributed among members. Among the Crow Indians, a successful warrior returning from battle after counting coup often brought an enemy's weapons, such as a gun. After a battle, "there was a hurrying forward and a scuffling among the people—men, women, or children—to seize and get possession of the implement. Whoever got to keep it [sic] as his own property," explained Thomas Leforge, a white Crow Indian. He added that horses captured were brought back and were "rushed after and led away as their own by people other than the one who had risked his life in their [the horses'] capture. He got acclaim, distinction, honorable mention, was serenaded, and perhaps his father gave away another horse or two in celebration of the glorious achievement of his son. . . . The point was, he proved that his motive for going out upon the hazardous undertaking had not been avarice, but merely for the honor of himself and the tribe."[16] All of this changed when the military forced the Crow and other tribes to live on reservations, as much of the cultural infrastructure was altered and the communities made societal adjustments. No outlets existed for bringing in acquired goods or any kind of surplus, expiring previous inroads of trade and acquisitions from hunting and raiding.

Maintaining positive relations with everyone in the family and in the community offered optimism in many circumstances, but for prisoners of war, it often created dissension and internal communal stress. Inwardness of kinship relations, however, united the factions as a collective community to oppose the outside. Solving the problems of factionalism, for example, called for Native leaders to deal diplomatically with outsiders. They cooperated with officials from the Bureau of Indian Affairs and accommodated them, often preventing strict measures toward anyone within the community. But restricted reservation living continually tested Native resilience. As a means to ensure positive relationships, giving and sharing remained pertinent virtues in many communities. Leforge recalled in his memoirs, "The giving to non-relatives at any time was looked upon as being a higher exhibition of generosity than the giving to relatives, although gifts to any one were regarded as proof of a good heart."[17]

As Native people learned to adjust to reservation life, missionaries of various denominations indefatigably proselytized Indians. Gradually and not so gradually, many Indians adopted Christian practices and became completely converted. Thus, traditionalists and new Christian converts existed in the same communities. Sometimes they married. Mountain Crow women welcomed marriage ceremonies conducted by preachers. Leforge, who was adopted into the Crow tribe during the late 1800s, related that "many Indians came to church for the apparent purpose of hearing the music. Little ones, wearing only a breech-cloth, would sit with shins in hands and listen rapturously to the unpolished harmonies. The Indian women like the church marriage ceremony, especially the clause, 'until death do you part.' Various ones dragged reluctant Crow husbands to the missionary for him to pronounce these binding words."[18]

Some people believed that, after someone died, the ghost or the spirit lingered among the family and relatives until it traveled westward to the other side of life into the afterworld. Leforge described the dead among the Crow during the late 1800s and the apprehension of the friends and relatives of the deceased. "Ghosts of dead people and spirits of all kinds," he said, "had a prominent place in the mental life of the Indians as they used to be—and many of them as they are to-day."[19] Beverly Hungry Wolf of the Blackfoot described her grandmother's talent as a medium. Her grandmother had the power to call and talk to ghosts. Hungry Wolf stated, "She was a very powerful person. She knew all our religious ceremonies and she doctored the people. . . . She had the Power to communicate with ghosts, and I once saw her do this."[20]

Communicating with spirits and the metaphysical forces remained an elemental part of Native life. Leforge described the Sun Dance as the central ceremony for worship; participants reached the threshold of sensing the supernatural power from the other side of life. Leforge said,

> The object of the sun-dance was to worship and to propitiate the "First Maker," or "Person Above." In preparation for the central event, many devout people went to hilltops each morning and each evening, they went to pray for the success of any coming enterprises or to ask favorable notice for the tribe in general. The prayers were addressed to the Sun, this material object, being looked upon as the substantial intermediary between the human being and the Person Above, who was too august to be addressed directly; or, by some people, the sun was supposed to be the dwelling-place of the "Almighty One."[21]

Leforge emphasized the importance of tobacco to his adopted people, the Mountain Crows. Held as a sacred substance, "tobacco was regarded as a gift of the Almighty—or First Maker, as the Crows used the designation [for Creator]."[22] Whether in small ceremonial groups or on an individual quest for a celestial blessing, the Crows used tobacco respectfully with canonical protocol for not abusing this gift from the Creator.

Indian ceremonies like the Sun Dance provoked public disgust and charges of savagism against Native people. Indian agents berated the dances and wanted them banished from reservations. As a young man, Leforge described the animus between whites and Indians with regard to the Sun Dance. He wrote, "How I wish I could see now [again] a genuine old-time sun-dance! To the businesslike white man, it was only an orgy of bloodthirsty savage paganism. To the spiritual-minded Indian, it was the supreme test of clean manhood and womanhood. It instilled into and stimulated in them the hardy and high qualities of character. The self-torturing that seems to us so revolting was to the Indians an occasion for cultivation of the spirit, for subduing the body until it was altogether governed by the higher faculties of the mind."[23]

Christian beliefs undoubtedly collided with Indian worldviews. The former denigrated the worship practices of the latter. Jim Whitewolf, a Kiowa Apache in western Oklahoma, remembered his youthful days on the reservation. He was a small child and his family lived east of the Indian agency near Anadarko. Some Catholic sisters sat under an arbor at a camp in the community, and someone called to Whitewolf and his parents. He recalled:

A fellow was there, named Bill Brownbear, who was interpreting for the Catholic sisters. There was another man with those sisters. This man who was with the sisters prayed, and then there was singing. He took out a black book; it was a Bible. He started reading from it. I didn't understand it at that time. The only thing he was doing that I knew was good was the praying because we had always had praying in the Indian way. Every now and then I could understand a little bit, like when he talked about "our Father," but the rest of the time I didn't know what he was talking about. When the service was over they said that they would give some of us rosaries.[24]

The reservation era began earnestly with the idea that federal officials would negotiate peaceful agreements with the western Indians. The officials also believed that the attitude of Indians needed to be changed, as well as the way they viewed things. In theory, Jeffersonian idealism held that Indian assimilation could happen, yet the reality of the West proved otherwise at the end of the nineteenth century. Eastern humanitarians, religious organizations, and idealistic reformers desired peaceful relations with the tribal nations. An earlier history of warfare with the Indian nations east of the Mississippi in the 1700s and early 1800s resulted in human destruction, including alcoholism from whiskey via trade and multiple foreign diseases introduced through contact with whites. Whether for guilt-ridden or purely humanitarian reasons, eastern reformers had an opportunity to help the disconsolate Indians in the West.

With persistent settlers on the frontier trails, hungry miners seeking gold and silver, and unscrupulous opportunists, accelerated change altered the gestalt of the West. During the mid-nineteenth century, the Plains Indian nations reached their zenith; it was the golden age of pursuing buffalo and a raiding economy to supplement their hunting. This resplendent epoch all changed irrevocably with America's westward movement inspired by Manifest Destiny. The vast plains environment hosted various commonly known and unknown species of life. Elk, antelope, beaver, bear, horse, and buffalo proliferated on the plains in numbers that non-Indian eyes could not believe.[25] As most of the land was devoid of trees, the Plains tribes were totally dependent on the buffalo and small game for food and shelter. The buffalo flourished in unfathomable numbers and had mysterious power, according to the Lakota and other plains people. And the horse had revolutionized the cultural ways of the Plains Indians—desired adaptation—when the Spanish introduced it to the West in the mid-eighteenth century. On the Plains alone, twenty-eight different tribes and their bands populated the infinite region covering 1.4 million square miles that would become ten western American states, while more Plains extended into southern Canada as well as into northern Mexico. Cold and warm fronts of air exchanged suddenly, causing extreme temperatures and drastic changes in the weather, including engulfing rainstorms, life-threatening tornadoes, cold sleet, and hard-driven winds. The Southwest offered an unenviable desert climate, bordered by the Colorado Plateau, and the high plains of the Northwest experienced severe, biting winters.

The Plains ruled. A demanding environment to live in, one had to be conscious of the weather at all times. People looked upward toward the skies to read the weather. To be wise was to study nature. The indigenous knew earth knowledge. The natural environment and climate dictated the lifestyle of the Plains Indians such that the people believed in supernatural powers of ethereal beings to help them. As a result, the reality of Plains Indians combined the metaphysical and physical. The people's spiritual acumen interpreted dreams and visions as an integral part of life.

The buffalo furnished many items to the Plains Indians. The Plains people discovered fifty-two different ways to use the buffalo—including its meat as a food source, its bladder as a water bag, its hooves to make glue, and its hump as the cover of a shield for warfare. A general estimate puts the population of buffalo at 18–20 million in the West at the time of European contact with the tribes. The buffalo dominated the plains with their prodigious numbers. With the Plains Indians domesticating the horse for their usage, they learned to hunt the buffalo with razor-sharp effectiveness. On average, a warrior hunter had up to twenty-five or more horses, and they were highly prized for their speed and endurance. On horseback, a warrior hunter could ride forty miles or more in a single day and kill a dozen or more buffalo in a day's hunt.[26] Tribes warred against each other—Lakota-Crow, Comanche-Apache, and Lakota-Pawnee—for dominance of hunting grounds and proclaimed fluidlike empires of tribal space. This prosperity, also known as the golden age of the Indian, horse, and buffalo in the West, declined sharply in the waning decades of the nineteenth century. One main reason for this rapid descent involved the coming of the railroads. Soon afterward, the once seemingly infinite buffalo population declined at an unfathomable rate. Railroad companies employed professional hunters to hunt the buffalo to provide food for their working crews.[27] Tanners followed the hunters.

Other hunters killed buffalo for sport, leaving their carcasses to rot on the plains, to the dismay of Plains Indians. In the 1870s, professional hunters used at least two big, 50-caliber guns, shooting easily more than a hundred to over a thousand buffalo per day, and so fast that one gun cooled down while the other was used. A buffalo hide fetched a three-dollar price in Dodge City, where railroad cars of buffalo hide stacks were shipped to eastern markets. A Kiowa woman described the last days of the buffalo when they were almost all gone: "Then the white men hired hunters to do nothing but kill the buffalo." Skinners followed the hunters in wagons. They piled the hides and bones into the wagons to the brim to ship east to the markets. The bone piles stood as tall as a man, "stretching a mile along the railroad track." The Kiowa tell the story that occurred on the north side of Mt. Scott in western Indian Territory:

> One young woman got up very early in the morning. The dawn mist was still rising from Medicine Creek, and as she looked across the water, peering through the haze, she saw the last buffalo herd appear like a spirit dream. Straight to Mount Scott the leader of the herd walked. Behind him came the cows and their calves, and the few young males who had survived. As the woman watched, the face of the mountain opened. Inside Mount Scott the world was green and fresh, as it had been when she was a small girl. The rivers ran clear, not red. The wild plums were in blossom, chasing the red buds up the inside slopes. Into this world of beauty the buffalo walked, never to be seen again.[28]

Hunting and the buffalo constituted the Plains Indians' economy and their religious beliefs, and helped to define their worldview. To the Lakota on the northern Plains, the buffalo stood as a mighty animal that was gifted to them by the White Buffalo Calf Woman in a vision to two starving hunters. Allies of the Lakota, the Cheyenne believed themselves to be one with the buffalo; when the buffalo went away, so would they.

Lakota, Cheyenne, Comanche, and other Native resistance to white expansion to the West provoked the U.S. military into action to protect settlers. White settlers had little idea that they had entered contested realms of a "raiding" economy on the plains and prairie. The tribal nations divided the vast region into territorial zones. Boundaries swayed according to power. Tribes with the most military strength, sometimes bolstered with allies, raided other Native communities for their horses, women, and young children. The American military intruded on this tribal raiding system. With the final defeat of the Lakota in 1890 at Wounded Knee, South Dakota, the Indian populace fell vulnerable to a terse reservation system that the federal government had devised. One hundred years later, 297 reservations and rancherías existed.[29] The most common—and most legally binding—way to create a reservation was through treaty negotiations where the United States and the Indian nations acknowledged each other's sovereignty.

In 1867 a joint special committee of Congress under Senator James R. Doolittle recommended inspection boards be created with authorization to oversee the supervision of treaties. The boards examined the conduct and competence of government-appointed Indian agents. From the end of the Civil War in 1865 until 1871, federal officials negotiated the last stage of Indian treaties, and these agreements still affect U.S.-tribal relations today. During these years, the government moved more and more tribes into Indian Territory. By the 1870s, an incredible number of sixty-seven different Indian nations congested the Indian Territory. In 1871, a rider attached to an appropriation bill permanently halted Indian treaty making, as government officials increasingly believed that all tribal nations of the West could be defeated and placed on reservations.[30] In 1907, Indian Territory became the state of Oklahoma. New Mexico and Arizona followed in 1912, thereby completing the political geography of the modern American West.

Forced to live in these restricted areas, the defeated Indian nations attempted to adjust to their enforced sedentary lifestyle. With the near disappearance of the buffalo and the army in pursuit of many tribes, the white man's diseases plagued various Native communities. On the Upper Missouri River, the Mandan initially suffered the most from smallpox when their population of 1,600 declined to 131 in 1837. From 1837 to 1870, at least four epidemics occurred among Plains tribes. Native peoples possessed no natural immunity to measles, scarlet fever, typhoid, typhus, influenza, tuberculosis, cholera, diphtheria, chicken pox, and venereal infections.[31] Tribal medicine makers tried to fight off the invisible microbes carrying lethal strange diseases. Foreign epidemics plagued Native peoples into the early decades of the twentieth century. Native cures and medicines could not heal Indian people against the white man's deadly diseases. At first, Native logic dictated the wrong ceremonies were being used, the Creator had taken away the healing powers of medicine people, or the people had failed to follow the prescribed way such as the Lakota pipe way and Sweet Medicine's Cheyenne way. Faced with the ineffectiveness of their medicine men and shamans, Indian nations began to search for new avenues.

In an effort to replace traditional beliefs, missionaries introduced various Christian denominations to Indians. Many American Indians converted to Christianity. Missionaries introduced twenty-two documented major religions among the western Native peoples. Marcus Whitman and his wife, Narcissa, started working in 1836 among the Cayuse and Nez Perce in the Oregon Country, and Henry and Eliza Spalding worked as Presbyterian missionaries among the Nez Perce. In Minnesota, Bishop Henry Whipple began his work in 1859 among the Ojibwa and later worked among the Dakota. Missionaries and Indian agents collaborated to introduce farming and civilization to Native people, who needed to rebuild their economies on their reservations. The steady influx of settlers and eager miners, as well as more railroads, increased the pressure on Indian-white relations. Could Indians adopt white ways? If so, how would they become a part of mainstream American society? Would they become U.S. citizens? These were questions that a group of people, called reformers, began to ask and venture their responses. By the late nineteenth century, the Indian reformers became known as Friends of the Indians. It was assumed that the Indians would convert to Christianity and white ways, or else they would perish as a race. Helen Hunt Jackson, an activist for Indians, urged an overall reform of federal treatment of the indigenous following the broad circulation of her book *A Century of Dishonor*, published in 1881. In fact, she took it upon herself to make sure that every congressman received a copy of her book.[32] Jackson blamed the U.S. government for its massive mistreatment of the indigenous race and argued that it should do something to correct this Indian problem in the name of reform.

The changing conditions in the late 1800s also brought the downfall of Indian leaders such as Sitting Bull of the Hunkpapa, Red Cloud of the Oglala, Crazy Horse of the Oglala, Geronimo of the Apache, and Chief Joseph of the Nez Perce. With the absence of influence of these noted leaders among their people, the tribes succumbed easily to reservation conditions. With their inherent sovereign freedom as hostage, too, they retained only hope to stay alive.

An Indian agent's report on the Blackfeet reservation in Montana disclosed the following account:

> 1884—When I entered upon the duties of agent, I found the Indians
> in a deplorable condition. Their supplies had been limited and many

of them were gradually dying of starvation. I visited a large number of their tents and cabins the second day after they had received their weekly rations. . . . All bore marks of suffering from lack of food but the little children seemed to have suffered most . . . [and] that it did not seem possible for them to live long. . . . So great was their destitution that the Indians stripped the bark from the saplings that grow along the creeks and ate the inner portions to appease their gnawing hunger.[33]

As the agent's report demonstrates, inhumane living conditions confronted the Indians. They now depended upon the federal government for daily subsistence due to treaty promises. This was an abhorrent life. Many deaths occurred during this labyrinth of cultural and psychological adjustments with a foreboding uncertainty.

During these ruinous years, Native peoples witnessed whites appropriate their lands in gluttonous quantities. For example, the Sioux (Lakota) Act of 1889 decreased the large reservation by about half of its size and divided the remaining land into five small reservations. This legislative blow humbled the Lakota, threatening the spirituality of the Lakota's heartland—the Black Hills.[34] The Treaty of Fort Laramie of 1868 had earlier carved out the Great Sioux Reservation from a much larger haven of indigenous life.[35]

With the Lakota and other Native nations placed within the institutional reservation system and under impudent control, the government accelerated its civilization program. The Indian Office assigned agents to the reservations with instructions to supervise Indians in a new agrarian lifestyle like white Americans. The government implemented a rigid plan for civilizing the Native peoples despite opposition from some tribal leaders, particularly Plains tribes who wished to continue their annual Sun Dances. In 1878 Congress established Indian police on the reservations. The government recruited the best prospects to become Indian police so that they could serve as role models to other Indians. By 1890 government agents utilized Indian police of 70 officers and 700 privates at fifty-nine agencies.[36]

To help maintain law and order, Secretary of Interior Henry M. Teller introduced the Courts of Indian Offenses in 1893. In an effort to help civilize the Indians, the government restricted the practices of polygamy, gambling, drunkenness, and the Sun Dance. Each court consisted of three judges who adjudicated offenses against the government's program. These court judges could be appointed from ranking officers of the reservation police or three Indians whom the Indian agent selected. The tribunal held the power to impose fines and jail sentences for crimes committed. In the process of preparing the Native peoples for civilization, the court system restricted the practice of Indian religious activities and ceremonies.[37]

Among the Pend Oreilles and Kutenais in Idaho, alcoholism became a serious problem. Chief Ronan stated, "In the days I speak of (early reservation time), my young men could get but very little whiskey—none knew the taste of it but those who hung around your settlements. It is different today! They have acquired the habit and love the influence of whiskey, and in spite of your laws can procure all they can pay for."[38] In the early twentieth century, alcoholism remained a problem on some reservations. John Saul, a Crow Creek Lakota, stated, "We should have a superintendent on the reservation, to take care of the reservation, the rulings and too, . . . much whiskey coming in, womens [sic] and mens [sic], who are drunken, all those should be prohibited, to make a better Indian, if the government wants to, but they don't care, it seems they don't care."[39]

Traditionally, spirituality bonded Native communities together, simultaneously connecting them to the environment. As the government insisted that Indians live increasingly as white Americans during the reservation era, spirituality diminished significantly. As mentioned, the ineffectiveness of medicine men added to the Indians' demise. A tribe's belief in spirituality demonstrated the strength, hope, and optimism of the people. With this ethos in decline, a growing number turned to a new utopian belief—the Ghost Dance.

The aberrant causes leading to this spiritual phenomenon of the late 1800s involved a desire to alleviate the dire reservation conditions. The government did not always deliver promised supplies on time, and poor-quality farmland added to the Indians' frustrating poverty. Government restrictions sabotaged Native life, and a yearning for the natural freedom of the old ways remained alive and well within many communities. Clinging to hope, a need for spiritual revitalization persuaded people to listen to and follow the teaching of Wovoka, a Native prophet from Walker River. The Paiute messiah's earth renewal prophesy prescribed a paragon and return to earlier times without white men.

Life after their forced migrations to the reservations as prisoners of war represented a final stage of the U.S. decolonizing of Indians' traditional cultures. In their eyes, Indians wondered if they were being punished by supernatural forces. Had they failed to heed some prophecy warning of the approaching evil of the white man? Had they violated a law of nature? With their spirits abased, they hoped that conditions would turn for the better; remembering better times, they prayed earnestly. As early as 1869, a Northern Paiute named Wodziwab or Tavibo envisioned a return to the old ways and began teaching the Ghost Dance doctrine. After very little success, years passed until his son Wovoka began teaching the Ghost Dance. In his younger years, the Paiute prophet worked for a rancher, but his personal experience in later years destined Wovoka to become well known as the Indian Messiah sent by ancestral spirits.[40]

The teachings of Wovoka called for revitalizing traditional beliefs and acknowledging the earth's importance. The Ghost Dance doctrine envisioned the earth's rebirth. Wovoka's vision called for his acolytes to dedicate themselves to this belief so that Divine intervention would restore the earth to green tall grass, flowing rivers from resplendent snow-topped mountains, and proliferating buffalo herds. While the Ghost Dance spread among Indians, an entirely different idea was spreading among federal officials. Many officials wanted to divide tribal lands into parcels to be farmed by the Indians. However, the idea of allotment made no sense to Native logic. Individuality ran counter to the Indians' communal way of thinking.

At Standing Rock Agency, the Indian agent and tribal police kept Sitting Bull under guard at his cabin. Correspondent James Creelman visited the noted Lakota leader. Sitting Bull told him,

> The fact of my existence entitled me to exercise any influence I possess. I am satisfied that I was brought in this life for a purpose; otherwise, why am I here? This land belongs to us, for the Great Spirit gave it to us when he put us here. We were free to come and go, and to live in our own way. But white men, who belong to another land, have come upon us, and are forcing us to live according to their ideas. This is an injustice; we have never dreamed of making white men live as we live. The life of white men is slavery. They are prisoners in towns or farms. The life my people want is a life of freedom. I have seen nothing that a white man has, houses or railways or clothing, or food, that is as good as the right to move in the open country and live in our own fashion.[41]

More than two dozen tribes and their communities joined in the belief that the ghosts of dead loved ones would return and the renewed earth would be rid of the white man. Many Lakota joined the ghost dancers, and locals feared that Sitting Bull would seize the opportunity to lead his people again. Agent James McLaughlin talked to the Indian police about arresting Sitting Bull, and some of them resigned. McLaughlin promised pensions to those who might be killed or wounded in the attempt to arrest

Sitting Bull. Bull Head, Red Tomahawk, and forty-one others were willing to follow through in arresting Sitting Bull. However, the legendary warrior had earlier stated his indifference in early December 1890: "I did not start this Ghost Dance, Kicking Bear came here of his own accord. I told my people to go slow, but they were swept into this thing so strong [that] nothing could stop them. I have not joined the sacred dance since I was told to stop."[42] With the arrest of Sitting Bull on December 15, bedlam broke out as other Lakota surrounded the famed leader, and Bull Head and Red Tomahawk escorted him from his cabin. One Lakota shot Bull Head, who turned and fired his revolver into Sitting Bull's chest; in the same moment, Red Tomahawk shot Sitting Bull in the head. The great leader's death did not stop the momentum of Native spirituality that seemed to rise, restoring hope to Indians.

In Indian Territory the Southern Cheyenne, not wanting allotment, protested against the division of their land. Old Crow spoke for the Cheyenne living along the Washita River: "The Great Spirit gave the Indians all the country and never tell [sic] them that they should sell it. . . . See, I am poor. I have no money; I don't want money; money doesn't do an Indian any good. Here is my wealth [pointing to the ground]. Here is all the wealth I want—the only money I know how to keep."[43]

Among the Blackfeet, allotment bifurcated two divisions of thinking. Two Blackfeet factions developed, one composed of truculent mixed bloods led by Malcolm Clark. The other side was led by Three Bears, who protested, "You fellows don't know what land is. The [white] people I saw are just like this water [the ocean]. They flood the country and I am afraid that some of these days that the people will flood our lands and there will be nothing left for us."[44] Simultaneously, Senator Henry Lane of Oregon sharply questioned Bureau of Indian Affairs officials about why they did not consider the needs of the Blackfeet over a long period of time.

As the halls of Congress filled with incessant debate over Indian allotment, many politicians supported it, and others claimed it to be tricky effrontery to obtain more reservation land. This controversial measure proved to be one of the most significant laws of Congress to impact Indians in history—the Dawes Allotment Act of 1887.[45] This landmark legislation reduced the tribal reservations in large portions and attempted to break the Indians' communal life existence. Conceptually, federal policy sought to individualize the tribespeople as landowners like the white yeoman farmers. This bureaucratic view represented a threshold for the American Indian to step over into a different world of civilization where a new life waited to be lived through the sweat of his brow by harvesting his own crops, building his own home for his family, and worshiping with his family in a church. Preserving any part of Native culture was not an option, at least among imperious bureaucrats.

Ironically, many tribes practiced successful agriculture before the allotment movement began in Congress. Evidence of this success was noted in the 1900 Census of Agriculture with the following observations. Traditional agriculturalists included the Pueblo Indian communities in New Mexico, the so-called Five Civilized Tribes in Indian Territory, and herders like the Navajo. The Oneida who were removed to Wisconsin grew gardens to support themselves as they had done traditionally in the upper New York area. A previous nonagricultural group, the Santee Sioux, soon adopted agriculture successfully on reservations in Nebraska, South Dakota, and North Dakota. At the Fort Berthold Reservation in Montana, the Mandan, Arakara, and Gros Ventre continued to practice old agricultural ways that were once supplemented by buffalo hunting. The Sac and Fox, Potawatomi, and Kickapoo continued their previous agricultural ways in Kansas, and the Yakama adopted farming and ranching, including fishing as a part of their new economy in central Washington. The Cour d'Alene established individual farms on their reservation in Idaho. East of the Yakama, Indians on the Spokane and Colville reservations adopted farming with relative ease in Montana.[46]

Successful ranching tribes before allotment included Lakota Sioux at Standing Rock Reservation, Pine Ridge, Lower Brule, Crow Creek, Rosebud, and Fort Berthold. In Montana, the Blackfeet proved to be successful ranchers. The Bannock and Shoshoni developed a cattle industry with relative ease in southern Idaho.[47] Raising livestock came easily to these groups prior to tribal land allotment, but these groups and the success of the farming groups mentioned did not halt the growing momentum for Indian allotment in Congress.

Distributing Indian lands to tribal members was not a novel idea when Secretary of the Interior Carl Schurz adopted it as a part of his Indian policy in 1887. As early as 1633, the General Court of Massachusetts authorized allotments to Indians who lived in a civilized way like English plantation owners. Indians and whites would become neighbors. Civilization and Christianity went hand in hand with allotment. In the early 1800s, some missionaries advocated allotment and preached that if Indians learned to own land, they would improve their livelihood like yeoman farmers and be peaceful during difficult times between the United States and England. Thomas Jefferson's plan for Indians to become farmers convinced Secretary of War William Crawford to recommend allotment for Indians in 1816. President James Monroe and Secretary of War John C. Calhoun supported the Indian allotment idea. By the early 1880s, the issue arose again in Washington. No one there considered asking the Indians what they thought.

Senator Henry Laurens Dawes of Massachusetts, a champion of the Indians' rights, grew angry with the Reverend Dr. Lyman Abbott and others who supported allotment with ulterior reasons. The idea of dividing reservations into parcels of land for Indians to cultivate did not sit well initially with Dawes. Abbott, editor of the *Christian Union* in New York, was a diehard reformer. He remained convinced that the reservations must go and that they prolonged the "Indian problem" of savagery and poverty.[48] To Dawes, Abbott's stubborn stand seemed absurd, as Abbott had never seen a reservation, and knew no more than ten Indians.[49] Furthermore, Abbott and other bureaucrats risked violating treaties made with the tribes, which would be another injustice in the prolonged enmity that the tribes were suffering at the hands of the white man. Dawes reminded his colleagues of the Friends of the Indians, such as the Women's National Indian Association that had petitioned Congress to uphold its treaty obligations to the Indians.[50] Under the leadership of Mary Bonney and Amelia Stone Quinton, the Women's National Indian Association became the staunchest supporters of Indians and their legal rights.

Railroad companies also stood to benefit from Indian allotment, due to their connection with the bill's proponents.[51] Following the first transcontinental railroad established in 1869 at Promontory Summit in Utah, the railroads' attitude toward the passage of the allotment act remained supportive of the Dawes legislation. The railroads needed land grants and land adjacent to the tracks for lumber to make ties. Furthermore, white settlers on Indian surplus land left over from allotments would help the railroad business, as towns would be built. In fact, some argued that the railroad companies were the real beneficiaries of Indian land allotment. The Council Fire, an Indian support organization, printed an article in its June 1885 newsletter asserting that allotment was for the benefit of neither the Indians nor the American people, but for the advantage of ascendant railroad companies. An estimated 23,800,000 Indian acres would be made available to railroads.[52] The railroads did not need to lobby extensively to promote their interests for the allotment bill. They could depend on eastern philanthropists, western land seekers, and others to pressure the bill before Congress.[53] By the end of the allotment era, four transcontinental railroads would cross former Indian lands in the West.

As the momentum for Indian land allotment seemed certain to make the bill into law, Dawes himself joined the effort to produce a less damaging measure for Indians. Dawes realized that he could not stop the allotment momentum among his colleagues, so he tried to exclude some Native groups from discussion by arguing that they were already good farmers. The Dawes legislation carried forward in Congress; the act excluded the Five Civilized Tribes of Indian Territory, as well as the Osage, Miami, Peoria, and Sac and Fox of Indian Territory. Under section 8 of the law, the Seneca Nation of New York was excluded.[54] However, amendments to the Dawes Act in 1898, 1901, and 1903 enabled the allotment of the Five Civilized Tribes in Indian Territory.

On February 8, 1887, Congress passed the Dawes Act, one of the most damaging laws to Native people. It stated:

> Be it enacted . . . , That in all cases where any tribe or band of Indians has been, or shall hereafter be, located upon any reservation created for their use, either by treaty stipulation or by virtue of an act of Congress or executive order setting apart the same for their use, the President of the U.S. be, and he hereby is authorized, whenever in his opinion any reservation or any part thereof of such Indians is advantageous for agricultural and grazing purposes, to cause said reservation, or any part thereof, to be surveyed, or resurveyed if necessary, and to allot the lands in said reservation in severalty to any Indian located thereon in quantities as follows.[55]

The amounts were 160 acres to a head of a household and 80 acres each to single persons and children. The Dawes Commission was set up to establish tribal rolls to carry out allotment and the surveying of tribal lands. Two years later, Congress passed the Nelson Act. This measure led to the allotment of Minnesota Indian lands, primarily involving timberlands.[56] In 1891 Congress passed an amendment to the Dawes Act, affecting other Indian reservations. The amendment altered section 1 of the Dawes Act that authorized the president "in his opinion, to order [any] said reservation surveyed and the land to be allotted to the tribe's members."[57]

In 1894 a paternalistic Congress made leasing restrictions more flexible and permitted any allottees "unable" to work to lease their land for five years to farmers and ranchers and for ten years to miners and businessmen. Newly chosen Secretary of Interior Hoke Smith authorized Indian agents to approve leases, resulting in 295 leases in 1894, 1,287 in 1897, and 2,590 in 1900.[58] The Indian Bureau controlled the leases, and Bureau of Indian

Figure 1.2. Members of the Dawes Commission Henry L. Dawes, S. McKennon and Meredith H. Kidd (left to right) who assigned allotments to members of the Choctaws, Creeks, Chickasaws, Cherokees, and Seminoles. Courtesy of Western History Collections, University of Oklahoma.

Affairs officials negotiated leasing Indian lands to earn revenue to tribes and allottees.

The federal court followed Congress by adding to the momentum to reduce tribal lands in the famed *Lone Wolf v. Hitchcock* case of 1903. In 1892 the Jerome Commission negotiated with the Kiowa for the allotment and cession of their lands, but the Treaty of Medicine Lodge established their reservation, and Article 12 of the agreement required at least three-fourths of all the Kiowa men to approve of any surrendering of land, and they refused. In early October, government officials claimed a majority of the Kiowa agreed to land allotment. This illegal taking of Indian land led to the court case. In this ruling, the Supreme Court established plenary power in Congress of Indian affairs and with the authority to abrogate Indian treaties.[59] In the Indian mind, a treaty represented an agreement of words from the heart. But, the desire for surplus lands from tribal allotments became a driving force for white settlement in Indian Territory.

One person who rose to challenge the allotment process was Chitto Harjo of the Muscogee Creeks in the newly formed Indian Territory. Chitto Harjo, whose name translated to mean Crazy Snake, represented a faction of mostly full-blood Creek traditionalists who wanted the old ways. His loyalist actions represented the sentiment against allotment of tribal lands. Many traditionalists felt the same, and these acolytes joined Harjo and voiced their support to recruit other kinsmen.

Harjo represented those Creeks who believed that traditional values and ancient ceremonial rituals should be maintained. Chitto Harjo was born about 1846 and grew up among the Upper Creeks or Loyal Creeks, who had sided with the North in the American Civil War. Primarily, the Loyal Creeks fought to protect themselves against Confederates, who invaded Indian Territory and the Creek Nation. In an attempt to revive traditionalism against the allotment momentum, Harjo led the Crazy Snake Rebellion. Considered a leader by the traditional system of clans and towns, Chitto Harjo was also known as Wilson Jones. He was a town *mekko* (Creek king) and represented his town as a member of the House of Kings in the Muscogee Creek National Council. As he realized the plenary power of the United States to force allotment onto his people, Harjo led a protest of ninety-four "Snake" followers. They took the name from one of the Creek clans. Harjo gathered the Snakes at Old Hickory stomp ground, six miles south of Henryetta, Oklahoma, and twelve miles east of Tiger Mountain.

A special Senate investigating committee surveyed the old Indian Territory to evaluate Indian progress, and officials agreed to hear the dissident

Creeks. On November 23, 1906, the Senate committee held a hearing at the Elks' Lodge Hall in Tulsa. A large number of people gathered at the hearing, and many supported Harjo and his Snakes. Chitto Harjo spoke against the allotment program. With his hat in his hands, his face full of sorrow, he stood before the committee and spoke about the treaties and his beliefs:

> Now I hear the Government is cutting up my land [and] giving it away to other people. . . . It can't be so for it is not the treaty. These people who are they? They have no right to this land. It never was given to them. It was given to me and my people and we paid for it with our land back in Alabama. The black and white people have no right to it. Then how can it be that the Government is doing this. . . . It wouldn't be justice. I am informed and believe it to be true that some citizens of the United States have title to land that was given to my fathers and my people by the government. If it was given to me, what right has the United States to take it from me without first asking my consent?[60]

Alarmed about the meeting of the Snakes, local officials believed that more Indians would join the traditionalist bastion, and they petitioned Governor C.N. Haskell for immediate protection on March 27, 1909.[61] Before help arrived, the Snakes killed three deputies. The U.S. Eighth Cavalry, federal marshals, and troops from Oklahoma City, and the towns of Shawnee, Muskogee, Durant, and Chandler were ordered to the area to suppress Harjo and the Snakes, plus an estimated sixty-five Creek freedmen (freed African American slaves) who had joined Chitto Harjo.[62] The Snakes fought the troops and marshals in two small exchanges of gunfire near Seminole and Wewoka. Choctaw traditionalists, who also opposed allotments, began to organize themselves, and federal officials had to use force to defeat them as well.[63]

Panicking authorities called for more outside help to deal with the bellicose Snakes. The authorities feared that all of the traditionalists would join Harjo, but not all did. One Creek traditionalist recalled,

> The Snakes were against the new treaty and wanted to stay with the old treaty. That was the cause of the Snake uprising. [Chief Pleasant] Porter made a complaint, and the government sent soldiers in here. The soldiers didn't know whom to get nor where to find them, so they had some Indians to go and help them. I rode with them about a month, and we gathered a whole lot from Wetumka, Henryetta, Sasakwa, Okemah,

and the last at Eufaula. When they were all rounded up they were loaded in a boxcar and sent to Muskogee to the jail. The soldiers were of the cavalry. We camped around and graded them before they were sent to Muskogee. Soldiers, big tents, horses, and we Indians made quite a camp. The Snakes didn't like me to this day for my part in it.[64]

Many full-blood Cherokees joined a secret society called the "Pin Indians" for the insignia they wore in their opposition to allotment. The membership of the Pins reached approximately 5,000 full-bloods under Cherokee leader Red Bird Smith, and they officially called themselves the Keetoowah Society. Undoubtedly the Native patriotism of Chitto Harjo influenced Indians of other tribes. One Cherokee recalled, "The Cherokees among the full-bloods protested the [allotment] law. . . . The government of the United States had broken so many treaties with the Cherokees that they at that time did not have anything to do with this law. They were called the Nighthawks."[65]

Born on July 19, 1850, Red Bird Smith was a traditionalist and called for his followers to walk the "White Path," a balance that stood for harmony in keeping the sacred fires of the Green Corn Dance to preserve the old ways. This movement resulted in an estimated 12,000 Cherokee allotments going unclaimed. Smith opposed allotment of tribal lands until he died in 1918. The Keetoowahs' anti-allotment feelings spread to the Muscogee, Choctaw, and Chickasaw. Eufaula Harjo, a Creek traditionalist, helped Smith to organize other Creeks, Cherokees, and supporters from the Chickasaws and Choctaws to join them. With members from all four tribes, they changed their name to the Four Mothers Society. Trying to find a solution to get out of their allotments, the Four Mothers Society sent a delegation to Washington to try to convince the federal officials to change federal plans to allot the lands of the Choctaws, Chickasaws, Creeks, and Cherokees. Federal officials refused the delegation's request for Four Mothers members to sell their allotted lands to anyone interested. In return, the Four Mothers wanted to take the proceeds from the sales to purchase land in Mexico. The Four Mothers Society had made an agreement with Mexico to buy land, but the U.S. government rejected this proposal.[66]

The Dawes amendments affecting the Five Civilized Tribes caused profound changes among the tribal nations and their communities, with a land grab occurring. The Cherokee owned 19,500,000 acres in 1891, but eight years later they had only 146,598 acres.[67] On March 4, 1907, the U.S. government closed the tribal rolls, and many people disputed the tribal memberships.[68]

Figure 1.3. Jackson Barnett, Muscogee Creek, wealthiest American Indian in the 1920s, due to oil. Courtesy of Western History Collections, University of Oklahoma.

Tribal land allotment led to much fraud and corruption committed against Indian allottees. This exploitation has been well documented in historian Angie Debo's classic, *And Still the Waters Run: The Betrayal of the Five Civilized Tribes*.[69] Shrewd politicians, watchful settlers, and impudent opportunists of all kinds exploited and even murdered Indians for the control and ownership of their allotted lands. The worst case was that of Jackson Barnett, a full-blood Creek. In 1842 along the Canadian River in Creek country of Oklahoma, Jackson Barnett was born to Siah and Thlesophile Barnett at Buzzard Hill. Barnett had a half-brother named Tecumseh. The brothers grew up during arduous times. Jackson Barnett received an allotment of 160 acres. He is listed on the Dawes Rolls as number 4524, 48 years of age from the Tuckabatchee town of the Muscogee Creek Nation.[70] A traditional full-blood, he joined the Snake faction at some point. Later he moved on his allotment outside of Henryetta, and his life changed. Jackson Barnett obtained his riches in 1912 when an oil company discovered oil beneath his otherwise worthless allotted land that was said to be so rocky that it could not feed a jackrabbit.[71]

In the same year, a field clerk negotiated to lease Jackson Barnett's allotted land to an oil company. A competing oil company also wanted Barnett's land for drilling rights. The competition proved too much for Barnett to handle, and a judge declared him legally "incompetent." The Okmulgee County court appointed him a "guardian" named Carl J. O'Hornett. The two oil companies negotiated an agreement, and the drilling began on Barnett's land located in the Cushing oil field. Both companies paid royalties to the Creek agency to be invested in Liberty Bonds or paid to O'Hornett for Barnett's welfare. Becoming wealthier each day, Jackson Barnett continued his humble life, living near Henryetta.[72]

The rest of the Jackson Barnett story is a tale of woe and corruption. One Annie Laurie Lowe, a black-haired big-city prostitute, married the full-blood twice, in Missouri and in Kansas, for his wealth and bilked him until his death. Barnett's sad story is the worst of many oil-rich Indians whose allotted land by happenstance contained vast amounts of oil below ground.[73]

The allotment years made things even worse on reservations for American Indians. After the devastation of allotment, traditional Indian life ended, and it had to be replaced if Native people were to survive. As Thomas Leforge described in his memoirs,

The Indians as a tribal whole were not the same. Their lands had been allotted in part and some of the former exclusive residence of the Crows had been sold and was occupied by bustling white men. These irreverent newcomers were plowing up and utterly ruining thousands of acres of good grazing-land! They were paying no heed whatever to the fact that this, only a few years before, had been the home of the deer, the elk, and the buffalo. To complete the desecration, a railroad now had its thundering trains tearing along through the very heart of the old-time rich hunting-grounds.[74]

At the turn of the twentieth century, reservation adjustments meant drastic changes for Indian people. They had to come to accept reservations, and by and large they did. Wooden Leg of the Cheyenne, who lived well into the twentieth century, described this adjustment. He lamented,

> It is comfortable to live in peace on the reservation. It is pleasant to be situated where I can sleep soundly every night, without fear that my horses may be stolen or that myself or my friends may be crept upon and killed. But I like to think about the old times, when every man had to be brave. I wish I could live again through some of the past days when it was the first thought of every prospering Indian to send out the call: "Hoh-oh-oh-oh, friends: Come. Come. Come. I have plenty of buffalo meat. I have coffee. I have sugar. I have tobacco. Come, friends, feast and smoke with me."[75]

The struggle of Indians on reservations after 1900 would help to redefine their postreservation heritage and identity. As they gained increasing control over their communities, they would rise from the ashes of conditions of poverty and poor health. But it would take time, and hardship persisted. World War I interrupted the continuity of life on reservations, although reservationhood would still remain separate from other kinds of Indian life, such as the emergence of the urban Indian and the increase of mixed-blood identity. Ironically, many of the 10,000 Indian men who fought for the United States in the Great War were not citizens of the United States. Congress rushed the Act of 1919 through in time to declare that all honorably discharged Indians from World War I would be automatically granted U.S. citizenship.[76]

In the remaining decades of the twentieth century, the reservation Indian retained the mindset of his and her ancestors. The vast openness of reservations continued to be a luxury that urban Indians and quasi-assimilated American Indians would not experience as they drew closer to the mainstream culture. Maintaining a connection through physical contact with the earth remains important to Indians. Of the earth, it was and remains important for them to maintain this connection. This was the way of the past that had always sustained them. And they feel that this needs to be continued, not just for their own sake, but for the future of their young people as well.

The openness of brown-green earth and blue sky created a home space in the Indian mindset. This vastness of the sky and landscape permeated the Native peoples' souls, creating a spiritual worldview. Through Indian eyes, the view reveals that people are one with the earth. Indian inherent sovereign ways had never known such restriction of life until the U.S. government forced the indigenous to live on reservations. This inherent sovereign freedom was their right to live as they wished. In the developing modern West, Native peoples struggled to regain their right to live as they wish against a strong federal paternalism exercised by Indian agents, the Bureau of Indian Affairs, and Congress.

The reservation represented a place that reservation Indians could call homeland, and it was theirs. This was their domain, although reduced in size from their original hunting areas and original territories via treaties. Enduring reservation life represented the strength of the people, and it remained an integral part of them as they made these chastised areas into new homelands. Constant pressure from westward settlement forced continuous encroachments in the American West. Urbanization of eastern cities and untamed growth influenced the West. The sunset of the nineteenth century closed the ages of Thomas Jefferson and Andrew Jackson and the age of Sitting Bull.

CHAPTER TWO

Missionaries and Boarding Schools

Education as a Tool

I can never forget the confusion and pain I one day underwent in a reading class. . . . A paragraph in the reading book was selected for the experiment. . . . My time came and I made no errors. However, upon the teacher's question, "Are you sure that you have made no error?" I, of course, tried again, reading just as I had the first time. But again she said, "Are you sure?" So the third and fourth times I read, receiving no comment from her. For the fifth time I stood and read. Even for the sixth and seventh times I read. I began to tremble and I could not see my words plainly. I was terribly hurt and mystified. But for the eighth and ninth times I read. I was growing more terrible. Still the teacher gave no sign of approval, so I read for the tenth time! I started on the paragraph for the eleventh time, but before I was through, everything before me went black and I sat down thoroughly cowed and humiliated for the first time in my life and in front of the whole class! Never as long as I live shall I forget my futile attempts to fathom the reason of this teacher's attitude. Out on the school grounds at recess I could not join in the games and play. I was full of foolish fears.

LUTHER STANDING BEAR (LAKOTA), CA. 1932

Numerous other Indian boys and girls had experiences similar to those of Luther Standing Bear. Confused and scared, taken away from their parents, and feeling lonely, they faced the strange white man's world. In 1877 a young Santee boy named O-hi-yes-a walked up the few stairs and stared at the wooden door that he had seen other Indian children enter after a bell had rung. He had seen such wooden houses, but he had never been inside of one. With his hand shaking, he reached for the handle on the door. He hesitated, pushed his long black hair aside with his hand, looking far over his shoulder toward where he had come from and where his grandmother remained. He had traveled far from his home and his people. Unsure what to do, he summoned his courage and pushed the door to the boarding school open, slipped in quietly, and sat on a back bench. From that moment onward, his life and those of many other Indian children who entered such classrooms changed forever. No one would have expected that this young Native lad would become Dr. Charles Alexander Eastman, graduate of Dartmouth College and Boston University School of Medicine. Most Indian children did not fare as well. Furthermore, Eastman voluntarily chose to attend the boarding school, whereas the majority of Native kids were seized from their families and forced to attend various institutions.

Native logic conflicted with the white teachers' linear instruction in boarding schools. Additionally, Christian ideology contradicted Native perception; the two mindsets viewed the world differently. This incongruence had been evident since the arrival of Columbus, leading to the incessant effort to colonize the minds of Native youth. Native ethos composed of tribal values and circular philosophy conflicted with the Christian linear approach of Western knowledge imposed in Indian boarding schools. In the same light, the typical approach to studying and writing Indian history has been from the Western paradigm. Equally important is the indigenous paradigm in the history of Indian-white relations. It is in this indigenous paradigm that the full complexity of the American Indian mind can be realized.

The general boarding school idea intended to change the lives of Indian youth so they could assimilate white ways. Dartmouth College, founded in 1769, originally started as a school for Indians. Even earlier, Harvard University, founded in 1636, devoted a part of its efforts to schooling Indian youth, as did William and Mary College, founded in 1693. In Indiana, the University of Notre Dame, founded in 1842, included the education of local Potawatomi Indians as a part of its mission in return for land that the school received north of South Bend. Early educators viewed Native youth as illiterate, born of savage ways, and culturally inferior to American students. Educating Indians represented the first important step toward civilization for the indigenous population.[1]

Western education has a long legacy among Indians, and the school is a powerful institutional memory. From 1870 to 1934 an estimated five hundred boarding, mission, and day schools existed.[2] Elders recalled having their hair cut short and their Native clothes burned and being punished for speaking their tribal language. Still, the Indian kids persisted in speaking their languages secretly to each other. The schools introduced alien life to them, without asking most, thrusting them into a brainwashing colonization process. Upon arrival, students were informed by school officials that they had to become like white men and women. In order to have any hope for the future, they had to acculturate by learning to read, write, and speak English on a daily basis. School officials and the U.S. government deemed that Indian youths had to undergo a radical transformation.[3] They said nothing about what was to be lost—the ways of one's people.

The drastic disjuncture between Native logic, meaning how Indians conceptualized, and the Western logic demanded in schools perplexed Indian youth and turned their lives upside down. How Indian people think and how non-Indians think are very different. In fact, Allen Chuck Ross, a Native scholar, theorized that Native people are right brain oriented, with strong characteristics of nonlinearity, creativity, spirituality, holism, perception, imagination, dance, art, music, and feeling. Linear thinkers are left brain oriented and are logical, scientific, analytical, and mathematical. They read left to right, and writing is often a strong trait.[4] Ross's view of the human brain's hemispheric halves divides Indians and whites. Ross hypothesized that Indians were more artistic and able to process abstract thought much more freely than mainstream Americans, who were more scientific and stressed empirical evidence. The boarding school experience proved that Native youth could learn to think like mainstream Westerners, although they were not initially inclined to do so.

Through the centuries, Native people had learned to think in a reciprocal relationship with their natural surroundings. Based on tribal traditions, Indian people think in an inclusive manner, drawing in their environmental influences and tribal heritages. This inclusion involves all things that are known to the Native world and that might be. In this way, all things are related and belong in what has been called a natural democracy. In a natural democracy, all things are recognized to exist based on mutual respect for everything and acknowledgment of all things.[5] All of this is Native logic.

Traditionally, Indian people learned via four different ways. Typically, one learned from observations, like an apprentice from a master craftsman. A young boy might watch his uncle make a bow by carving and shaping the bow from bois d'arc or some other kind of appropriate wood, soaking it in water to create the arc, and stringing sinew from the muscle tissues of an animal into a cord for the bow. Through observing the construction of several bows, the young hunter learned the art of bow making. Then he would be able to pass this knowledge to the next generation of relatives. By observation, this knowledge was carried onward. More broadly, as a student of nature and the environment, an Indian person observed happenings around himself or herself. This kind of visual logic developed a historical consciousness of how things happened in the natural world and are meant to be.

At unpredicted times, metaphysical occurrences presented information or knowledge to a person in an experiential manner. Like Moses and the burning bush of God narrated in the book of Exodus in the Bible, visions and dreams bestowed knowledge on Indian people. Such aberrations are important to Native people, and these visual sightings become a part of tribal knowledge. Typically, a person might request the assistance of a wise elder or medicine person to interpret the ethereal experience.

The experiential way, or learning on one's own through trial and error and learning from one's own efforts, was a third means of obtaining knowledge. From a basis of known knowledge, a person tried a new trail or path, or decided to do things differently, which added new experiences. Wisdom usually followed from collective experiences. Sometimes forced into a situation, for example, a hunter had to be resourceful to find his own way out of a predicament, such as finding a new route back to camp. This personal quest of obtaining knowledge through experiences is like being self-taught.

The fourth method of obtaining knowledge involved oral tradition. Elders shared myths, legends, songs, and parables. They shared this information and knowledge as a means of passing time to entertain young ones or as a part of the coming-of-age ceremonies. Sharing stories was a means of passing information and knowledge, thus teaching the next generation, while perpetuating Native logic and enhancing indigenous ethos. This cycle of oral tradition informed tribal members about community heroes, famed battles, crises, and prophecies. In spite of the boarding school training, oral tradition remained within the communities throughout Indian Country as long as someone remembered the stories.

Since community values and the environment influenced the Indian mind, Native people naturally learned to think in a holistic manner as a community member and contextualized the nonhuman and the human community in the same space.[6] Recognition of the importance of relationships augmented the significance of kinship. In their ethos, Native people humanized all things and valued things most important to them. By calling a mountain or a river by a name, for example, Indians created a community of their natural surroundings like a kinship network. This Indian thinking often extended to all things in the universe. Each important piece of knowledge represented an integral part of a story that recorded the details, served a purpose, and highlighted certain characters and a place. This indigenous contextualizing connected knowledge in a home space that can be called a bioregion.[7] Such a region consisted of the community and natural world with the people respecting and depending on the earth's resources of the area. Where the oral tradition served Native people sufficiently, the American mainstream developed differently, emphasizing pen and paper.

In white schools, education and learning was assumed to operate in one direction, whereas the Indian experience has centered on learning from another culture in a venue of cross-cultural thinking. At the same time, many non-Indian people have become a part of tribal communities to learn quid pro quo, although this is not normally discussed in any forum. Even anthropologists and ethnologists who learned about Native ways by visiting and living in Indian communities approached their experiences from a Western paradigm, and they still do. Learning is only perceived to be meaningful in the Western-minded way, a biased ethnocentrism that substantiates the subaltern—the voiceless minority.

John Riley, a superintendent of an Indian school in 1885, described the necessary transformation of the Indian child as "a prickly thorn that must be made to bear roses; he is a twig bent out of the perpendicular, and he must be straightened so that the tree will stand erect, inclining in no way; he is a vessel of bronze that must be made bright by constant rubbing."[8] The incongruence of the Indian mind and the white man's mind encouraged the latter to strive to change Native logic to an altered state. In order to accomplish this task, English had to be taught, and only English. To say the least, Native students had to change how they thought and how they saw things, meaning to forsake their Native perception. For the majority of Indian students, this did not happen. Instead, the Native youth incorporated the white perspective into their own perceptions. The ability to include another way of perceiving their surroundings made the Indian students bicultural, with a dual vision of the world. After leaving school, most former students reached a crossroads at which they had to choose which vision appealed to them.

Over the years, Native people have been impressed with the white man's educational system in the pre- and post-boarding school era. This intrigue compelled Native communities to send their youth to eastern schools during the early 1800s and start their own tribal schools during the mid-nineteenth century. Charles Eastman, a Santee Sioux, followed his father's wish to attend a boarding school, and he did this without any sense of how much his life would change. After advancing through a series of boarding schools, he graduated from Dartmouth College and medical school, becoming a doctor in 1890. Carlos Montezuma (Yavapai) experienced a similar fate, also becoming a medical doctor a year before the infamous Wounded Knee massacre took place.

In Indian Territory, the Choctaw started Fort Coffee Academy in 1843 and initiated several public schools, including Elliott Mission School, and opened Spencer Academy and New Hope Academy in 1844. The Seminole started a mission school at Oak Ridge, Oklahoma, in 1844. The Chickasaw started Bloomfield Academy in 1852, as well as McKendree Academy and Manual Labor Academy about the same time. Chickasaw schools included Wapanucka Institute, Collins Institute (later called Colbert Academy), and Burney Institute, a Presbyterian-supported school.[9] The Cherokee male and female seminaries are examples of tribal educational goals during the late 1800s. The Muscogee Creeks started Nuyaka Mission School and a boarding school of their own that became known as Bacone College, named after Almon C. Bacone, a missionary.[10] In other parts of Indian Territory, government agency schools such as Seneca Indian School, Chilocco, and Fort Sill Indian School opened for operation in the late 1800s.[11] The movement to educated Indian youth in the West continued, and by the 1860, forty-eight day schools existed near Indian reservations so that the children could return to their families every afternoon.[12] In ten years, the federal government replaced the day school with more boarding schools as the most effective means for educating Indian children. The government believed that family influences distracted the children and that they needed to be fully immersed in boarding schools to become completely civilized and educated.

The Indian Bureau assigned the Indian agent in charge to operate the schools on a daily basis, and later a superintendent was put in this position. Normally, the schools had four primary grades and four advanced grades, with half of the school day focusing on English and basic academic subjects, and the other half concentrating on vocational training such as stock raising and blacksmithing. Instructors and older boys taught male students carpentry and harness making. For girls, teaching focused on domestic responsibilities such as laundry, cooking, and sewing. School officials required the students to be educated to read and write, as well as learn vocational skills, while daily maintaining the school by cleaning floors, doing laundry, raising livestock, repairing buildings, and whatever else that was needed.

Figure 2.1. Carlos Montezuma (Yavaipai) became a medical doctor in 1889 and member of the Society of American Indians. Courtesy of the Hayden Arizona Collection.

The funding of Indian education grew proportionally with the accelerated policy of trying to assimilate indigenous people into white ways of life. In 1877, Congress appropriated $20,000 for Indian education and increased this in large amounts yearly, so that $2,936,080 was spent in 1900. Bureau of Indian Affairs officials counted Indian student enrollment to be 3,598 for 1877, and that number increased to 21,568 by 1900.[13]

Congress proved willing to fund Indian education, but this also required having sufficient enrollment at schools. The government allowed school officials to remove Indian children from their families and put them in schools. Indian youth taken from their families became common practice. In doing so, school officials and Indian agents severed the connection between Indian youth and their elders. This meant disconnecting the traditional pathways for the transmission of knowledge. Once such connections were severed, it was expected that Native youth would begin to think like white men. But this did not always happen. Rather, Indian students incorporated this new thinking but did not dismiss their Native ethos.

The decision of Indian families to send their children to boarding schools tested the love of the parents, especially when they had been recently at war with whites. One Cheyenne man lamented this difficult, emotional experience. He surrendered his child to Agent John D. Miles and explained that "the Whites killed my father and mother at Sand Creek and last summer took my only brother and sent him away from us. My heart had felt bad towards whites many years but today I have thrown that feeling all away. Take my child as proof of my sincerity."[14]

At the decision-making crossroads, other Native parents welcomed schools. This enormous decision presented itself to almost all Native parents and their communities. The Flatheads of western Montana desired a school for their boys. Upon arriving at the reservation, Indian agent David Shanahan found himself sought out by Chief Arlee, who said, "There is a school at the mission seventeen miles away but it is of no benefit to the tribe. They educate girls there but no boys. We want our boys educated, not our girls. We want a school at the agency according to our treaty."[15]

Richard Henry Pratt has been popularly noted as the major figure for starting Indian boarding schools when he opened the doors of Carlisle Indian Industrial School in Pennsylvania.[16] Born in New York in 1840, Pratt had only a common school education, which ended at thirteen years of age. His father was murdered while returning from the gold fields in California. During the Civil War, Pratt served as a cavalry officer, and when his postwar business failed, he reentered the army as a second lieutenant.

The military assigned him to the Tenth Cavalry, an African-American regiment that he led in fighting Indians on the southern plains in 1868–1869 and in the Red River War of 1874–1875.[17]

While fighting Comanche, Cheyenne, Arapaho, and Kiowa in the Red River Wars, Captain Pratt became familiar with Indians. In April 1875, his next assignment entailed escorting seventy-two Indian prisoners to Fort Marion in Florida. At the fort, he allowed the Indians to guard themselves since they had nowhere to escape and they were so far from home. Pratt then thought that the Indian youth could become educated. He escorted several Indian children to Hampton Institute, an African American boarding school in Virginia. From this visit, Pratt became convinced that the Indian youth could become educated and that they needed their own school for his experiment.

Pratt believed it was both essential and possible for American Indian youth to change. He stated,

> It is a great mistake to think that the Indian is born an inevitable savage. He is born a blank, like the rest of us. Left in the surroundings of savagery, he grows to possess a savage language, superstition, and life. We, left in the surroundings of civilization, grow to possess a civilized language, life, and purpose. Transfer the infant white to the savage surroundings, he will grow to posses a savage language, superstition and habit. Transfer the savage-born infant to the surroundings of civilization, and he will grow to possess a civilized language and habit.[18]

In 1879 Pratt petitioned Secretary of Interior Carl Schurz several times, and the badgered official finally gave authorization to move the potential Indian students to a site to begin the Indian education experiment. Carlisle, Pennsylvania, became the residence for a new Indian school. Dilapidated barracks had to be repaired, and Pratt had to hunt down potential teachers. More than any other Indian boarding school, Carlisle has had the greatest impact in Native history. The ascendancy of Carlisle Indian Industrial School epitomized the institutionalization of young Indian minds. Other schools soon followed Pratt's military-like school with its rigid instruction. An estimated 1,200 Indian students regularly attended Carlisle from 1879 to 1918, when the federal government needed the school buildings due to World War I. For thirty-nine years, an impressive number of alumni attended Carlisle, although less than eight percent graduated.[19]

Luther Standing Bear, an eleven-year-old Lakota, described his changed life traveling to the East to be at Carlisle. He said,

At once I was thrust into an alien world, into an environment as different from the one into which I had been born as it is possible to imagine, to remake myself, if I could, into the likeness of the invader. . . . On our way to school we saw many white people, more than we ever dreamed existed, and the manner in which they acted when they saw us quite indicated their opinion of us. It was only about three years after the Custer battle, and the general opinion was that the Plains people merely infested the earth as nuisances, and our being there simply evidenced misjudgment on the part of Wakan Tanka [the Creator in the Lakota religion]. Whenever our train stopped at the railway stations, it was met by great numbers of white people who came to gaze upon the little Indian "savages." . . . In my mind I often recall that scene–eighty-odd blanketed boys and girls marching down the street surrounded by a jeering unsympathetic people whose only emotions were those of hate and fear; the conquerors looking upon the conquered. And no more understanding us than if we had suddenly been dropped from the moon.[20]

The initial curriculum involved vocational training and civilization practices. Furthermore, the pedagogy of instruction consisted of cruel discipline. Strict rules had to be obeyed. All of this was preached to the Indian students in English, forcing Native students to learn by total immersion without regard for the damages from losing their traditional cultures.

Carlisle pg 54

Pratt devised his outing system as a way to provide students with a practical education after they completed their training. The program involved placing the students with white rural families near the school for three years. The federal government paid the host family $50 a year for the student's medical care and clothing. For the student, he or she learned the agricultural lifestyle from the farmer and his family. Ideally, the host family served as a model of civilization and the Native youth became a part of it.

Boarding school life proved to be demanding and hard on the students. Ted Lunderman (Brule Sioux) attended Rosebud Boarding School. He remarked,

Them was [sic] rough days then, boy. We went to school half day and then we worked half day, kind of vocational. Well, they gave us six weeks to work [at] one place and then six weeks [at] another place [un]til, keep a going [un]til where we started from. Carpenter work and farm work and we worked at the dairy for six weeks and then we worked at the kitchen six weeks, boys building six weeks, and then we got back to where we started like engineers.[21]

At many schools the students wore cadet wool uniforms, marching to class at the ringing of a bell or at a teacher's command like at the Citadel or U.S. Military Academy at West Point. A typical schedule until lunch was as follows:

5:30	Rising bell
5:30–6:00	Dress and report for athletics
6:00	Warning bell
6:00–6:20	Setting-up exercise
6:20–6:25	Roll call
6:25	Breakfast bell; raise flag
625–6:30	Line up; march to dining hall
6:30–7:00	Breakfast
7:00–7:25	Care of rooms
7:15	Sick call; bugle
7:25	Work bell
7:25–7:30	Line up; details report
7:30–8:00	Industrial instruction
8:00–8:15	Academic division
8:15–8:25	Prepare for school
8:25	School bell or bugle
8:25–8:30	Line up; march to school building
8:30	School application industrial division
10:00–10:15	Recess; five minutes breathing exercise
11:30	Recall bell; all departments
11:30–11:45	Recreation; details return to quarters
11:45	Warning bell
11:45–11:55	Prepare for dinner
11:55–12:00	Line up; inspection march to dining room
12:00–12:30	Dinner

The afternoon had every activity scheduled so that the students knew what to expect and where they would be. In this rigid manner, many Native youths learned the white man's time, according to a clock. Bells and bugles regulated their new lives.

Lunderman described the school to be military oriented, complete with stuffy uniforms. He said, "We had uniforms. We had to drill every morning before breakfast and in the evenings. It went over pretty good. Yeah, because when we went in the service, why, then we knew how to drill and everything. [It] helped us a lot while the other kids didn't know first thing about drill[ing]."[22] George Dennison, a Navajo, attended Inter-mountian Indian School in Brigham City, Utah, with about 2,300 Navajo kids ranging from seven to twenty-three or twenty-four years old. He recalled that the school had five-year, seven-year, and ten-year programs as an elementary and vocational school. He missed his home and family, stating, "Oh boy! Was I ever homesick! Regimented. From 6:00 o'clock in the morning until you go to bed at night, everything was regimented. You get up, you do this, you do that, do that, so I begin makin' plans to run away again. I took off seven times in that spring and I was successful four times."[23]

In order to keep their doors open for business, the early boarding schools had to maintain a stable Indian enrollment. School officials trav-eled to the reservations to kidnap Indian children in order to put them into the schools. Numbers rose and fell, and were even falsified, as many Indian children ran away, trying to find their way home. It would not be presumptuous to say that students went AWOL at all Indian boarding schools. Some children never made it home, but even when they did, officials found them and returned them to the schools. Some died from the journey during wintertime.

Indian students at mission and boarding schools received new names that their instructors could easily remember. Tribal names were foreign to the white instructors, and they forced the students to take Christian first names from the Bible such as Luke, John, and Peter. Peter MacDonald, chairperson of the Navajo Nation in the 1970s, recalled that a trader had told his father about a famous person in the Bible named Peter. His father discussed the name with his mother, and they gave him the first name of Peter. A teacher could not pronounce his last name, "Hoshkaisith" in the Navajo language, so he was called "MacDonald" from the nursery rhyme "Old MacDonald Had a Farm."[24]

The greatest problem for Native students at night was loneliness—missing their loved ones. After many days, the loneliness would pass and the youths would adjust and often continued to rebel. Lunderman said, "It [loneliness] did [begin] from the start, but we got used to it. Yeah, they used to run away all the time when they get lickings. They used to use some regular, oh I don't know, tugs off a harness on us. Yeah, we used to really catch it. [They] brought you back and make you wear a dress and shave you bald head[ed] and you walked the campus every weekend. That was our punishment. Oh, we'd run away and come up town, Mission [South Dakota], and they'd catch us and we'd be punished for a couple weekends."[25]

The initial encounter with the white man's boarding school shocked Indian children. Charles Eastman describes his first day at Flandreau Boarding School in South Dakota as a harrowing experience.

> By this time we had reached the second crossing of the river, on whose bank stood the little mission school. Thirty or forty Indian children stood about, curiously watching the newcomer [me] as we came up the steep bank. I realized for the first time that I was an object of curiosity, and it was not a pleasant feeling. On the other hand, I was considerably interested in the strange appearance of these school-children. . . . The hair of all the boys was cut short, and, in spite of the evidence of great effort to keep it down, it stood erect like porcupine quills. . . . When the teacher spoke to me, I had not the slightest idea what he meant, so I did not trouble myself to make any demonstration for fear of giving offense. . . . He then gave some unintelligible directions, and, to my great surprise, the pupils in turn held their books open and talked the talk of a strange people. . . . I had seen nothing thus far to prove to me the good of civilization.[26]

Only English was spoken as the official language at the schools. If Indian students did speak their Native languages, school officials washed their mouths out with soap, struck their hands with rulers, assigned them extra chores, and other punishments. Francis La Flesche, an Omaha, described his schoolboy years at the Presbyterian mission school on his reservation in the 1860s: "Like the grown folk, we youngsters were fond of companionship and of talking. In making our gamesticks and in our play, we chattered incessantly of the things that occupied our minds, and we thought it a hardship when we were obliged [to speak English] in conversation." La Flesche added, "When we entered the Mission School, . . . we encountered a rule that prohibited the use of our own language, which rule was rigidly enforced with a hickory rod, so that the new-comer, . . . was obliged to go about like a little dummy until he had learned to express himself in English."[27]

One former student said that he and other students spoke their tribal language when no one else was around. He recalled, "They wouldn't let us [speak tribal languages], but we always sneak around and speak it. . . . A lot of them couldn't even speak a word of English when they came there. Well, they were with boys that talk English to them all the time, you know, other boys that knew how to speak English, why, they got them to talk to them all the time, speak English. They caught on pretty quick though."[28]

As the last decades of the nineteenth century reached their end, Native people increasingly recognized that they would need to learn the ways of the whites in order to survive. On one occasion in 1886, school officials invited the noted Lakota leader Sitting Bull to visit the industrial boarding school at Devil's Lake to observe a class taught by priest Jerome Hunt. Given a chance to say something to the students, the great leader said,

> My dear grandchildren: All of you folks are my relatives, because I am a Lakota and so are they. I was glad to hear that the Black Robes had given you this school where you can learn to read, write and make things. You are living in a new path. When I was your age, things were entirely different. I had no teachers but my parents and relatives. They are dead and gone now, and I am left alone. It will be the same for you. Your parents are aging and will die some day, leaving you alone. So it is for you to make something of yourselves, and this can only be done while you are young. . . . Now I often pick up papers and books with all kinds of pictures and marks on them, but I cannot understand them as a white person does. They have a way of communicating by the use of written symbols and figures; but before, they could do that, they had to have an understanding among themselves. You are learning that, and I was very much pleased to hear you reading. In the future your business dealings with the whites are gong to be very hard, and it behooves you to learn well what you are taught here. But that is not all. We older people need you. In our dealing with the white men, we are just the same as blind men, because we do not understand them. We need you to help us understand what the white men are up to.[29]

Native youth responded with their own strategies to survive boarding schools. They learned English yet continued to speak their Native language to other tribal members late at night or when school officials could not see them. They used their imaginative ways to remain connected to their traditions and even secretly held dances when they could.

No doubt some lost hope, and others became vulnerable to the mistreatment at boarding schools. Far away from home, many Indian children cried at night for their families, and many never saw their mothers and fathers again. Some students were even sexually abused by their instructors. Helen Sekaquaptewa wrote in her autobiography that as a student at Phoenix Indian School, a male teacher regularly "called one of the girls to stand by him at the desk and look on the book with him." The teacher proceeded to "fondle this girl as she tried to read to the class."[30] In the 1970s, Indians in South Dakota reported to the Bureau of Indian Affairs that well over a hundred physical and sexual abuse incidents occurred involving Catholic teachers harming their children in schools.[31] Other kinds of abuse and problems occurred at schools. At Santa Fe Indian Day School, male and female students consuming alcohol ran into trouble with school officials.[32] Terrance F. Leonard, who was born on the Salt River Pima-Maricopa Reservation in Arizona, attended a boarding school for Indians. He recalled that "the boarding school student can be the loneliest person on earth. Even to make it through the year takes a lot of guts."[33]

Irregular attendance occurred with high dropout rates. Indian children were criticized for "returning to the blanket," meaning failure and regression to old ways upon returning to the reservation. Yet these children preferred their tribal ways to those of boarding schools. School officials felt frustrated that after graduation many students did not use their education to secure a job and join the mainstream, although others did. A lack of motivation existed among students, and they resigned themselves to a general defeatism. Others defied authority, not fully realizing that the white man's ways of learning would become their future tools for rebuilding their tribal communities and governments. School officials believed that education for American Indians was the key for survival in the twentieth century, not realizing that it would be more than that.

In 1891 a presidential executive order placed Indian school personnel, including superintendents and agency physicians, under the classified civil service. The measure scrutinized those individuals in charge of reservation schools. This resulted in employees being removed from the kinds of spoils systems that were in place in which the only qualification for reservation employment was a stated intent to work among Indians. The year before, the commissioner of Indian affairs replaced the position of Indian agent with school superintendent, but the implementation of this long process took fifteen years. Meanwhile, mission schools remained at work, and missionaries proselytized to American Indians. Jim Whitewolf, a Kiowa Apache, recalled when Christianity came to his people's reservation in western Oklahoma during the late 1800s when his tribal land was still a part of Indian Territory. As he explained,

> I remember that, before the country opened up, there was a Kiowa man named Joshua who went to school. When he came back, he preached against the Indian ways. Some of the Apaches went and listened. He said that the Indian ways belonged to the Devil. He preached that

Figure 2.2. Indian students in uniforms leave Phoenix Indian School dining hall through separate doorways. Courtesy of the Heard Museum.

> Christ had made everything in the world for us and that we should believe in Him. Some of the Apache and Kiowa began to believe in it. He said to quit marrying more than one wife or we would go to hell. He preached against peyote, too.[34]

Wooden Leg, a warrior among the Northern Cheyenne, described the influence of Christianity and its impact on him personally. He recalled,

> I was baptized by the priest at the Tongue River mission when I was almost fifty years old. My wife and our two daughters were baptized too. I think the white people pray to the same Great Medicine we do in our old Cheyenne way. I do not go often to the church, but I go sometimes. I think the white church people are good, but I do not believe all of the stories they tell about what happened a long time ago. The way they tell us, all of the good people in the old times were white people. I am glad to have the white man churches among us, but I feel more satisfied when I make prayers in the way I was taught to make them. My heart is much more contented when I sit alone with my medicine pipe and talk with the Great Medicine about whatever may be troubling me.[35]

The struggle between the old medicine ways of Indians and conversion to Christianity still continues. In the late nineteenth century and early decades of the twentieth century, Indians were introduced to various Christian denominations. Jim Whitewolf seemed somewhat confused by the many white man's religions. He recalled,

> We didn't know the difference between Baptists, Methodists, and Presbyterians. They were just church people to us. All except the Catholics. We knew them by their robes, and because they gave us rosaries with beads on them. The Indians said the others were no good because all they wanted was money and gave us nothing. It seems to me that the Catholics quit coming around later, but the others kept on. . . . [An Indian woman] said that Catholics were good because they gave them things, but the others made you pay for your religion. I guess the old people knew that when they prayed in the Indian way they didn't have to give anybody any money, and that was why they disliked the churches that asked for money."[36]

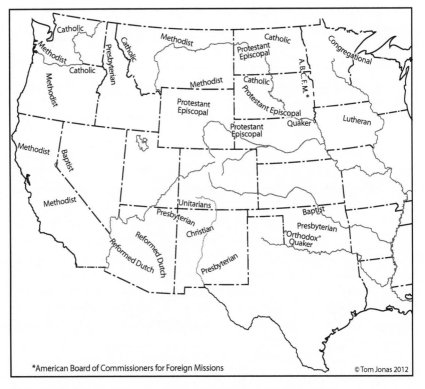

Map 2. Christian religions in Indian Country from 1870 to 1934.

The Bible did not make an immediate impact on some Indians, because they did not really know what it was. Whitewolf recalled, "Sometimes when the missionaries gave the Indians Bibles, they liked them because the paper was thin, and they could use the pages to roll cigarettes. They didn't know the Bible contained good words for them."[37] The introduction of Christianity to Indian students by missionaries caused confusion among Indian children, even into their young adult life. For example, Soaring Eagle, a twenty-six-year-old warrior of the Cheyennes, described this effect:

> It is good to go to church. When I was at my home, I did not know about church. When I was at home, I did not wear good clothes. My hair was long. I know now to spell and read a little, and will know more. When I go home, I hope to sit down and sing God's hymns . . . at home I did not know who Jesus was, I loved to hunt, shoot and sleep on Sundays like other days, but the Bible God's book has told me it was wrong. I now look up to Jesus who has been so good to me and pray to him to forgive all my past sins and make me his child.[38]

The Bible remains as the most published book in history and a popular book among Indians. As more Native people understood the Christian God, they believed Him to be the same Creator of their indigenous world. Through Christianity, Indians learned about white ways and how to read and write.

By the late nineteenth century, an off-reservation boarding school movement had burgeoned. By 1900 no less than twenty-four federal boarding schools had opened. Following the establishment of Carlisle Indian Industrial School in Pennsylvania in 1879, Chemawa Indian School opened in 1880 in Salem, Oregon. Four years later, four more schools opened: Chilocco, Oklahoma; Genoa, Nebraska; Albuquerque, New Mexico, and Haskell in Lawrence, Kansas. A school opened in Grand Junction, Colorado, in 1886. In 1890 three schools started in Santa Fe, Mexico; Fort Mojave, Arizona; and Carson, Nevada. Two schools opened their doors in Pierre, South Dakota, and Phoenix, Arizona, in 1891. Two more began operating at Fort Lewis, Colorado, and Fort Shaw, Montana. Local officials established four schools in 1893 at Flandreau, South Dakota; Pipestone, Minnesota; Mount Pleasant, Michigan; and Tomah, Wisconsin. Two more opened in 1895 at Wittenberg, Wisconsin, and Greenville, California, and another at Morris, Minnesota, in 1897. In 1898 three schools operated at Chamberlain, South Dakota; Fort Bidwell, California; and Rapid City, South Dakota.[39]

At boarding schools, illnesses periodically struck, resulting in many Native students getting sick and even dying. Following World War I, the flu was a major killer at Rosebud, Haskell, and other schools. Ted Lunderman recalled, "Let's see, I was there right after the flu that was in 1918 when we had that flu going around [at the boarding school]. We were lucky though. We only lost about two kids out of that [epidemic]."[40] Survival depended upon the spiritual strength of the students.

The resilience of the Native youth at schools enabled a continuance in learning, establishing an exigency—education—for the future. Dr. John Tippeconnic III was born in 1943 in Oklahoma, and he is Cherokee and Comanche. He was a product of boarding schools, and so was his father. He described his father's advocacy for education:

> My father stressed education and I think he stressed this because he was a product of the government's educational policy. He too went to the bureau boarding school and the approach then was assimilation into the mainstream as soon as possible. The school reflected this. Anything Indian was downgraded, was not to be done in the school setting. . . . They [administrators] aimed at "De-Indianizing" the students. . . . He [John's father] had a lot of unpleasant memories of that process.[41]

Figure 2.3. Graves of children who attended Haskell. Courtesy of the author.

John's surroundings were difficult, especially the non-Indian people. John remarked,

> In Oklahoma, just being an Indian, at times I felt discriminated against. Sometimes it was quite open. One example, in a small town in Oklahoma a couple of friends and I were refused service in a restaurant. Being away from the family was hard. Our family had close relationships and it was bad going away to boarding schools. Once I graduated from college and was working as a professional, people did not look at me just for what I could do. Perhaps they looked at me as what I represented as "an Indian." In order to be accepted I had to perform at or beyond the level of others. I had to prove myself.[42]

The memories of boarding school life remained etched in the minds of many Indian people. Most memories were about the difficult times, but some times were good.

At Carlisle Indian Industrial School, the Indian student athletes excelled. Louis Tewanima, a Hopi, was an excellent long-distance runner in track. Tewanima, who came from Shungopavi, Second Mesa of the Hopi people, weighed only 110 pounds, but the coach found that he ran like a deer. Coach Glenn Scobey "Pop" Warner would become famous leading the Carlisle Indian players to victories in football, and he later moved on to coach football at Stanford University.[43]

Tewanima defeated all challengers in the ten- and fifteen-mile races. Pop Warner continued to describe the talent of Tewanima. He said, "Once I took him to New York for a 10-mile competition in Madison Square Garden, and after he looked at the track, he turned to me and said: 'Me afraid get mixed up go round and round. You tell me front man and I get him.'" Warner described the event as a challenging race for Tewanima. He said, "About the middle of the race I managed to catch his eye and point out the runners who led him, and one by one he picked them up, finally finishing in a burst of speed that established a new world's record."[44]

Jim Thorpe, the famous Sac and Fox athlete, remembered his teammate in 1940. Thorpe stated, "I recall the day Carlisle had a dual meet with Lafayette College. They had 20 men on their track team. We had only three Indians, Frank Mount Pleasant, Louis Tewanima, and myself." Thorpe continued with a smile, "A big crowd turned out for the meet. Mount Pleasant and I won the sprints. Tewanima and I took the middle-distance events. And I was lucky enough to win most of the field contests. THE THREE OF US LICKED LAFAYETTE."[45]

Later, Tewanima, Thorpe, and Mount Pleasant defeated a talented Syracuse University team in another dual meet. Tewanima and Thorpe were so fast on the track that both athletes were selected for the Olympic team without having to undergo national trials—an extraordinary honor demonstrating a lot of confidence placed in the two Indian athletes. Tewanima and Thorpe participated in the Olympics in Stockholm, Sweden, in 1912. The "Flying Finn," Hannes Kolehmainen, who was considered the greatest distance runner in the world, took first place in the demanding 10,000-meter race, and Tewanima finished in second place. Tewanima's extraordinary performance at the Olympics in Sweden stood as a record for fifty-two years as the best time for any American in that event. Years later, U.S. Marine Billy Mills, a Lakota, eclipsed Tewanima's record at Tokyo in 1964.[46]

Jim Thorpe attended Carlisle two different times and during that brief span he brought a considerable amount of media attention to the small Indian school in Pennsylvania.[47] "The Greatest Athlete in the World" is the way King Gustav V of Sweden described James Francis Thorpe. The king of Sweden was referring to America's greatest all-round athlete, a champion at football and track and a baseball star. Jim Thorpe was another one of Pop Warner's products.[48] Interestingly, many football players since then have played their early years in Pop Warner football leagues for boys, which started in 1934, and they might not know of Warner's legacy with Carlisle.

James Francis Thorpe, born in small-town Prague, Oklahoma, on May 28, 1888, played football at Carlisle Indian School in 1907 and 1908. He left Carlisle to play baseball for the Fayetteville and Rocky Mount teams of the Eastern Carolina League. For his playing, Thorpe received $15 every week. In 1911 Thorpe returned to school at Carlisle. In the greatest football game he ever played, he scored a touchdown and dropkicked field goals of 23, 45, 37, and 48 yards to help Carlisle Indian School beat Harvard College 18 to 15. The next season Thorpe scored 25 touchdowns and 198 points for Carlisle in 1912.[49]

As mentioned before, the Olympic Games were held in Sweden that year. Thorpe performed spectacularly, winning both the decathlon, consisting of ten events, and pentathlon, consisting of five events. Unfortunately, his medals were taken away because he played (like a lot of athletes did at the time) semi-professional ball for a summer baseball team. A newspaper reporter discovered that Thorpe had received money for playing baseball, making him a professional athlete before the Olympics.[50] Stripped of his gold medals in the Olympics, Thorpe tried to get them back. In a letter to the Amateur Athletic Union, he wrote, "I hope I will be partly excused by the fact that I was simply an Indian schoolboy and I did not know all about such things."[51] Ironically, Thorpe went into the Major Leagues the year after the Olympics. He played in the outfield for the New York Giants. He also played for the Cincinnati Redlegs and for the Boston Braves. In all, Thorpe played professional baseball from 1913 through 1919, batting .252 in 289 games.[52]

Jim Thorpe also excelled in professional football. He played for the Canton Bulldogs, Cleveland Browns, Oorang Indians from Marion, Ohio, and New York Giants. His last game was with the Chicago Cardinals in 1929. As football was developing as a new professional sport, Thorpe was named the first president of the American Professional Football Association in 1920. The association became today's National Football League, making him the first NFL president. In 1950 the Associated Press voted Thorpe the best athlete of the first half of the twentieth century. Thorpe was also named to both college and professional football halls of fame.[53]

On March 28, 1953, Jim Thorpe died at his home in Lomita, California. To commemorate the famous Indian athlete, Mauch Chunk, a town in Pennsylvania, changed its name to Jim Thorpe in 1954.[54] Senator Quentin Burdick of North Dakota and Senator Charles Percy of Illinois were convinced to look into the issue of Jim Thorpe's amateur status during the years 1901–1912. The U.S. Olympic Committee and the Amateur Athletic Union reevaluated Thorpe's case, although the final decision was made by the International Olympic Committee in Switzerland. President Gerald Ford added his support in writing to the committee, "I hope the Committee will consider this request and act with a sense of equity in the light of history and of the contribution that Jim Thorpe has made to the world of sport." Thorpe's three daughters, Grace, Charlotte, and Gail, actively lobbied for the return of the Olympic medals to their father.[55] Their efforts and the time and energy of others succeeded in the return of the two gold medals to the Thorpe family in 1982. In April 2013, a federal judge ruled that Jim Thorpe's body be reburied in Oklahoma.

Jim Thorpe was a unique case among Native youth attending boarding schools. While many did and continue to excel in sports, the majority of Indian students struggled to succeed in their studies. Jim Whitewolf described his days at the Kiowa boarding school in 1891:

> In school they watched you pretty closely to see how you behaved and how you caught on to things. When they thought you knew how, they would give you different jobs to do. . . . I didn't like the jobs they gave

me, but I knew that if I did them all right they wouldn't bother me. But if I didn't, they might whip me. I kept that first job three weeks. They would change you over to a new job every few weeks. My next was to help wait on the table I sat at during meals. At each table there were two boys, one at each end, who had to go to the kitchen and bring the food. Then when everybody had eaten, those who did that work for the different tables got together to eat. . . . My next job was in the kitchen where they threw away the garbage. . . . All of these jobs were in addition to going to school all day. Later on I worked half a day and went to school half a day.[56]

Whitewolf's many jobs helped the school to be self-sustaining as boys and girls worked as they learned.

The introduction to boarding school life remained a cultural shock even in the late twentieth century. As one contemporary Native person described,

The summer I got out of junior high I started to experiment with drinking and marijuana. I started getting into a lot of trouble. My mom finally told me she thought I should go to boarding school and get straightened up. I agreed because I was afraid I was going to end up another statistic on the rez, like maybe get killed or something because of the drinking and stuff. . . . I still remember the day because it was the saddest day of my life. I had never been away from my family, and I remember getting on the bus behind the police station, and my mom and sister were crying. I was really sad, and my mom was crying so hard she had to turn her back towards me. It felt like I was being kicked away and abandoned. I felt lost. My first few days at school, I just laid in my room and thought about home. Then, as I started to know more people, I really got used to the school and actually started to like it, kind of like a whole new world. It was pretty much effort on my part to make me stay at Chemawa [Salem, Oregon].[57]

The majority of boarding school experiences were hard lessons for Indian youth and such memories have become a part of many personal histories of Indians.

Another young Native person stated, "A lot of kids have it hard. They don't really learn well out of books. I know I don't learn that well out of books, but I learned enough to pass the course. But if they show you something, so your eyes can see it, then you can really learn it. Indian students in general can learn better like that."[58] It seemed that the Native youth who struggled were close to their tribal traditions. As a result, their way of logic was different from that of the mainstream and the textbooks that they were assigned to use. This has been the struggle for Indian students since the inception of boarding schools, and they struggle in mainstream schools as well. As Indian students became more accustomed to mainstream life and adopted white values, they succeeded in graduating from high school and obtaining higher education in colleges and universities.

At this date, American Indians are in the fourth and fifth generations of enrollment at boarding schools. Ironically, boarding schools have become a positive experience in the lives of many Native youth, and elders remember good times at Haskell, Sherman Institute, and other schools. Many times there were also bad memories. They endured. The students' success has led to enrollment in junior colleges, universities, or at one of the nearly forty current tribal colleges in the United States and in Canada. Resilience meant being strong to not only endure but also to take from the white man's world what was needed to build an Indian future. To remain in control of their own lives has been the mantra of Native people.

The important conclusion is that Native people have gained control over their own educational needs and are working with boarding school officials throughout Indian Country. The mainstream tool of education, like the horse, became a part of Native people as they realized its importance in dealing with the rest of the country at all levels. Education was a vital key to their future. Simultaneously, they added Christianity to their Native beliefs, although many dropped their traditional ways. Little did the churches know at the time that many Indians would embrace Christianity and start their own churches—First Indian Baptist, First Indian Methodist, and so on. Such Indian churches are located throughout Indian Country in the modern West. Little did the white churches know that some converted Indians would become electrifying fire-and-brimstone preachers at the pulpit. Some Native groups formed communities around churches, while many Christian Indians continued to practice the old ceremonial ways. In fact, many non-Indians attend Indian churches and are members. Indians saw no conflict and decided to practice both, as well as adopting the white man's education, to navigate the course of Indian-white relations. In fact, this adaptation became a sine qua non for survival of their identity and for sustaining hope for the future.

CHAPTER THREE

The Indian New Deal and Tribal Governments

Flexibility of Adaptation

This was the new deal for the Indians. Nobody really understood it. They knew that they were going to have to vote on whether they wanted it or not. Of course, it was very difficult many times to get things accurately to them. It was a matter of communication—very difficult because they would interpret in many ways the minor things. They had all kinds of stories going about the new program. Many were against, and many were for it. From what they understood of it, it was very difficult because it was such a radical change from their way of life.

ALFRED DUBRAY, LAKOTA, CA. 1960

What was it like, even today, to be a part of a tribal community, that is, being on the inside? Being a member of a tribal community is like living two lives, one being a member according to kinship relations of some sort, and the other being a citizen of the United States and living in your town, city, or residing in a rural area. Indian and non-Indian are different realities with different sets of values, and they possess their own histories. For Indians who are close to their traditions, they are on the inside of their communities.

On reservations and in rural areas, tribal communities continued to function in a parallel existence to the mainstream. Communal coherence held people together in spite of the allotment policy attempting to individualize Native people. This infrastructural cohesiveness based on kinship enabled traditional governments to persist and simultaneously transition into another state of Native authority. This "flexibility of adaptation" was the heart of indigenous communities, to endure and include change. Indeed, flexible adaptation had sustained the Indians through centuries, long before allotment or the Indian New Deal.

Outside of Indian Country, fecund technologies, including the auto-mobile, interchangeable parts, and the radio, rapidly created a modern American West in the early decades of the twentieth century. Following World War I, the country entered into a false sense of prosperity that has been called the "Roaring Twenties," but only a small percentage of the nation actually enjoyed this euphoria. Following the laissez-faire capital-ism of the early 1920s, the rich got richer and those below the standard of living plodded along toward an unexpected forthcoming disaster caused by a collapsed national economy.

At this time, Indian Commissioner Charles Burke assembled a team of experts to conduct a national survey of Indian conditions. The Meriam Report, published in 1928, shocked federal officials. The report consisted of a task force led by Lewis Meriam, a staff member of the Institute for Government Research, with nine technical specialists in law, economic conditions, health, education, agriculture, family life, and urban commu-nities and one Indian person serving as an adviser. The task force surveyed living conditions for seven months on ninety-five reservations.[1] Among this ten-member team, Henry Roe Cloud, an Omaha and graduate of Yale University, served on the task force and helped produce the Meriam Re-port. He sought to encourage educational authorities to understand Native people rather than teaching through force and discipline.[2] This ubiqui-tous fieldwork produced a final report of 23,069 pages definitively proving that the Dawes Allotment Act of 1887 had failed. Overall, Indians did not become successful individual landowners and assimilate into the Ameri-can mainstream like bureaucrats had predicted. The alarming conditions on reservations compelled the Bureau of Indian Affairs (BIA) to change federal Indian policy as soon as it could. But the BIA moved forward with desultory reform for the next few years.

While the nation found glory and experimented with new social values in the 1920s, the majority of Indians remained poor; the oil-rich Osages were an exception, including some Creek families like Berryhill, Rich-ards, Deer, and Fixico in Oklahoma. In South Dakota, Oliver Eastman, a Sioux Wahpeton, recalled that "there was nothing for the Indians in 1920, there was nothing . . . for the Indians. We had to survive."[3]

In 1928 roughly 55 percent of the Indians had a per capita income of less than $200 per year, and only 2 percent had incomes greater than $500 per year. Another study in 1933 conducted by the Civil Works Administra-tion found that 49 percent of Indians on allotted reservations were landless and that the per capita value of those lands remaining in Indian hands was approximately $800. Living under the trust relationship, Indian welfare continued to decline under the guidance of the new commissioner of the BIA, Charles J. Rhoads, who served from 1929 until 1933. A Quaker from Georgetown, Pennsylvania, and a devoted member of the Society of Friends, Rhoads held membership in the Indian Rights Association. Prior to working for the government, he was active in banking and religious activities.[4]

During his brief administration, Commissioner Rhoads succeeded in acquiring a limited amount of additional lands for tribes who needed it to sustain their people. Under President Herbert Hoover's "rugged individualism" philosophy, Rhoads believed only those Indians who could apply the Republican laissez-faire philosophy would become self-sufficient. He tried to reorganize irrigation projects to improve the tribes' agricultural economies and attempted to eliminate loans from the government, which obligated the tribes to pay back all funds. Rhoads attempted to strengthen programs in education and health, two areas that concerned him the most as the Indian problem proliferated. In addition, he wanted to improve the BIA's personnel by appointing competent and concerned individuals who were sensitive to Indian exigencies. His philosophy stressed individualizing Indians in preparation for assimilation into the mainstream society.[5] However, the idea of individuality ran counter to Native stick-to-itiveness values that emphasized the importance of community. As Rhoads attempted to ameliorate Indian livelihood, the entire country slipped into an unpredicted epoch.

On October 29, 1929, Black Tuesday made history in America and caused the world to change. On this infamous date, stocks immediately lost 13 percent of their value. The crash on Wall Street replaced general prosperity with nationwide financial failure. Ironically, for the majority of Indians, nothing had changed much. The vast majority of Indians remained poor, although the Osages and some oil-rich Native people like Jackson Barnett, dubbed the richest Indian in the world, and a small number of Creeks and Seminoles enjoyed bizarre prosperity. The rest of Indian Country remained stagnated in third-world economic conditions and languished in poor health. Things could only get better.

Federal policy under Charles Rhoads attempted to determine the direction of tribes' self-sustainability. In the process, the federal government would assume a lesser role in Indians' lives. As a part of the policy philosophy, Secretary of Interior Ray Wilbur advocated the transfer of federal responsibilities to states. Wilbur also suggested accelerating programs of reform and supported the Swing-Johnson Bill when it was introduced before Congress in 1930. The bill requested the interior secretary to con-

tract with state agencies for providing state services of health and education to Indians, but it died in the House of Representatives.[6] Gaining new
momentum, the Swing-Johnson bill was opposed only by the Eastern
Association on Indian Affairs and Mrs. Joseph Lyndon Smith, a very influential member. The association had supported the Pueblo communities
in regaining their land and believed that the communities were ill prepared for such legislation.[7] Secretary Wilbur disagreed. Wilbur believed
that within twenty-five years the BIA could be abolished, as there would
be no need for it.

Another bill that would allow tribes more self-direction soon gained
attention. The BIA drafted the Leavitt Bill, H.R. 7826. The measure remained on the floor of Congress for periodic discussion for four months
and became law on July 1, 1932. It sought to improve tribal lands that
were related to irrigation. The Interior Secretary also had the right to
adjust or eliminate debts against individual Indians or tribes due to certain circumstances not under their control.[8] In support of the Leavitt
measure, Congress passed the Indian Irrigation Act on January 26, 1933.
This law authorized the Interior Secretary to defer payment on construction costs involving irrigation projects supervised by the Bureau of
Indian Affairs until problems were resolved among all those parties
involved.[9]

Familiar problems continued to plague Indian Country. For example,
Indian health continued to be a major concern for Commissioner Rhoads.
In a report to the President, he stated that 140 physicians worked in Indian
health, including 15 specialists in eye, nose, and throat disorders. More
than 400 field nurses covered most rural communities. A total of 96 hospitals existed with a total bed capacity of 3,600 patients. Congress authorized another six hospitals to be built. Responding to these services, more
than 37,000 Indians received treatment during 1929.[10]

In Native reality, medicine makers were hard pressed to cure their sick
tribal members. Their ancient cures that had always worked failed in the
face of white man's illnesses. New cures had to be found from herbs and
plants. Going to government hospitals was the alternative, thus testing the
people's faith in Native medicine making versus trying the white man's
health treatment.

In spite of government efforts, conditions for Indians turned worse in
1931. During the summer a drought and swarms of grasshoppers devoured
crops in Nebraska, North and South Dakota, and eastern Montana. Starting in November, the Red Cross contributed $192,260 over several months.
The U.S. Army, called upon by the BIA, sent fifty-five train cars full

of surplus supplies, consisting of overcoats, jackets, gloves, wool trousers, underwear, shirts, socks, shoes, and blankets. Working during the winter months, the Army distributed approximately 6,190,000 pounds of flour and 5,500,000 pounds of crushed wheat for stock feeding. The western states did not escape nature's wrath. In the Southwest, an unprecedented series of storms pummeled New Mexico and Arizona during November and persisted until January. Hazardous roads forced an airplane drop of 30,000 pounds of food to the Navajos, whose reservation was mostly engulfed by a large blanket of snow.[11] Freezing cold gripped the Southwest. Although difficult to imagine, the living conditions on reservations and in rural communities had taken another despairing turn for the worse. Declining hope threatened the resilience of the people.

The commissioner's annual report disclosed that the total Indian population represented 320,454 persons, who lived predominantly in four states in the West—Oklahoma, New Mexico, Arizona, and South Dakota—comprising 199,388 persons or 62.2 percent of the total Indian population.[12] These weather-fragile areas possessed the largest indigenous communities, and they existed in some of the most difficult terrain and challenging climatic conditions. A desolate landscape colored Indian Country.

Commissioner Rhoads found his job difficult to perform under the micromanaging Interior Secretary Wilbur. Rhoads tried to conduct his business, but Wilbur's ideals for Indian reform usurped his efforts. An experienced business executive with administrative abilities, Rhoads did not possess an important ingredient: cultural acumen about Indians and their lifeways. In fact, he had no practical ideas on how to work with Indians, and the intricacies of Indian affairs perplexed him.

Politically, the Depression produced an unpredicted transition in the presidency from Republican to Democrat when the American people elected Franklin Delano Roosevelt in 1932. A savior needed, the United States pinned its hopes on FDR. In Oklahoma, a very large percentage of the Indians went out to publicly rally support for Roosevelt. On May 15, 1932, the tribes selected their own delegates to represent them, and they organized at the famous 101 Ranch in western Oklahoma to lobby votes for Roosevelt.[13] Major reform measures were needed to rid the country of notorious Hoovervilles, as some economically depressed areas were worse than Indian communities, if this could be imagined—most brothers did not have a dime to spare. The FDR administration's optimistic agenda for national improvement included a plan for a better livelihood for Indian Americans. Everyone needed hope, thought FDR: "When you get to the end of your rope, tie a knot and hang on."[14]

People had new expectations of the Democratic administration. FDR represented liberal thinking with heart, and Indians seemed destined for a better future while Roosevelt remained in the White House. But the immediate question that concerned Indians was who would become the next Commissioner of Indian Affairs. First the new president would select a secretary of interior, and then followed a new commissioner of Indian affairs. FDR selected Harold Ickes, a progressive Republican from Pennsylvania with a law degree, as the new secretary of the Department of Interior. The bipartisan-thinking Roosevelt believed that Ickes's appointment would appease undecided voters, and he needed public approval.

The candidates for Commissioner included Senators Sam G. Bratton, Burton Wheeler, Harry Mitchell, and Reuben Perry.[15] All participated in Indian reform but were affiliated with the Republican Party. The previous commissioner, Charles Rhoads, stood a fair chance of being reappointed, and Assistant Commissioner J. Henry Scattergood also gathered sufficient support to be considered a serious candidate. Ickes narrowed the list down to three candidates—Lewis Meriam of the Institute for Government Research; Nathan Marigold, a New York lawyer who served as legal adviser to the Pueblos; and John Collier, president of the American Indian Defense Association (AIDA).[16] The same association petitioned FDR to select the right person to save the Indians from cultural, political, and economic destruction. Naturally, the AIDA championed John Collier as its clear choice.

One meaningful Indian response for commissioner came from the All Pueblo Council. The council sent a delegation to Washington to endorse Collier as the new commissioner. On various occasions, Collier had helped the Pueblo communities, and he had earned their respect. His bond with the Pueblo groups produced a reciprocation of Pueblo support for him. Collier had great respect for Pueblo people since he first visited Taos and referred to their community as a "Red Atlantis." He admired their communal work as a whole, based on traditional values, and realized that their *longue durée* history had recorded many triumphs over tragedies.

Secretary Harold Ickes proved to be a New Dealer. Progressive minded, Ickes was a reformer and a member on the board of directors for the AIDA[17] and thus knew Collier very well. Ickes's wife, Anna, had also heard about John Collier as a champion of Indian interests, and she lobbied her husband that he would be the right person for the job. Convinced about Collier, Ickes chose him and leaned toward William Zimmerman, Jr., as the assistant commissioner. The new commissioner appointed his own men, many of whom had served in the AIDA. They included Ward Shepard, Walter V. Woehlke, and Jay B. Nash.[18]

In spite of the skepticism toward him from Congress, Collier brought a fresh attitude to the BIA, and its agenda would be totally different while he held this office. In his work with the AIDA, Collier had antagonized some people due to his singular belief in Indian interests. He believed in fighting for Indian rights and their religious ceremonies, which ran counter to the work among the tribes by missionaries. His support of American Indian concerns called for action, and his views of reform demanded immediate results.

From Atlanta, Georgia, and educated at Columbia University, Collier was the son of a prominent banker and former mayor. As the FDR administration introduced the New Deal programs for the betterment of American people, Commissioner Collier outlined an aggressive reorganization of tribal governments. At the same time, something had to be done about the horrible squalor on reservations. On the last day of March 1933, Reverend Dr. Dirk Lay, who had lived on the Pima Reservation for sixteen years as a missionary, described the destitute situation there. He disclosed to Collier that in one township, which constituted a third of the tribe, one-fourth of the Pimas had died of starvation in the last four and a half years. This fatality rendered "ACUTE CONDITION OF UTTER HOPE-LESSNESS AND HEARTBREAK."[19]

Collier had lived among the Pueblos in the southwest; he admired and knew their culture thoroughly. His annual report for 1933 revealed his liberal and vigorous approach: "If we can relieve the Indian of the unrealistic and fatal allotment system, if we can provide him with land and the means to work the land; if, through group organization and tribal incorporation, we can give him a real share in the management of his own affairs, he can develop normally in his own natural environment."[20]

Collier's plan to reform Indian conditions began to take shape. This aggressive approach would later become known as the Indian New Deal. Programs included reform measures that proved valuable to Indian progress during the 1930s as the nation struggled to rise from its knees. For example, the Indian Timber Contracts Act of March 4, 1933, permitted the interior secretary, with the consent of Indians involved, to modify the terms of uncompleted contracts of timber sales. A similar provision was made with respect to allotted timber, and the modified agreements stressed the preference for Indian labor.[21]

Figure 3.1. Navajo Council Chairman Henry Taliman (left) and Bureau of Indian Affairs Commissioner John Collier (right). Courtesy of the Navajo Nation Museum, Window Rock, Arizona.

On June 16, 1933, the National Industrial Recovery Act initiated public works projects. Indians worked on Public Works Administration projects, building schools, hospitals, libraries. The new legislation supplied jobs for people out of work, some of whom were Indians. Three days later the Emergency Appropriation Act of 1934 established the Civilian Conservation

Corps (CCC). Collier pushed for Indian participation in the CCC, and the director, Dr. Jay B. Nash, responded with an Indian Division with $5,875,000. Nash's staff assigned Indians jobs in seventy-two work camps in fifteen western states. Plans for Indian work included building roads in reservation forests for fire control, constructing storage dams to prevent erosion, and erecting fences and wells in the states of Arizona, Oklahoma, Montana, New Mexico, South Dakota, and Washington. For their work, the program paid Indian enrollees a salary of $30 per month, a handsome sum for people who had been trying to scrape by.[22] Hunger compelled the Indians to adapt, leave homes, enter the government labor force, and return home with checks to purchase food for their families.

During these enterprising years Collier published *Indians at Work,* a small informative magazine that publicized American Indian progress. In summarizing the CCC program, the commissioner reported that the Indian CCC program affected seventy-one reservations. In New York on the Onondaga Reservation, Indian boys working for the National Youth Administration cut down trees, shaped logs, and developed a summer camp for children. Dams and irrigation projects were constructed, and the Indian workers built and maintained 7,000 miles of telephone lines and more than 1,000 bridges and operated twenty-five Indian CCC camps.[23] In Arizona, 60 percent of the Tohono O'odham job incomes came from this program.[24] Harold Schunk, a Yankton Sioux and a BIA superintendent for many years, commented: "This gave the Indian the opportunity to go to work. I actually knew a great many fellows who had never had a steady job."[25]

Collier advocated numerous reform measures to help American Indians. His most successful measure proved to be the Indian Reorganization Act (IRA). President Roosevelt signed this pivotal measure on June 18, 1934, and it became the heart of Collier's Indian New Deal. Introduced as the Wheeler-Howard Bill in the House, the combined efforts of William Zimmerman, Nathan Marigold, and Felix Cohen produced the original draft. Surely none at the time realized that the IRA would set the foundation for present-day tribal governments. BIA wisdom divided the bill into four sections, and in total it proved exceptionally long, forty-eight pages.[26] Representative Edgar Howard sponsored the bill in the House, and it passed 258 to 88. Senator Burton Wheeler followed, introducing the bill in the Senate.[27] The IRA became the high point of Indian reform during the New Deal legislation and halted the previous land allotment policy. The preamble described the IRA as follows: "An Act to conserve and develop Indian lands and resources; to extend to Indians the right to form business and other organizations; to establish a credit system for Indians; to grant certain rights of home rule to Indians; to provide for vocational education for Indians; and for other purposes."[28]

Certainly Collier was a reformer, a rogue one indeed; he was his own Indian New Dealer. The early 1930s brought hope with new Indian legislation being considered in Congress. Anything new was better than the crushing poverty that the Great Depression wrought. Congress entertained one of the most radical bills in the history of American Indians by restoring tribal communities. As Robert Morrison, a Lakota, remembered,

> In the year of 1930 [1934] when the bill of the Howard and Wheeler Act was in action, the people of the Rosebud, also of the Pine Ridge, were all excited about the New Deal that was coming up. At the time why we had Indians that were promoting for the bill, [we] thought that it would be alright [*sic*] to take the bill, and that we'd be better off. And the promoters of it at that time was [*sic*] Tony Roubideaux and John Crazy Bull, Felix Crazy Bull, Charles Brooks, who was the Chief Clerk of the Rosebud office.

Morrison recalled distrustful confusion surrounded the provisions of the bill:

> There were minor people that were trying to encourage other people to better themselves. There were a lot of, many things, that was said, and so it came to time, in about the year after when it came up for the vote of the people. The voting, there was quite a voting problem there. They used a system there that, so it would pass the voting. It seems to me like it wasn't the majority of population. I think it was just $\frac{1}{3}$ of the people that voted on that. . . . Every community in our, on the Rosebud reservation had to act on it. But we acted on it wrong in the beginning.[29]

The loan provision caused further confusion as everyone thought they would get one. Issues of competency and tribal membership exacerbated communal dissension as officials sought to determine who might be eligible for IRA assistance.

Richard LaRoche, a Brule Sioux, recalled the discussion surrounding the IRA many years ago. As he explained,

Well, I was just a young boy, but I can remember it [IRA]. My father was on the council. There was quite a little, you know. I think the vote, I think at the time was pretty close, but the tribe did accept the Wheeler-Howard Act. . . . It was mostly the old timers wanted to hang on to the old ways. Then at the time there was a good many promises that the government had made to the people that they hadn't kept. . . . Everybody carried a pair of soles in his hip pocket made out of cardboard, you know, and then when that old one wore out in his shoe, why he'd just sit down and take out a cardboard sole and put it in and that was in '34. So, naturally the people were grasping at any kind of a deal that they could get.[30]

Many years later Alfred Dubray, a Lakota, recalled his people being nonplused over the IRA. Commissioner Collier visited the reservation and sent his officers to convince Dubray and his community to accept the IRA. Dubray was undecided. More important, he did not fully understand the Wheeler-Howard Act. Many of his suspicious kinsmen called it another white man's trick. Others, many mixed-bloods, fell under Collier's persuasion and wanted the provisions of the law to help their people, but mainly themselves. Alfred believed that the most serious problem was the bickering and arguments among his people that Collier and his law had caused. No one wanted to be told what to do by a white man, and the government had been doing this for too many years.

The IRA proved to be prickly, confusing, and controversial among the Lakota. Dan Clark, a Crow Creek Lakota, recalled, "Full bloods [were] the ones against it [IRA]. . . . I was not for it because I am a full blood. So, I'm on that side and the half breeds on the other . . . and they're the ones who accepted it. . . . They wanted the constitution and bylaws." Clark further explained, "Older people were against it and younger people for it."[31] The IRA proved to be the most radical law to affect tribes in the twentieth century, thus dividing communities, even family members.

John Saul, a Crow Creek Lakota, remembered his people rejecting the IRA: "This Wheeler-Howard Act, we didn't accept that because the government had not fulfilled their promises. That's the way we understood it and we didn't want to vote for it. We wanted the government to square up with us and then [they] attacked us with something new, that we won't know much about."[32] Plethoric pages of political jargon posed too much to digest, much less to understand, even its important provisions. Mostly the Indians wanted ironclad promises to help them that the government would not dare to break.

Among the Blackfeet in Montana, the members of the tribal council expressed concern for the protection of the oil on their tribal land. One leader, Bullcalf, said, "We have oil possibilities here on the reservation, and we should look forward to getting developments on our oil resources, and this timber, and these canals, and things of that kind. If we could get these developments done, and [sic] then I am sure we would be self-supporting. Then we would have plenty of money to put in our pockets."[33] The oil issue did not dissipate as other tribal members expressed concern. Mountain Chief Black Weasel, an eighty-five-year old full-blood, stated, "We are tired of the leasing of our grazing lands and tired of outside sheep companies. We want to utilize our own resources and develop our oil companies. We want to utilize our own resources and develop our oil lands."[34] Blackfeet elder Rides at the Door addressed the Collier delegation and said that it would be best for his people to accept the IRA. Rides at the Door stated, "My people now own a large area of oil land as we have now on our reservation three producing wells, and that is the reason I came here, and I want some law or protection whereby I can always hold that property intact so that no white man can take it away from me." His listeners applauded, including the BIA delegate standing near Rides at the Door.[35]

As the IRA proved to be controversial and was opposed by some Indians, Collier grew angry with some tribes for not accepting the new law, and he threatened them. A Yankton Lakota, Cecil Provost, recalled the short, slender commissioner coming to the reservation:

> John Collier came down and was very much upset over the fact that the Indians are slow in adopting this, when the other reservations have already gobbled it up. In the process of interrogation, Collier was pretty much upset, and he said, "All right, boys tighten up your belts. You're going to get under the Indian Reorganization Act whether you like it or not . . . you come crawling to us . . . we'll starve you to death!" So he did. John Collier starved us to death. And I was one of them. I remember that, and I'll be darned if I'll ever go under the Indian Reorganization Act as long as I live, for the fact that I was [felt] starved to death.

Collier made this threat at Greenwood, South Dakota, at a meeting with Native people. Provost described that the weather was against them just like Collier and the BIA:

> There was nothing. No rain, dust, grasshoppers—day after day. . . . You couldn't buy work even if you wanted work. Relief was handled by the

Bureau of Indian Affairs. Apparently, just from my own thinking, Collier must have stopped all this, because my Dad and many others were refused relief. And for two weeks at a time, I had nothing to eat, just drank water, straight through. And, I have never forgotten that to this very day.[36]

The IRA provided several important provisions, including the cessation of the allotment program. Tribes were to receive an annual $25,000 to help reorganize tribal governments, although a lesser amount was actually provided. Indian business enterprises were encouraged. A program would be started for college education or vocational training for Indian Americans. Indian religions would be restored. A "revolving" loan fund of $10 million would be set up for chartered tribal corporations. From 1935 to 1944, the government loaned $5.6 million to tribal groups. The BIA encouraged Indian arts and crafts. Officials encouraged the conservation of Indian lands to help the communities develop. And the IRA authorized an appropriation of $2 million a year to purchase additional lands for tribal use.[37]

The new IRA aroused controversy and provoked criticism. Some bureaucrats argued that the new legislation allowed American Indians to live as "traditional Indians" and undermined any progress or civilization that had been made under the previous Indian policy. U.S. Representative Theodore Werner from South Dakota questioned the bill in committee hearings, stressing that it would segregate and reisolate Indians, preventing them from assimilating into the mainstream. Oklahoma Representative William Hastings claimed that it would perpetuate indefinite hegemonic control over American Indians.[38] Furthermore, the tremendous expense of federal appropriations provoked additional criticism of the IRA. Nonetheless, this measure proved to be one of the most reformative bills in history to affect the Indian population, as it began to reverse the tide of damage caused by the allotment policy.

Missionaries and religious organizations protested that the IRA hindered their work to Christianize and civilize the Indians. Most of all, they argued that the IRA reversed the prime federal objective of "assimilating" Indians into the mainstream society, especially when the traditional Native way of life was no longer viable. Ironically, many Indians became Christian Indians and embraced the religious beliefs of the mainstream. All across Indian Country in the West, some Indians retained traditional ways, and others wanted to become like whites. This did not diminish Native identity; these conversions stressed that Native people could also be

Christian Indians. Dedicated IRA opponents like Flora Seymour, a former member of the Board of Indian Commissioners, argued that communal life as emphasized in the traditional Native worldview no longer existed; it was socialism and linked to communism.[39] Indian community life opposed Amerocentricism and was deemed fundamentally un-American. With Indian communalism under attack, Native people stubbornly continued their lifeways in their communities with or without the IRA. Yet the people realized that they had to be flexible to changes. They learned to navigate the maelstrom of criticism and cross-culturally embrace what they needed of the IRA. In the Southwest, Native leaders like Fred Mahone and elders of the Hualapai realized that their new political situation affected their traditional cultures. They discussed in-depth how to use the law and obtain legal allies like the Indian Rights Association to help defend their land rights against the powerful Arizona Senator Carl Hayden and railroad and mining interests. After four years of continual discussions among themselves, the Hualapai voted to accept the IRA.[40]

Supporters of the IRA included social scientists who were knowledgeable about Indians and their cultures and were concerned about Indian welfare. Anthropologists, sociologists, and other scholars believed that the Indian way of life was disappearing but could be revitalized to save the Indians. They deemed that the Indian cultures and the people could be simultaneously preserved. Federal officials like Interior Secretary Harold Ickes and Assistant Commissioner William Zimmerman concurred.

From the outside of Native communities, the decline of traditional cultures appeared to be happening. But from the inside of Indian communities, the general response was "what else is new?" The IRA simply appeared to be a new wrinkle in federal-Indian relations. As the discussion continued in the various tribal communities, the Blackfeet remained divided over the IRA, and many were irate about it or just confused. Blackfeet elder No Coats expressed his feelings in a letter to Ickes, stating, "I am confused about the Wheeler Howard Act. I do not know what it means. If you could tell me what we may expect from it, I would appreciate it."[41]

Another Blackfeet tribal member, John Brown, said, "[The IRA] gave us powers that we had never had before. It gave us the chance to use our funds; it gave us the chance to get credit and we have under it all of those things and they have helped us, and we fear that if the act were thrown out and we had to go back to the old system that we could not get the advantages that we have now."[42] On the other hand, some tribal members disagreed. As a group, the Blackfeet full-bloods spoke against the IRA. In the

Figure 3.2. Navajos dipping their sheep to prevent diseases. Courtesy of Special Collections of Cline Library, Northern Arizona University.

voting on the IRA, twenty-eight of the thirty-four delegates voted to accept the IRA provisions, and to many people's surprise, many full-bloods accepted it. Six full-bloods rejected it. One of the pro-IRA full-bloods, Juniper Old Person, received criticism when he said, "My children got a start under the Wheeler-Howard Act and I feel proud of them and they will feed me."[43]

Within ten years after the passage of the Wheeler-Howard Act of 1934, tribal communities held 258 elections to accept or reject the IRA. In 1936, Congress amended the IRA to include Alaska Natives and Oklahoma Indians. Some large tribes like the Crow, Iroquois, Menominee, and Navajo rejected the IRA. A total of 192 tribes accepted the IRA; 88 tribes produced constitutions, and 68 tribes adopted charters of incorporation, affecting 129,750 Indians.[44] The IRA was rejected by 77 tribes totaling 86,365 Indian people, which included the Navajo population of 45,000. Significantly, the law required the votes of only one-fourth of a tribe's adult members for approval.[45] In 1938 a total of 85 tribes had reestablished IRA governments, affecting 99,813 Indians. By 1946 a total of 161 tribal constitutions and 131 corporate charters had been adopted under IRA guidelines. For charters of tribal incorporations, only one-third of the tribal members were required to approve this IRA provision at the tribal council meetings.[46]

Although the Navajo voted against accepting the act, something else influenced them. Between 1933 and 1947, the Navajos' more than half a million sheep became an overgrazing problem, and the federal government put a stock reduction program into effect. Sheep are known to graze about seven hours daily, and they eat grass so close to the ground that they need to be rotated to new grassy areas. The sheep reduction program proved devastating. Many years later, former Navajo Chairman Peter MacDonald described, "Some families like mine, suddenly poor after the livestock reduction, had to make do with whatever we had. We children then had to wear our clothes until they were so tattered and raggedy that they could not be mended. I don't know why I was embarrassed by this. So many families suffered during the livestock reduction that I shouldn't have felt that way. But something about the circumstances made me feel humiliated."[47] The majority of Navajos felt wronged by this action, eschewing cooperation between the tribe and federal officials.

Collier's Indian New Deal called for reform, which meant solving problems *for* Native people. One area of concern involved raising livestock according to a land base sufficient to support the animals. The Soil

Figure 3.3. The Navajo tribe developed their tribal government after rejecting the Indian Reorganization Act. Courtesy of Special Collections of Cline Library, Northern Arizona University.

Conservation Service imposed a permanent reduction of the Tohono O'odham's cattle herds and the removal of approximately one-half of the Indians to the Pima and Colorado agencies. This government action galled the Tohono O'odham. Relations went further awry when officials announced that local disease required a horse herd reduction.[48] These actions put Native pastoral groups at loggerheads with the government.

Throughout Indian Country, tribal leaders and their communities attempted to politically organize themselves according to federal regulations. Felix Cohen, a Jewish lawyer from New York, aided in creating and restructuring tribal courts under the IRA. Through new tribal ordinances, Native courts adopted codes similar to those of the Western legal system.[49] Alfred Dubray, a Lakota, described the Indian New Deal years for his people: "This was the new deal for the Indians. Nobody really understood it. From what they understood of it, it was very difficult because it was such a radical change from their way of life."[50] The Lakota refused to surrender complete autonomy and fought to retain control over their own lives and do things the Lakota way.

The combined support of experts to help the tribal communities led to an infusion of people with scholarly backgrounds into the federal government. The academic experts were much more familiar with Indian conditions and Indian cultures than the previous officials in charge of Indian affairs. Furthermore, they proved to be more sympathetic toward Indians than previous bureaucrats in the Indian Service. The more that Indians voiced their concerns, the more the government— which Indians thought had no ears—began to listen.

The Indian response to the IRA was mixed. Some tribes rejected the IRA because they were suspicious of the federal government. Some skeptics believed that despite government promises, they might lose the remainder of their lands. Mixed-bloods who had done well with their allotments did not want to return to the old cultural ways and therefore opposed the IRA. Some believed that the IRA meant additional government restrictions. The biggest rejection of the IRA came from the Navajos, who voted down the act on June 14 and 15, 1935. Of 15,600 votes cast, the margin of defeat was only 134 votes.[51]

The essence of the IRA was self-government, based on federal guidelines. Its heart lay in sections 16 and 17: "Any Indian tribe, or tribes, residing on the same reservations, shall have the right to organize for its common welfare, and may adopt an appropriate constitution and bylaws."[52]

Collier's prime objective in the IRA was to reestablish Indian tribal authority, but according to federal guidelines. The act was designed to assimilate Indians into the mainstream, but through tribes that were self-governing, self-sufficient, self-sustaining, and economically independent. At this point they would no longer require the aid of the federal government, and individual Indians could then integrate themselves into the mainstream based upon their own choice. At such a time, federal responsibilities and the BIA could be reduced. Actually, John Collier was one of the few BIA commissioners who entered office with knowledge of Indians and their diverse cultures. In addition to cultural ignorance, most ethnocentric commissioners held Indians to a lower level of society and imperiously believed that Indian ways had to be ended. Collier realized that Indians would assimilate when they themselves desired to do so, but he wanted them to move faster.

Yet Collier was trying to accomplish something that many Native people were not ready to accept in toto. He tried to force change on them yet again, much as the allotment policy had tried to do. He did not realize that their "flexibility of adaptation" worked only when individual tribal communities wanted it to. The Crow tribe rejected the IRA and wrote a letter to Senator Burton Wheeler, one of the sponsors of the bill. It read, "That under the Collier, chartered community plan, which has been compared to a fifth-rate *poor farm* by newspapers in Indian country, the Indian is being led to believe that they, for the first time in history, would have self-government."[53] Most Indians did not understand Indian reorganization, according to the government, and they did not want to be duped again, recalling that the rivers could be stopped from flowing and the grass could be stopped from growing, in treaty-talk jargon.

In retrospect some years later, Indian leaders charged the IRA with federal paternalism. Ramon Roubideaux, a Brule Sioux trial lawyer in South Dakota, claimed, "It's not self-government, because self-government by permission is not self-government at all. Everything that the Indian Reorganization Act brought in under the guise of self-government was subject to the approval of the concurrence of the Secretary of the Interior." His final point was that the act kept the Indian as a perpetual "ward of the government."[54] This Indian generation of many boarding-school-educated individuals rejected federal paternalism.

At the same time, some people just did not like Collier, who was a peculiar person, even to those who thought he was right in supporting Native people. Supporting independence for Indians, the *Baltimore Sun* described Collier as "a small slender man in gold spectacles and with a lock of brown hair over his right eye. . . . He had on a black suit . . . loose knot of his gray tie [that] keep slipping." Collier was an unimpressive character, but no one should underestimate his influence and stubborn determination. He did not want Congress to take "most of his power away from him . . . over 350,000 Indians" because he sincerely believed that he could help them in his own way.[55] Under his supervision, the BIA became a growing bureaucracy, and some critics viewed this trend as a power grab by Collier. He was short, slender, and underweight, yet he was a despotic force to be reckoned with, and most people tried to avoid his evangelical desire for Indian reform. Behind the glasses of Collier's myopic eyes, if you were not for him, you were against him.

Congress also approved the Johnson-O'Malley Act on April 16, 1934. This act supplemented the IRA by giving the secretary of the interior the authorization to enter into contracts with states and territories "for the education, medical attention, agricultural assistance, and social welfare, including relief of distress, of Indians in such State or Territory, through the qualified agencies of such State or Territory."[56] Its goal was for Indians to have the same state services as other citizens and to prevent discrimination against Indians in receiving the described services. The Johnson-O'Malley

Act was an endeavor to make Indians apply to state service programs rather than federal programs.

The IRA encouraged additional legislation to be passed during the early 1930s in order to better Indian livelihood. Another important measure was the Indian Arts and Crafts Board Act approved on August 27, 1935. Urged by Collier, it was "An Act to promote the manufacture of Indian arts and crafts to create a board to assist" Indian people in protecting their production of traditional artifacts.[57] The board consisted of five commissioners who engaged in research and experimentation to establish market contracts to aid in securing financial assistance for the production and sale of Indian products. This would create and administer government trademarks for Indian products. Members of the board also organized the Indian craftsmen and supervised the merchandizing operations. In addition, the board conducted research on production techniques.[58]

Since the Oklahoma Indians were originally excluded from the IRA, they could not apply for loans from the revolving loan fund.[59] The IRA, consisting of nineteen sections, had six sections that did not exclude the Oklahoma Indians: sections 2, 4, 7, 16, 17, and 18.[60] Two years later, Congress passed the Oklahoma Indian Welfare Act which applied all IRA provisions to Oklahoma Indian communities.[61] After 1936, the BIA received an appropriation of nearly $30 million to help destitute Indians in Oklahoma and all Indian people. An estimated 2,200 new overall BIA employees were hired, and salaries were raised 25 percent. This created a ratio of one BIA worker to every thirty-six Indians.[62]

During October, Oklahoma tribes were given assistance from the Federal Farm Board. The tribes accepted used clothing from the U.S. Army and received loans from the Department of Agriculture. The Red Cross provided food for approximately 3,000 Indian families during the winter of 1931. December was the worst month when Congress had to provide an emergency appropriation of $1 million for the destitute Oklahoma Indians.[63]

In 1936 Congress passed two acts that affected Oklahoma Indians and Alaska Natives. The latter had been left out of the original IRA of 1934. The IRA also excluded the Oklahoma Indians on the basis of their progress as individuals possessing allotments and without reservations. Representative Will Rogers and Senator Elmer Thomas cosponsored the measure; however, it excluded the Osages. Like the Five Civilized Tribes, the Osage were progressive and sometimes referred to as the sixth civilized tribe. The Oklahoma Indian groups staunchly viewed themselves as separate Native nations fighting their own fight against a paternalistic federal government and confronting state and local political interests. Of grit and stubborn pride, the Oklahoma Seminole passed a tribal resolution requesting a special U.S. marshal's office to protect its people, which they got. Seminole determination resulted also in Congress legislating $7,787 to fund construction of a community building for the tribe.[64]

A total of eighteen Oklahoma Indian groups organized under constitutions and thirteen gained corporate charters.[65] The Oklahoma Indian Welfare Act authorized $2 million for loans to Oklahoma Indians. Nationwide, 372 Indian students received loans for higher education, and 146 students went through vocational training. Under IRA provisions, sixty-five tribes representing a population of 86,238 adopted constitutions and by laws. Thirty-two of the groups ratified charters of incorporation. In addition, ninety-three hospitals and sanitariums for Indians now existed throughout the entire country.[66]

The acceptance of the Indian Welfare Act by the Oklahoma Indians presented a dilemma, especially for those who were not recovering on their own. The allotment program had been a success for many mixed-bloods, who favored assimilation and supported the IRA. Tensions between mixed-bloods and full-bloods bifurcated Oklahoma Indians and those on reservations like the Crow and Blackfeet reservations in Montana. Overall, conservative-minded traditionalist full-bloods viewed mixed-bloods and the mainstream as being more progressive. This polarized factionalism haunted tribes and organizations for the rest of the century, even during the cooperative times of indigenous progress. In an even stranger irony, the dissension within tribal politics united Native communities in dealing later with outside political threats. This was the internal nature of Indian politics and finding resolution to bond tightly, thus resulting in a powerful inner strength that could thwart most any threat from outside of the community.

Joseph Bruner (Creek) was the president of the American Indian Federation. Founded in 1934 at Gallup, New Mexico, the federation built up a membership of approximately 3,500. The American Indian Federation opposed the IRA's emphasis of forming corporations and reestablishing tribal governments. Bruner likened this emphasis to "Russia and in Mexico communism."[67] At the same time, some members of the American Indian Federation disagreed with Bruner because he came from Oklahoma—a sign of political distaste of an Indian from a different tribe being in charge. Political jealousy, especially deriving from longtime tribal rivalries, often served as an obstacle for any organization of Native people coming from various tribes.

On the other hand, many western Indians in Oklahoma were still very much dependent on the federal government. Tribal groups like the Cheyenne, Arapaho, Kiowa, and Comanche still lived in communities like they did historically.[68] Over 100,000 Indians resided in Oklahoma, and twenty-nine former tribes were officially represented. A few groups were considered successful farmers. For example, Kiowa farmers earned an average profit of $1,200 for each forty-acre farm in the fertile Washita Valley.

The status of the majority of Oklahoma Indians depended on seasonal employment. They picked cotton for 75 cents per day. Malnutrition, starvation, and diseases, including pellagra (a disease caused by vitamin B deficiency) and tuberculosis, affected the people. Three-fourths of the children were undernourished. The diets of those fortunate enough to have food consisted of dry salt meat, beans, and bread. The Cheyenne even resorted to using diseased horses for food. The Depression had devastated Oklahoma, causing a large number of people to journey to California, as described in John Steinbeck's *The Grapes of Wrath*. Poor Okies often stole chickens and whatever else belonged to Indians as they passed by. Dust bowl storms during the 1930s added to Depression suffering, convincing some panicked people that the earth was coming to an end.

Like the Oklahoma Indians, Alaska Natives found themselves excluded from the original IRA legislation through section 17. Under their own IRA measure, Congress passed the Alaska Reorganization Act on May 1, 1936. Some 2,063 Alaska Natives lived on 126 reserves, containing 1,338,700 acres that executive orders had created. In 1884 the Alaska Organic Act had allowed the Natives to remain undisturbed on land they occupied until future legislation. The people remained ensconced in isolated fishing villages instead of tribal communities. After becoming convinced that the Alaska Natives did not need the IRA of 1934, Anthony J. Dimond, an Alaskan politician and member of the Territorial Senate, was instrumental in getting the 1936 measure passed to provide the villages with loans. The BIA persuaded 10,899 Natives out of a population of 29,000 to draw up constitutions and charters of incorporation for forty-nine villages.[69] Prior to the IRA, members of the Alaska Native Brotherhood and Sisterhood had already achieved a fair amount of success. The Brotherhood was founded at Sitka in 1912. Many of its members had attended Sitka Training School, where they were influenced by Sheldon Jackson, a Presbyterian missionary. Both organizations were pro-assimilation and supported education as the keystone to the Alaska Natives' future success.

During the 1930s the population consisted of 4,462 Tlingit, 588 Haida, and 466 Tsimshean Indians in southeast Alaska. This count included

4,028 Aleut, 4,935 Athapaskan, and 11,000 Eskimo on the Aleutian Is-
lands, in the interior, and along the coastal regions of the territory.[70] In
another area, the growing reindeer herds bolstered the economy of Alaska's Natives and Eskimo. During the 1890s, the people had almost exhausted their food supply, and reindeer was introduced to feed them. This
animal produced meat for food, skins for clothing, and a small export and
trade of goods resulted.[71]

The situation in Alaska exemplified life and the general conditions
throughout Indian Country. From 1935 to 1938 the total appropriation for
the Indian Service to Alaska Natives rose from $28,146,105 to $47,942,541.
Most of the increase was for emergency relief funding. After 1941, the total
amount decreased, and $28 million was spent in 1944.[72] The BIA reported
in 1937 that the total of Indian lands had increased within two years to 2.1
million acres. Indians were also included in the Housing Act of 1937. Indians could participate in the low-rent public housing program, and the
tribal groups were permitted to form housing authorities. This enabled
them to become eligible for federal loans to finance housing for their
people. The average income for Indians rose to $600 per year, which was
a remarkable improvement.[73]

The effects of Collier's Indian New Deal reforms rippled in many directions. As of December 31, 1940, sixty-seven Indian chartered corporations had loan funds amounting to $4,777,861. Under the Oklahoma
Indian Welfare Act, thirty-four Indian credit associations had borrowed
$667,000, and $275,000 went directly to individuals.[74]

In 1944 and 1945, the Department of Interior exercised its authority
under the Alaska Reorganization Act of 1936 to establish reservations. The
Alaska Natives had the final approval. They rejected three reservations
and accepted six.[75] The Alaska Natives adopted forty-four constitutions,
and other Indian groups adopted 106 constitutions.[76]

With American interest in the war in Europe, Collier's Indian New
Deal struggled in the 1940s. Toward his last years as commissioner, Collier grew frustrated, although he stayed in office until the end of the war,
resigning in 1945. A good part of Collier's twelve years as Indian Commissioner involved responding to critical missionaries like Gustavus Lindquist
of the Home Missions Councils of Churches.[77] Lindquist was a longtime
critic of Collier who believed that the IRA reorganization policy to help
tribes to work in their communities went against the grain of Christian
instruction, especially when the head of the BIA supported tribal religious
ceremonies. Upon learning of Collier's resignation, the Southwest Indian
Superintendents Council expressed its regrets to the commissioner. The

council passed a resolution that said, in part, "During his tenure of office the Social and economic welfare of the Indians of the country has been improved to such a marked degree as to create in all of us a real feeling of pride."[78] In other regions, Blackfeet community leaders made their voices heard as they helped to reorganize their nation.[79] Reinvention of culture occurred as the Niomlacki and Pit River people and the Yuki and Wailacki of Round Valley Reservation worked in the California labor economy. The Indians made this a part of their lives, and it developed into their new labor economy—one example of what began to happen in tribal communities throughout Indian Country in the modern West.[80] One might conclude that traditionalists in tribal communities began to reach out to embrace modernity on their own and at their own rates across Indian Country. More important, how did the community leaders do this?

Collier's efforts had produced a series of significant reforms for American Indians accompanied by federal paternalism. Indians saw in Collier a friend and sometimes foe in the federal government whom they could usually trust, and he was confident that they could earn their own livelihood with federal assistance. The difference was that they would employ traditionalism as their basis of operation for business enterprise, self-government, day schools, and health improvement. Oddly, Collier helped to sustain the heart of the Indian people—their community identity—as they progressed under the Indian New Deal. But for some Indians, Collier represented BIA hegemony, and his efforts to control them provoked criticism. They called Collier paternalistic and refused to accept the IRA wholesale. Reacting against Collier's headstrong approach, they opted to do things their own way. They would take what could be used from the Indian New Deal programs and begin to rebuild their communities. In this Native logic, it was survive first, imagine rebuilding, and then do it. Interestingly, Collier appreciated Native communities, and he wished them to remain intact, but at the same time he wanted their leaders to accept his IRA provisions. And he wanted Native people to change at his pace. Collier's Indian New Deal was a contradiction to Native people, and they had learned long ago how to live with contradiction. Being inclusive by nature, Indians could embrace incongruent entities and make them work in their societies. For example, their flexible adaptation had allowed them to incorporate dichotomies of light and dark, male and female, right and wrong, war and peace, and other opposites into their worldviews, philosophies, and realities. They saw the IRA as another form of government, and they combined it with their traditional government to forge a new one of their own.

The collective philosophy of Native ways and Collier's support for Indian communities proved to be mostly positive for Native people. The traditional majority of tribal elders went along with the federal policy to continue Native communities under federal guidelines, but they did not see the future as Collier did. Some tribal members were even contentious with Collier. As a result, the Collier New Deal for Indian life disrupted the historical continuity of tribal communities and traditional identities. Rather than helping them to restore tribal cultures, the IRA irrevocably undermined traditional Indian life, although Indians viewed this as a compromise. Collier wanted tribal reorganization to mimic how the federal government was set up with a constitution and government to govern its people. But Collier and other bureaucrats underestimated tribal infrastructures, which were based on clans or societies for the various tribes— these systems were centuries old and could not be dismissed overnight. Collier's Indian New Deal represented change forced upon the tribes, and Native people would only change when they wanted to. While the nation had lived vicariously in the Roaring Twenties and suffered in the 1930s, America's indigenous people continued in their own existence—a world apart that included cultural borrowing from the American mainstream. Their next generation would move away from an isolation existence and begin to rebuild traditionalism toward an Indian paradigmatic new traditionalism of old and new ways while using IRA provisions. Essentially, they would retain the core identity of their tribal cultures and borrow new mainstream cultural ways in what might be called Indianization. Rebuilding upon resilience required imagination on the part of tribal leaders and cohesive cooperation from tribal communities. But Indians' lives would be interrupted by war. This transition of one generation to the next did not preclude a total loss of culture, but actually maintained continuity as the seeds of a new Indianness would be sowed.

Retaining their communities helped Indians to face the unfolding decades of indifference. Secure in their tribal groups, Indian people survived the tests of cultural alienation, imposing policies, and sociocultural discrimination. The majority of American Indians stood apart from the mainstream. In addition to this parallel existence with the mainstream, the strength of community life proved itself again after World War II, when the relocation program produced urban Indians who began to cluster into communities. Thereby, Indian America consisted of tribal communities on reservations and on traditional lands and of Indians moving to towns and cities. Native leaders learned a key tool of flexible adaptation to adjust their ways in navigating within the terrain of federal bureaucracy.

They adapted to acquire what they needed for their communities as their resilience had sustained them during the early hegemonic decades of the twentieth century. Under the Indian New Deal, tribal leaders would make their own deal and use IRA provisions to rebuild, and they were more in control than Collier and other bureaucrats believed.

CHAPTER FOUR

Relocation and Urban Indian Communities

Navigating Cultural Systems

In Daly City, I was getting ready to enter the seventh grade. The thought of that depressed me a great deal. That meant having to meet more new kids. Not only did I speak differently than they did, but I had an unfamiliar name that the others ridiculed. We were teased unmercifully about our Oklahoma accents. My sister Linda and I still read out loud to each other every night to lose our accents. Like most young people everywhere, we wanted to belong. . . . I was also growing like a weed and had almost reached my full adult height. People thought I was much older than twelve. I hated what was happening. I hated my body. I hated school. I hated the teachers. I hated the other students. Most of all, I hated the city.

WILMA MANKILLER, CHEROKEE, CA. 1992

Many people reading this page will likely recall their difficult junior high or high school years of peer pressure, not having the right clothes, not being of the right class background, or not being a part of the in-crowd. Junior high and high school years can be difficult for any student, but Native youth experienced additional hardships. Outside of the norm of the 1950s and 1960s, Indian students like Wilma felt peer pressure plus cultural pressure. Wilma and her sister tried very hard to fit in and wanted to be accepted, but they could never change their brown faces. They faced the color barrier and felt the numbing pain of prejudice. They felt unwanted, in the way, and rejected by their mainstream white peers. From hurt develops hate, and Wilma hated her white high school for rejecting her and her sister. While the government tried to forcibly assimilate Indians with its new relocation program, Wilma never forgot this hurt, while her white peers never understood what she was going through, for they were the cause of much of the pain. This inflicted suffering knows no time, and people usually hurt others when conditions are difficult overall, due to bigger problems.

The Great Depression waned due to the development of something even worse. The outbreak of World War II inspired by Germany's aggression for more *Lebensraum* produced chaos and conflict. Adolph Hitler's invasions with his Nazi *blitzkrieg* warfare engulfed much of Europe. American involvement followed quickly when the Japanese attacked Pearl Harbor on December 7, 1941. In the succeeding weeks, Germany declared war on the United States, and America found itself embroiled in a global conflict on two fronts.

Analogous to participation in World War I, Native peoples responded patriotically to the call to arms, and 25,000 Indian men joined the U.S. Army. Others joined the Navy and Marines, and several hundred Native women served in the armed forces. Indian participation attracted attention with the Navajo Code Talkers, who used their tribal language to send coded messages on the battlefields. Other tribal code talkers were used as well, and the Thunderbird 45th Division became filled with young Native men from the Southwest. A number of awards were earned for exemplary service, including six Medals of Honor awarded to Thomas Van Barfoot, Choctaw of Mississippi; Pappy Boyington, Coeur D'Alene of Idaho; Ernest Edwin Evans, Muscogee Creek and Cherokee of Oklahoma; Roy W. Harmon, Cherokee of Oklahoma; Jack Montgomery, Cherokee of Oklahoma; and Ernest Childers, Muscogee Creek of Oklahoma.[1]

Following World War II, the world changed and bureaucrats altered their positions toward American Indians. With so many Native men and women participating in the armed services, the government realized that they could be integrated into society. This new view reintroduced the idea of assimilating Native peoples into the mainstream. Government officials wanted Indians integrated into urban areas, forcing them to move from their reservations and rural homes to cities. Again Indians felt the firm hand of federal paternalism changing—and ostensibly improving—their lives. Instead, numerous problems occurred during the transition from the traditional culture of reservation living traditional to dealing with an urban mainstream culture. Even more, a hidden agenda could be speculated that involved the securing of tribal lands. First of all, the encouraged removal of Native peoples to cities raised serious questions about the larger historical context of U.S.-Indian relations. With the displacement of Indians from their tribal homelands on reservations to urban areas, who stood to benefit the most? American Indians in new urban homes with unstable jobs, or non-Indians who saw capitalistic gain from the natural resources on reservations with fewer Indians there? Indians became victims in the relocation program as they in fact became something of a disappearing race by becoming invisible among other ethnic peoples in the city streets. Those left on reservations carried on and had to endure bleak economic years for at least two decades. The people with the most potential tried relocation; thus, the best and the brightest sought urban promises as the Indian population tilted from reservations toward cities.

Relocation pushed Indians into a situation of new adaptation. They learned a new tool of navigating within a cultural system. Much of this learning, however, came via the school of hard knocks, making mistakes due to their naiveté, and their resilience saved them. In much the same way, the relocated Indians were like newly arrived Europeans being continually processed at Ellis Island as they entered a cold sociocultural system that was more likely to reject than to accept them. Living and working in foreign urban environments, Indians learned where they were not wanted and where they were accepted. They became bicultural and bilingual as they learned to move back and forth between their Native realities and that of the mainstream. Operating between two different value systems gave them knowledge of how the mainstream worked, but the learning curve was steep.

The idea of Indian relocation originated with the Navajos suffering from blizzards that struck many people and livestock during the winter months of late 1947 and early 1948. The military made airdrops to keep sheep and horses from starving to death. Government officials conceived of the idea of moving Navajos from the reservation to jobs and housing in three principle cities: Denver, Salt Lake City, and Los Angeles. From the Navajo experiment, Bureau of Indian Affairs (BIA) officials believed that it was promising to relocate Indians from economically collapsed reservations to urban areas.

President Harry Truman appointed Dillon S. Myer as the new commissioner of Indian affairs to introduce both the relocation program and the new termination policy that would become a critical part of the whole change in Indian policy. Myer, a conservative Republican from Ohio, had recently left the directorship of the War Relocation Authority that coordinated the relocation of an estimated 120,000 Japanese Americans from the West Coast and Hawaii to internment camps during the war. In his new appointment as Indian commissioner, Myer likely was not expected to be a friend to Native people but rather to get a difficult job done. Myer served as Indian commissioner for less than three years. On July 28, 1953, President Dwight Eisenhower appointed a former banker from New Mexico, Glenn Emmons, as the new head of the BIA.[2]

Generally, the relocation experience frustrated many Indians who moved to urban areas during the period from the Korean War years to the end of the Vietnam War. In the early 1950s, McCarthyism and the Second Red Scare exacerbated problems for relocatees. Senator Joseph McCarthy from Wisconsin started what became known as McCarthyism, and he was eagerly supported by FBI Director J. Edgar Hoover. In the eyes of McCarthy, Hoover, and others, anyone who did not look American was perceived to be a communist. McCarthy and his followers blacklisted over three hundred individuals in the film industry and an estimated 3,000 seamen and longshoremen, as well as professors, teachers, lawyers, and people in other professions. The paranoia and fear of the Cold War enabled McCarthyism to destroy the careers and lives of many Americans and simultaneously made the public skeptical of Indians.[3]

Multiple experiences of relocation occurred involving those who became quasi assimilated to form a new identity called the "urban Indian." This cultural transition from reservation to urban living exemplified sociocultural adaptation at a high cost of cultural confusion. The off-reservation paradox represented a critical means of survival after relocation officials persuaded many individuals to take their families from dilapidated homelands to a presumed better life in cities.

The U.S. government introduced "relocation" as a federal program officially offered to all qualified American Indians. This innovative program tried to accomplish two goals: help them find jobs and help them find suitable housing in cities, mainly in the western half of the United States. More important, the federal government convinced Indians to leave their homes, their reservations, and their traditional areas that they had come to love.

Simultaneously, the federal government enacted the termination policy. The BIA had introduced the termination policy based on House Concurrent Resolution 108 approved by Congress in 1953. Representative William Harrison from Wyoming introduced HCR 108 in the House, and Senator Henry Jackson sponsored it in the Senate.[4] The resolution called for terminating the "trust" relationship with tribes, thereby ending federal responsibilities described in the treaties once and for all. The resolution stated: "Whereas it is the policy of Congress, as rapidly as possible, to make the Indians within the territorial limits of the United States subject to the same laws and entitled to the same privileges and responsibilities as are applicable to other citizens of the United States, and to grant them all of the rights and prerogatives pertaining to American citizenship."[5]

The Eighty-Third Congress approved of the resolution using rhetoric that assimilation was best for American Indians. This policy of paternalistic "withdrawal" from Indian affairs would enable Native peoples to assimilate productively into the American mainstream. This did not happen as planned. This new Indian policy ended the federal trust relationship with many tribes, communities, and individuals. In all, 109 termination cases occurred, the Menominee tribe being the first in 1961. Termination threatened to remove all federal protective measures from Indian lands, including those trust properties of individuals, and this dreadful policy finally ended about the same time as relocation ended, in 1973 with the introduction of Indian self-determination. Until then, BIA officials and congressmen argued that both relocation and termination liberated Native peoples to enjoy all the privileges of full citizenship like everyone else.[6]

Relocation officers processed Native applicants like numbers through an urbanization experiment, moving them to cities where nobody cared about Indians.[7] During these years, Native people became just another group in cities, much like European immigrants and others who came to the United States who were taken advantage of and cheated by American capitalists. As a result, Indians became like the unwritten chapter in the fictitious saga *The Jungle*, by Upton Sinclair. They experienced hardship and social alienation from the urban mainstream. Like the European immigrants, Indians were resilient; many stayed in cities to establish new homes despite the fact that they were novices to urban ways.

Former Cherokee Principle Chief Wilma Mankiller described going on relocation as a child with her family: "I never liked the idea of moving away. I can still remember hiding in a bedroom in our house of rough-hewn lumber, listening while my father, mother, and oldest brother talked in the adjoining room about the benefits and drawbacks of relocating our family. We younger children tried to listen through the door. We were terrified. They were talking about possible destinations. They spoke of places we had barely heard of—Chicago, New York, Detroit, Oakland, and San Francisco."[8] This sense of home space for young Wilma was so great that her child mind could not imagine living anywhere else, especially so far from rural Oklahoma.

A large family of nine, the Mankillers decided to go on relocation. The entire family took a train from near Tahlequah in Oklahoma to Kansas

City. They had never ridden a train before, and after some confusion, they transferred to another train to San Francisco. As Wilma Mankiller described,

> My folks had the vouchers the BIA officials had given them for groceries and rent. But when we arrived, we found that an apartment was not available, so we were put up for two weeks in an old hotel in a notorious district of San Francisco called the Tenderloin. During the night, the neighborhood sparkled with lots of neon lights, flashily dressed prostitutes, and laughter in the streets. But in the morning we saw broken glass on the streets, people sleeping in doorways, and hard-faced men wandering around. The hotel was not much better than the streets. The noises of the city, especially at night, were bewildering. We had left behind the sounds of roosters, dogs, coyotes, bobcats, owls, crickets, and other animals moving through the woods. We knew the sounds of nature. Now we heard traffic and other noises that were foreign.[9]

The hardness of the urban world intimidated Wilma and her family. Urban brashness surrounded them, and their new hotel home did not offer security in their minds as they saw strange sights and heard overwhelming sounds that threatened their spiritual balance. All points of reference for life had been left behind in Oklahoma, and they would need to chart new references to know where they were safe and where danger awaited. This meant learning a new urban culture and new means of survival.

For Indians the new life in cities proved to be confusing and harmful. An article in the *Christian Science Monitor* described the reality of a Native family relocating to a city. The story itself depicted a true picture of what relocation was probably like for a Native family in an unfamiliar situation:

> Tony and Martha Big Bear and their family had just arrived in Los Angeles from the reservation. Everything was new to Martha and she never said a word and scarcely raised her eyes while holding the children during the bus ride to the relocation office. The first thing the relocation officer did was to advise Tony about spending money wisely. A $50 check was drawn up for Tony and he was told how to open a bank account. The Big Bears were then temporarily lodged in a nearby hotel. Although Tony wanted to be a commercial artist, he settled for a job in

an aircraft plant. The Indian Bureau placement officer persuaded Tony to accept this job first and then he could check into the art field later after he became familiar with Los Angeles and when his family had a more permanent place to live. Everything was moving too fast for the Big Bears. The field office helped Tony find an apartment—a "slum," according to most people, but it was better than anything Martha was accustomed to.[10]

The Big Bear family struggled to navigate the urban hardships. For many families, it was even frightening. McCarthyism closed factories and welfare agencies had to aid relocated families. Promised jobs fell through. Nearly all relocatees experienced difficulties of one kind or another in the uncharted waters of urbanization. The first relocatees were sacrificial lambs for others who would follow.

A writer for the *Atlantic Monthly* magazine described an account of an Indian family of seven, struggling in the city. The situation involved Little Light, her husband, Leonard Bear, and their five children. From a Muscogee Creek community in Oklahoma, they found city life harsh. "Today they are slum dwellers in Los Angeles, without land or home or culture or peace." In response to the interviewer's questions, Little Light spoke of how her husband went out drinking every night, of people in stores laughing at her, and of the need for a doctor for her sick child. She wanted to return to Oklahoma, but there was not enough money to go back. The woman stared solemnly, and her face became distorted as she lamented, "They did not tell us it would be like this."[11]

Most Indians did not understand relocation. They could not believe that the government would pay them to move and find jobs for them. Lakota activist Russell Means, who lived in southern California, exclaimed, "What the hell was relocation? The idea was to integrate Indians into urban ghettoes so that in a few generations we would intermarry and disappear into the underclass. Then the government could take the rest of our land and there would be no one left to object."[12] This design had the brain-drain effect of leaving the reservations with less effective leaders to defend the tribal lands and natural resources.

At first, the BIA offered relocation services in Oklahoma, New Mexico, California, Arizona, Utah, Colorado, and Chicago, with the first official relocatees arriving in Chicago in early 1952. The number of Indians relocating increased rapidly by the mid-1960s. By 1973, perhaps as many as 100,000 American Indians relocated to metropolitan areas and later to Plains states, Oklahoma City and Tulsa in Oklahoma, and Wichita in

Kansas. Some people relocated on their own expense.[13] The West Coast attracted many relocatees, making Los Angeles the urban Indian capital of Indian Country. Indian populations in San Francisco, Oakland, and Seattle were not far behind. Means described that "relocation applicants ostensibly were limited to three preferences among seven cities—Los Angeles, San Francisco, Denver, Chicago, Saint Louis, Dallas, and Cleveland. . . . In general, most people were lucky if they ended up with their third choice, unless they were willing to wait—sometimes years until the quota for a particular city opened up."[14] Within one decade, a major demographic shift began to occur with more Indians living in cities than on reservations.

The federal government made it easy to qualify for the relocation program because officials wanted the program to succeed. A person had to be between eighteen and about forty-five years of age and in good health. The applicant had to be capable of working and learning a job skill. Any prior job experience in the mainstream proved to be helpful, although it did not guarantee successful job placement by relocation officials. The government began to learn that its plan was not working out like it was supposed to. Oliver Eastman, a Sioux Wahpeton, recalled very clearly being discriminated against at work. His relocation to California did not work out for him. He said,

Figure 4.1. Los Angeles Indian Center. Courtesy of the author.

No, it [relocation to California] really didn't [work out] because I was older for one thing [in 1957]. And I was a carpenter, I was a union carpenter; so when I got out there, why, it was just like in anything else, you're discriminated against because you happen to be Indian or because you don't belong to the clan. You know I worked with a group that was Italian, and when another Italian came along, they hired him and they removed me. You know, there was a Mexican guy working there, he [it] was the same thing and there was an ordinary white guy working there and he was gone after a while. They took Italians.[15]

In contrast, Eugene Wilson, a Nez Perce, found the relocation experience to be rewarding. After graduating from college, he completed graduate work at the University of Kansas and proceeded to work for the BIA in Wrangell, Alaska. After two years he and his wife and two kids moved to Arizona, where he worked in the guidance department at the Phoenix Indian School and then later moved to the Stewart Indian School near Carson City, Nevada. He supported the relocation program, stating, "There are many people who are ignorant, to put it mildly, of social programs, that say the Relocation Program or the Employment Assistance was a miserable failure. I differ with the people who make these statements about Indians. This did the Indians a lot of good. It developed independence, it gave many Indians skills, work skills, and certainly general education about what the rest of the world was like."[16] Undoubtedly Wilson's college experience and graduate school training made relocation a lot easier as he was already used to moving away from his homeland.

In the end many relocatees returned home to reservations penniless and filled with a plethora of stories about the big city. Some accounts were adventurous, and others were sad tales. Undaunted by urban frustration, some intrepid individuals felt compelled to try relocation again and this time went to visit other cities. In the end, many stayed permanently in new urban spaces, and some found that the big city life was not meant for them.

In the early years of the relocation program, 54 percent of the relocatees were processed at Indian agencies in Aberdeen, South Dakota; Billings, Montana; and Minneapolis, Minnesota. Another 46 percent, including my relatives, came from the South and Southwest from Anadarko and Muskogee, Oklahoma; Gallup, New Mexico; and Phoenix, Arizona. The heavy migration of Indians to cities occurred from 1954 to 1961.[17]

The first relocatees felt cultural shock as they soon learned about telephones, clocks, elevators, stoplights, subways, and other items that they had never seen before. The constant thronging crowds made the relocated Indians apprehensive about what they were doing and what might happen next to them. In encountering such a foreign reality, they were on their own with little prior experience off their reservations, except in the case of the Indian veterans who had fought in the European or the Pacific theater. The relocatees felt abandoned by relocation workers, and they needed help on a daily basis for the first couple of months. In addition, they soon learned about prejudice, racism, and street life in the cities. By forcing Indians into new lives, the federal government exercised increasing control over Native people as a part of its plan to make Indians invisible via assimilation and to make them eventually lose their traditional identity. This did not happen. Frequent social rejection from other urbanites compelled Native relocatees to stick together, thereby forming an urban Indian identity.

Finding life hard in southern California with little job experience and almost no education, one angry Native woman called relocation an "extermination program" and said that President Dwight Eisenhower believed "the Indians would be integrated by taking all the youngsters off the reservation, the old would die off, the young would be integrated, and the land would become free for public domain, and all the people could grab it."[18]

Other new urban Indians found modern institutions too overwhelming. Duped into buying on credit, their inability to make installment payments caused indebtedness, possibly bankruptcy.[19] This immersion required learning things the hard way, by experience. Unfortunately for the relocatees, they had to learn from their mistakes.

Realizing that American Indians needed job training, Congress passed the Indian Vocational Training Act in 1956 to step up its efforts to help Indians.[20] The new law authorized loans and assistance to companies that would move or establish factories near the estimated 250 reservations. Indians received on-the-job training, pretraining for certain occupations, and job placement. After 1957, relocation became known as the Indian Employment Assistance program until it ended in 1973, and a new Indian policy called self-determination would replace it. In addition, the federal government funded urban Indian communities to start centers to offer counseling and opportunities to serve Native people as central points for socialization and community life. Such centers emerged along with other independently funded centers in Oklahoma City and Tulsa in Oklahoma; two sites in Dallas-Fort Worth, Texas; the Lincoln Indian Center in Lincoln, Nebraska; three Indian centers in Rapid City and one center in Sioux Falls, South Dakota; and the Mid-America Indian Center in Wichita,

Kansas. With all of this assistance, the first relocatees struggled to succeed in an urban world of congested buildings and different people.

Working with Indians arriving in Minneapolis, a social services director at the Minneapolis Native American Center witnessed their frustrations. The director lamented the disillusion of relocation goals and hopes, saying, "I think everybody who comes to the city has a dream—a dream of making it, a dream about improving their lives. But then prejudice slaps them right in the face and they're worse off. Call it culture shock. When your bubble is burst, there's nothing left but to go back home and start dreaming again."[21] While Indians struggled to urbanize, the mainstream urban Americans seemed distrustful of them and other people of color. Bear in mind that this occurred in the midst of the Cold War, when society retrenched to protect American idealism and democracy.

Amidst this hardship, one Native woman received unfortunate news about her brother and lost control. She shared an apartment with another Native woman who said the stricken woman "tried to commit suicide and we had to rush her over to the hospital. . . . She was Blackfeet . . . from Montana . . . her brother got killed in Vietnam and when she got the news she kind of freaked out. And she stayed drunk for about three days and locked herself in the bathroom."[22] Suicide was one of the leading causes of death for American Indians; the statistic for Indian suicides continued to increase. Even at present, Native young people have a higher suicide rate than any other ethnic group in the United States.

Alcoholism and suicide destroyed many relocated Indians. Relocation robbed many American Indians of their confidence and self-esteem. Most of the time, Indians were the low man on the totem pole where they worked. They felt beaten down. They gathered at local bars to share their frustrations. Over the years, some establishments became known as Indian bars—for example, Columbine in Los Angeles, Red Race in Oklahoma City, and Warren's Bar in San Francisco. In the Twin Cities, bars lined Franklin Avenue where Indians drank. One might say that a bar culture developed among relocated Indians much like the Irish in Boston, Samoans in Seattle, and other ethnic groups. Sometimes turf wars occurred with other ethnic groups in the cities. In the bars Indians felt comfortable talking to other Indians about their families, concerns, and problems. Indians sought out other Indians for socialization. Oliver Eastman said, "So they had a way of finding each other, some way or other, they go to a certain bar and it becomes known as an Indian bar. And then when you start going there why you begin to find each other. It's a bad situation, looks like a bunch of drunks, you look like a bunch of drunks because that's your meeting place."[23] Being with other Indians and being Indian at these times could be mistaken for a form of intoxication. Many Indians in cities felt more like the Lone Ranger than Tonto.

Indians needed to talk to other Indians because they were lonely. And, they found other Indians often at Indian centers, churches, powwows, and bars. Eastman recalled, "Well, there's the hardships they get there, you know, criminals, and I would say that a lot of it is being lonesome. Because you can live next to a neighbor five years and you'll never get acquainted. And you know, Indian people are not forward people so they would never get [acquainted with neighbors] . . . so the Indian Center is a good thing . . . and then the only place they really meet is in their homes, . . . or they go down to some certain bar. You have Indian bars in every city."[24] Hanging out at bars became a kind of therapy for venting frustration and trying to navigate the urban cultural labyrinth. Confusion was the first stage of urbanization, followed by frustration and decision making of what to do about one's situation of living in a strange environment.

One relocatee described the confusion that was caused by such tremendous change:

It [confusion] really starts when we are born on a reservation, because while we are there, we are geared to a lifestyle that is not very comfortable

Figure 4.2. San Francisco Indian Center. Courtesy of the author.

to take along with us into the city. When we get there, we don't know really what do we leave and what do we pick up to develop a healthy personality and to develop some character out here, because we really haven't the kind of discipline and the kind of character built in and the kind of responsibility on the reservation that we need out here [in the city]. . . . I look at the self image, the self respect, the personal worth, this kind of thing, and I don't know what it was like before the reservation got here. This is one of the things that has done a lot to harm the Indian person.[25]

Some Native people who were first-generation relocatees began to feel disconnected from their identity. City life represented a new frontier for them, and they made tremendous adjustments to survive. For others, urban life was too overwhelming.

Many Indians felt humiliated in cities, and they opted to return to their reservations. This has been called "returning to the blanket" in a reference to Indians not being able to make it in the competitive urban white world. What might be overlooked is that any experience of urban frustration became told in stories and became knowledge for others who would relocate to cities. In this light, Indians broadened their worldviews to include personal experiences and those of friends and relatives about how to navigate between cultural systems. Their core belief systems of a circular perspective connected all things, human and nonhuman. In the Native paradigm of "relatedness," a natural democracy existed based on acknowledging all things being important in an inclusive worldview, according to each tribal community that now began to include Indian urban experiences. But Indians felt disrespected during the early years of urbanization and ignored by other people in the cities. Overcoming urban difficulties was the first major step toward reimagining and expanding Indian Country to include urban areas.[26]

This new "Indian problem" of relocation and urbanization had to be understood by Indians themselves and solved by them. Even with government assistance, no one else could do it for them. They had to gain information and knowledge about urban life and have courage to stick it out in the cities. Betsy Kellas (Hopi) grew up on one of the mesas in Arizona. Afterward, she lived in southern California during the 1960s and 1970s. She attended public schools. Betsy remembered feeling alone because she was an Indian, and she learned to deal with her situation. She graduated from California State University at Northridge and worked as a counselor at the Indian Centers Inc. in Los Angeles. She shared her experiences with other Indians and related to them about their Native identities:

> It is exciting to work in the Center because most of these [young] people have problems. Many of the parents work, and the children only have a mother. They have to work just to keep going. They are examples of the society, of persons shut out by society. They have not been given a chance. They need to be themselves, and they need more than skills. They need to have opportunities to express themselves. The children are so quiet. They cannot come up and tell you what is bothering them. They just hold it inside. They need people who will listen, and find out how they feel. The Indians need to find out how to express how they feel [about] themselves, and let it be known. . . . The Indian people need a chance to see what the world is about. They will know where they are at. They will know they are at the bottom, and how much they have to work to get up where they want to be.[27]

Indians were at the bottom of the totem pole, considering this country was once all Indian homeland. To succeed in urban society, they had to act like non-Indians, out of their element as Native people.

John Walker (Lakota-Ottawa) described the second generation of urban Indians. He was a former director of the American Indian Center in Chicago, the first Indian center established during the relocation era. "All of a sudden, we were left in a vacuum," said Walker. He was born and raised in Chicago, among the first urban born Indians. A new link was added to the continuity of tribal communities, the urban experience. Some elders from reservations were skeptical of urban Indians, even though their own relatives were becoming a part of the urban Indian communities.[28] Many Indians felt abandoned to find his or her own way in the big city. Education Director George Scott of the Chicago American Indian Center said, "Indians don't know how to deal with the cities. They need some basic orientation." Scott also felt that some Indians were fulfilling the stereotypes and expectations of others, since they had no guidance.[29] This general impression would change with time as relocatees learned to navigate the urban cultural system of cities.

Being Indian was hard, since mainstream racism and prejudice toward "Indian-looking" Indians still occurred, especially in border towns off the reservation. These towns were rougher for Indians, even more than the cities. Many border towns had prejudiced people who simply did not like Indians. Strangely, sometimes the biggest racists against Indians were mixed-blood Indians themselves, who looked more white than Indian. One might imagine the racists being men, but women were also prejudiced against Indians. A Native described a white woman, now a teacher, who was mean to her while she grew up. After a workshop years later for the Eureka City Schools, the offender burst into tears and apologized to the Indian woman, who described the scene: "She had big alligator tears, and she said, 'You know, I'm half Hupa and our folks were so ashamed of being Indian that we destroyed everything. Baskets, everything.' They were burned because they didn't want anybody to know that they were Indian. I understand now that that's just the characteristic of people. If you want to cover something up you make fun of somebody else."[30]

Racists in big cities intimidated Indians, especially if the relocatees had powerful assertive bosses or petulant landlords. Some relocatees failed to negotiate their way in big cities, but the struggle continued as more Indians began to arrive in urban areas because the reservations' economies offered too few jobs during these years. The first point of survival was for relocatees to understand that a cultural gap existed between Indians and most other people in big cities. In fact, most people knew very little about Indians. This cultural alienation would always be there, so the relocatees had to find a comfort zone in order to take on and navigate the urban mainstream and its ways. This was a matter of constant endurance and an individual battle for everyone almost at a primal level. Learning to be like others in the city was new for many, but some did have previous urban experiences. Russell Means sarcastically described being shown the simplest things like having an alarm clock to get up in time for work. Means replied that he had a clock, and

> then a huge fat woman came into the [relocation] office to teach me how to live in Los Angeles. She began with a telephone. She grabbed my right hand and shoved my index finger into the dial of a rotary phone and "taught" me how to dial. She told me about prefixes and made me practice dialing. I was thinking that those had to be the stupidest people I had ever met, but that was my first experience with government bureaucrats. While the fat lady was gripping my hand and showing me how to dial, I looked at her and the counselor. With all the sincerity I could muster, I said, "What will they think of next?"[31]

Means's sarcasm became a defensive tool that Indians learned to adopt to ward off prejudice and discriminatory remarks. Too often Indians faced these situations alone and recounted their experiences to other Indians later. Shared misery bonded Indians, filling them with grit as they encountered in-your-face attitudes on a daily basis.

Native communal ways did not work very well in the urban mainstream that emphasized individual desires and personal goals. Urban Indians had to think like white mainstreamers in order to learn the street knowledge of big cities. They felt disconnected from the other peoples in the cities and began to realize that they needed to talk to other urban Indians. Therapeutic conversations about being Indian and unwanted in cities rendered encouragement to all who faced a racist at work, riding a bus to work, at school, or at the grocery store. As they endured, they discovered other forms of discrimination. Silent racists who only stared could be tolerated, but outspoken racists tested urban Indians.

The welcoming idealism of "Give me your tired, your poor, your huddled masses yearning to breathe free" on the Statue of Liberty proved disheartening. In addition to this new socialization of "get with the program," they had to take on new attitudes, even adopt a jaded outlook on life, if they were going to survive in cities. In urban areas they had no land to call their own. They mostly rented apartments and houses. Only a small percentage could afford to buy homes.

Racial differences were an enormous problem during the 1960s and 1970s. African Americans, Mexican Americans, Asian Americans, and American Indians suffered tremendously because of mainstream racism. With little or no familiarity with indigenous Americans, the urban mainstream believed old stereotypes about Indians. Because Indians looked different and their skin was darker, they found themselves opposed by the urban mainstream. Wilma Mankiller described her school years after her family's relocation to Daly City, California:

> In Daly City, I was getting ready to enter the seventh grade. The thought of that depressed me a great deal. That meant having to meet more new kids. Not only did I speak differently than they did, but I had an unfamiliar name that the others ridiculed. We were teased unmercifully about our Oklahoma accents. My sister Linda and I still read out loud to each other every night to lose our accents. Like most young people everywhere, we wanted to belong. Also, there were changes going on inside me that I could not account for, and that troubled me very much. I was experiencing all the problems girls face when approaching the beginning of womanhood. I was afraid and did not know what to do. Besides having to deal with the internal changes, I was also growing like a weed and had almost reached my full adult height. People thought

I was much older than twelve. I hated what was happening. I hated my body. I hated school. I hated the teachers. I hated the other students. Most of all, I hated the city.[32]

During the mid-1970s, anthropologist Garrick Bailey of the University of Tulsa conducted a study of urban Indians in Oklahoma. He discovered public myths about Indians to be pervasive. According to Bailey, "The average non-Indian Oklahoman believes the Bureau of Indian Affairs spends vast sums of money on the Indian. They believe the bureau takes care of every need of the Indians and even gives him a monthly allowance check. The general consensus is that the Indian receives far too many benefits from the government and there is a great deal of resentment against Indians because of these alleged benefits. This resentment is strongest among the poor whites and other minorities."[33] Bailey refuted the public belief that the government took care of Indian people. In fact, the opposite was and remains closer to the truth. Ignorance can be dangerous, and the same state of mind fueled anti-Indian attitudes expressed to hurt and disarm Native people of their self-respect. Mostly poor working whites discriminated against Indians and other people of color, although they underestimated the resilience of Indians' ability to gain a tough exterior.

Relocation introduced a new opportunity for Indians to reinvent their tribal cultures to include urbanization. This new urban Indian culture consisted of navigating the city transportation system, reading bus and train schedules, and driving in the big cities on freeways and city streets. Relocation meant, in an Indian way, establishing a new home space and learning the ways of a new culture. Like warriors traveling centuries ago to provide for their people, the new urban Indian pathfinders represented the first generation of a new modern culture in American Indian history.

Urban Indians finding each other and finding housing represented another parallel with the past—that of "making camp" to establish a new home space. This went against the grain of a relocation program that attempted to assimilate Indians into the mainstream melting pot. Indians meeting other Indians began to dissolve tribal barriers that once stood as parameters separating tribal communities. In effect, such meetings initiated the development of a pan-Indian identity. The second generation of urban Indians began to realize that they faced many of the same problems as other people of color. Facing discrimination at work by their white bosses and landlords frustrated Indians, African Americans, and Mexican Americans. In some instances, they joined each other in coalitions to fight for their civil rights. In one protest at the Supreme Court in 1968, Mel

Thom, Ralph Abernathy, Hank Adams, and Reijes Tijerina led a joint demonstration for Indian fishing rights.[34] The protest movements of the 1960s carried over into the 1970s as unfair urban life disempowered people of color who sought a better life in the cities like everyone else. Placed in the same powerless position, Indians, African Americans, and Mexican Americans became protest partners as activism became a part of their new urban cultures.

By the 1970s the typical dichotomy of reservation and urban Indians had changed. Some Native people traveled back and forth in the reservation-urban scenario. Their frequent mobility connected urban Indians to the Indian Country. With the dual identity of reservation Indians and urban Indians, the federal government found itself involved in a trichotomy in Indian affairs—reservation Indians, the government, and urban Indians. This situation added to the complexity of federal supervision of Indian people. At the same time, the federal government under Jimmy Carter and especially under Ronald Reagan in the 1980s promoted privatization of industry and entrepreneurship. Before the end of the century, the mainstream would witness a rise of Indian entrepreneurship, not taught by Reaganomics but learned by Indians themselves.

The government's attention shifted from reservation tribes to the urban scene. Frustration with inadequate housing, low-paying jobs, and bad working conditions led to Indian protests. As more urban Indians voiced their concerns, the American Indian Movement became the source of a national Indian voice, forcing the federal government to listen through its protests and occupations in the late 1960s and early 1970s.

Relocation had a profound effect on American Indians. By the 1980s more than half of the Indian population lived in cities. Furthermore, cultural alienation proved to be a lingering problem as long as mainstreamers distrusted Indians and other people of color. At the same time, a small number of mainstream people felt sympathy for relocated Indians. Although these Indian supporters called relocation a form of Indian removal, the relocatees that persevered eventually survived the city life and began to develop urban Indian communities throughout the western cities and in other urban areas. The relocation plan had failed to integrate and dissolve Indians into urban communities, thereby semicolonizing the Indian identity but not controlling it. The population shift of the majority of Indians from reservations to urban areas finally resulted in about two-thirds of the total Indian population residing in cities.

Indian neighborhoods began to form in the poorer parts of cities, the ghettoes. Their new neighborhoods represented a new kind of home space without land. This was a new kind of tribalism or retribalization that formed new groups like Chicago Indians, Los Angeles Indians, Bay Area Indians, and Cleveland Indians. Los Angeles became the urban Indian capital of Indian Country. This newly formed identity was one that transformed from tribalism on reservations to Indianness in cities, while remaining connected to their people and traditions. This meant that Indians knew they were "Indian" and what tribe they were from. As most Americans did not know the many various indigenous groups by name, they called urban relocatees "Indians."

The effects of relocation caused a crystallizing of Indians in certain neighborhoods as relocatees lived near each other, especially if they were relatives. In Minneapolis and St. Paul, urban Indians regularly met socially and lived near Franklin Avenue. Tribal barriers began to dissolve such that Indians of different tribes began to form Indian neighborhoods. The Native neighborhood in the mission district in San Francisco was called the Reservation. Uptown became identified as the Indian area in Chicago's northside. As Indians identified with cities such as Chicago, Dallas, and the Bay Area, a new urban tribalism manifested itself. The common ground became the city as young Native men and women married people from different tribes and races. Tribal traditions became mixed, and cultural knowledge decreased. Unfortunately, tribal languages became lost with each generation of relocated Indians. By the end of relocation, less than one-third of Native people spoke their tribal languages. Using English every day made them forget those languages.

As urban Indians began to succeed in their new communities, they became justifiably frustrated for other reasons. As Indian children attended schools, they felt that they were studying a foreign culture, which was the mainstream. History textbooks used in classrooms neglected Indians. Values of the urban mainstream were different. Racism and discrimination against Indians and other minorities became obvious. As a response, Indian neighborhoods began to experiment with forming alternative schools. The Native people of Milwaukee, including the Ojibwa, Menominee, Oneida, Potawatomi, and other tribes formed the Milwaukee Indian Community School. In the Twin Cities, concerned Indians and all the American Indian Movement organized the Heart of the Earth School in 1972. In Chicago, the Indian community founded Little Bighorn High School. Also in Chicago, the first urban Indian college was founded in 1974. Native American Education Services, Inc., known as NAES College, closed in 2002.[35]

The establishment of alternative schools meant that Indians in cities wanted to invest in their children's future. They wanted to offer curricula in their own schools that would help prepare their children and offer courses that would help to teach their cultures and histories to their youth. These were mixed tribal schools, furthering the pan-Indian development in cities.

At least four generations of Indians had experienced urbanization by the end of the twentieth century. This process of cultural navigation continued into the twenty-first century. Five Indian generations attended boarding schools as both urbanization and boarding schools became a part of modern tribal cultures. Ironically, such schools used to be institutions that Native people dreaded. Threatened and mistreated in these school institutions, now urban Indians created institutions of their own. Education became a tool for Native people who realized its usefulness to improve their communities.

Following the Indian activism years of the 1960s and 1970s, Native people asserted more control over their lives. Many graduated from college and worked as teachers and in other professional areas. By the 1980s an Indian middle class emerged. Professional Indian teachers, lawyers, doctors, and others formed a small core that associated with others who wanted a better life for their families. Toward the end of the twentieth century, the numbers of Indians in professional areas increased, but they were still small compared with other minority professional populations. At the end of the 1980s only an estimated 250 Indians, for example, held a Ph.D., a small number, but this represented a start in higher education.

The survival of the first two generations in cities consolidated an urban Indian identity. As a part of urban families, city Indians also became increasingly individualized. They learned to adapt to urban life but also surrendered much of their cultures, tribal values, and languages in the process. This provoked the question of what kind of new Indians they had become. Were they now more like the mainstream person? How did they survive the domination of federal paternalism? Urban Indians had forged a new identity of their own. For each relocatee, moving to the city for the first time became a haunting memory. Learning to become an individual displaced tribal emphasis on communalism. They had to adapt to new surroundings and learn how to navigate within a new cultural system as a new dimension of urbanization became a part of Indian Country.

While many Native people learned how to navigate the urban mainstream, some could not make the adjustments required. Perceiving themselves as social and cultural outcasts, mainstream pressure proved to be too great. They lost their internal spiritual balance, allowing prejudice to make them feel unwanted. In time, most urban Indians would regain this balance.

For example, in Minnesota more than 700 foster homes kept Indian children in 1969. A survey five years later showed that of 159 Native children in the state of Washington's care, 114 had been placed in foster non-Indian homes. Former South Dakota senator and chairman of the Oversight Hearing on the Welfare of Indian Children, James Abourezk, stated that

> 25 percent of all Indian children are either in adoptive homes, foster homes, or boarding schools. In Minnesota one out of every four Indian children was removed from their [sic] home to foster care; in Montana, the rate was 13 times that for non-Indian children; 16 times higher in South Dakota; and in the State of Washington, 19 times higher. In Wisconsin it was 16 times more likely for an Indian child to be removed in comparison to non-Indian families.[36]

In 1978 Congress passed the Indian Child Welfare Act that prioritized Native children being adopted by relatives of the same tribe. The law stipulated an Indian family but of a different tribe would be the next option for adopting Native children. Finally, a non-Indian family could adopt an Indian child.

Many non-Indians adopted Native children. Many mixed marriages occurred with other races, Mexican Americans, African Americans, and especially white Americans. Many young Indian men and women married whites, resulting in biracial children who often suffered from bicultural problems. Social acceptance of mixed marriages and mixed-blood children proved to be a challenge for the mainstream.

Mixed marriages often succeeded if the Native parent lived according to mainstream norms. One Native woman recalled that she arrived in the city at age eleven and grew up urbanized. As a young woman, she married a white man and felt no obligation toward her tribal relatives. The woman felt assimilated and rejected her relatives and tribal heritage.[37]

In San Francisco, however, 71 percent of Indian mothers with a high school education or more wanted their children to marry Indians. The same preference held for 59 percent of Indian mothers with less than a high school education.[38] At the same time, the percentage of Indian and non-Indian marriages continued to increase, producing one-fourth of the Indian youths in San Francisco to be mixed-bloods. This occurrence often caused an identity crisis. As a youth, the child might be taught tribal values by one parent, even a Native language, while the other parent used English. Biculturalism resulted, and if a child could handle the situation, he or she would be well prepared for future challenges.[39]

The impact of urbanization tested the core identity of many Indians. A Navajo from Gallup, New Mexico, asked, "What is in store for us in the future? Because we have lost most of our traditional values which bonded us together in the past, we must find new ways, new values and new customs that will restore the stability and the respect in our relationship. Otherwise chaos will continue to rule, destroying the fiber of our society, leading to moral decline and eventually to the disappearance of us as a people and a nation."[40]

Navigating the white urban mainstream proved to be both threatening and advantageous. As urban Indians reinvented themselves to take on mainstream practices at work and home, they had to realize what was happening and to remain in control. In 1976, Pat Locke, a Chippewa-Sioux and director of Planning Resources in Minority Education for the Western Interstate Commission for Higher Education, stated: "Today's Indians must learn to walk both the white path and the red path. Both are important for survival."[41]

The first relocatees enabled the following generations to have an easier time in making adjustments to living in cities. This led to Indians moving to urban areas on their own as the indigenous population increased. For example, in 1960 the Indian population was 551,669, and in 1970 it was 827,091.[42] During the 1970s the number of Native people increased three and a half times faster than the mainstream. This pattern continued for the rest of the twentieth century. By 2012, the population of American Indians and Alaska Natives reached nearly 5 million.

Urban Indians demonstrated a stubborn persistence to make it in the cities as a radical demographic shift occurred. By the 1980s well over half of the total Indian population lived in urban areas, not on reservations. One might surmise that the reservation system weakened, but both reservation and urban communities crystallized into stable sociocultural units that enabled them to develop in the following decades. Urban Indians, indeed, learned how to navigate other cultural systems. They embraced the contradiction of an alien city culture and their reservation culture to form an urban Indian identity. By becoming bicultural and often bilingual, they learned the values of urban America and practiced them on a daily basis. The ability of Indians to use their ancient means of flexible adaptation involved cultural incorporation to live better lives. One might argue that urban Indians represented a modern example of colonialism, but the reverse argument can be made, too. For example, in the *longue durée* of Indian history over centuries, Native groups had colonized each other and endured colonialism from the French, Spanish, and Russians. But, if one retains autonomy and the power of decision making, then Indians from reservations began to colonize American cities with assistance from the relocation program. Colonialism implies a greater authority oppressing another people and changing them, but arguably Indians re-created their identities and changed themselves as they navigated the urban cultural system.

PART TWO

Rebuilding

Imagination

Imagination is everything.
It is the preview of life's coming attractions.
(I am enough of an artist
to draw freely upon my imagination.)
Imagination is more important than knowledge.
Information is not knowledge
and yet knowledge is still limited,
for knowledge of what is
does not open the door directly to what should be.
Yes, logic may get you from A to B,
But Imagination encircles the world.
Imagination is everything.

Albert Einstein

Rebuilding a nation requires considerable imagination on the part of the people involved. Here the relentless pursuit of imagination saved the future of American Indians. From imagination springs fresh ideas to difficult questions and challenging situations, and the indigenous people within the United States faced impossible odds as they witnessed their Old World approach its end. They took stock of their resources. One may possess or borrow the right tools, even more than those needed, but an idea and a plan come from visionary thinking within, not from thoughts of the outside. Inside of the communities and inside of the minds of leaders, native people applied themselves to reinvent themselves, alter their cultures, and apply a new logic born of Indian thinking and mainstream values. This is how they would rebuild their nations by adjusting again and again. Indeed, they proved that imagination is everything.

CHAPTER FIVE

Red Power Activism, the American Indian Movement, and Wounded Knee

The Rise of Modern Indian Leadership

We contacted all of our relatives, friends, acquaintances, and people from the reservations as well as from the Indian slums in the city. We went from house to house with five hundred leaflets we had printed, handing them out to every Indian we could find. . . . Our first meeting was set for eight o'clock on the evening of July 28, 1968, in the basement of a rundown church. . . . Almost two hundred people had gathered to listen and to begin making their voices heard. . . . As the meeting went on, people began to speak up. One man spoke of the police brutality and said, "When do you propose to go down there to Franklin Avenue, to all those Indian bars where the cops inflict abuse on our people every night?" I told him, "We could go down there tomorrow night." He said, "Hell No, let's go down there right now, tonight!" . . . In that moment, AIM was born.

DENNIS BANKS, OJIBWA, 1968

"I can't get no satisfaction. I can't get no satisfaction. 'Cause I try and I try and I try and I try," sang Mick Jagger in June 1965 as the world and the United States rocked and rolled in turmoil and confusion. If you recall this song, then you are a baby-boomer that lived during these years or you like 1960s music. This tumultuous decade witnessed pivotal changes in politics, society, and culture, and more change appeared on the horizon. Change seemed to rush forward like a tide, compelling Americans to re-examine their core values. The country had not encountered such havoc since the economic suffering of the 1930s, the Civil War of the 1860s, and the colonial revolution that founded the United States.

The protest movement of many organizations in the Cold War 1960s proved mostly to be destructive, pulling society apart, except for the fact that the tempestuous energy forged a modern Indian leadership. This was a time of the youth movement that challenged old conservative thinking, creating a generation gap. One could argue convincingly that this fresh leadership derived from Indian activism during the civil rights era and protests against the Vietnam War. But in examining the periods of the twentieth century to the present, one could also point out a broader scope, suggesting the seeds of this leadership emerged as early as 1911 with the founding of the Society of American Indians in Columbus, Ohio. A group of fifty frustrated, educated Indians included a core of leaders: Dr. Charles Eastman, Dr. Carlos Montezuma, Henry Standing Bear, Laura Cornelius, Charles Dagenett, and Thomas L. Sloan. This brazen group advocated the abolishment of the Bureau of Indian Affairs (BIA) for its paternalism and pressed for the protection of Indian legal and cultural rights until the organization fell by the wayside in the 1930s. Although the society was not founded in the West, it operated on a national scale.

In Denver, Colorado, an intrepid gathering was held of Native leaders who arrived from various parts of Indian Country with one goal in mind: to protect the rights of tribal communities. Native Flathead scholar D'Arcy McNickle was a core leader, as well as Judge Napoleon B. Johnson, a Cherokee, who served as the first president of the National Congress of American Indians in 1944. One of the founding delegates, Ben Dwight (Choctaw), metaphorically explained that the group had to find common ground: "Now I know that you can't put the same blanket over everybody because when you do that you are going to pull it off of somebody else. The same blanket won't go over everybody at the same time, but if you use some judgment you can spread the blanket out so that the one that is a little bit colder can get warmth from it."[1] Indian groups would need to work together, forgoing tribal differences, to stand shoulder to shoulder to protect their interests and rights. Later decades witnessed the founding of the National Indian Education Association in 1970, National Tribal Chairman's Association in 1972, Council of Energy Resource Tribes in 1975, and several regional intertribal organizations.

In 1961, with tireless work, professors Sol Tax and Nancy Lurie, Robert Thomas (Cherokee), anthropologist Alice Marriott, and others organized a pan-Indian conference held at Midway near the University of Chicago. This weeklong American Indian Chicago Conference brought together frustrated Indians and produced a Native consensus that vented against the government's termination and relocation policies. From June 13 to

June 20, the gathering produced a fifty-page document known as the "Declaration of Indian Purpose: The Voice of the American Indian" that articulated an Indian policy by Indians. The Creed in the Declaration stated:

> WE BELIEVE in the inherent right of all people to retain spiritual and cultural values, and that the free exercise of these values is necessary to the normal development of any people. Indians exercised this inherent right to live their own lives for thousands of years before the white man came and took their lands. It is a more complex world in which Indians live today, but the Indian people who first settled the New World and built the great civilizations which only now are being dug out of the past, long ago demonstrated that they could master complexity.[2]

But some attendees were not satisfied with so much talk but little action—the young Indians. While the Chicago conference produced its own Indian policy to present to President John Kennedy, the frustrated youths left and called for a meeting later in the summer for themselves and other interested Native youths.[3] In two days, they formed the National Indian Youth Council (NIYC) in Gallup, New Mexico, to plan their own agenda of activism. Both sets of Indian activists realized that the timing was right to take action against the colonialist U.S. government, if Indians were going to remain Indians, as they wanted to be. Representing a younger generation, Clyde Warrior, a charismatic Ponca from Oklahoma; Mel Thom, a Walker River Paiute from Nevada; Shirley Hill Witt, Mohawk; Herbert Blatchford, Navajo; Karen Richard, Tuscarora; Viola Hatch, Arapaho; Della Warrior, Otoe-Missouri; and other young upstarts became disenchanted with tribal elders and wanted action immediately. Some had attended college, and many were products of the white man's boarding schools. NIYC became involved in the Poor People's Campaign and advocated the protection of Indian fishing rights in the Pacific Northwest. NIYC leaders broadened their concerns to protect Indian treaties and hunting and fishing rights.[4] A new urban Indian population forged its way in the city streets, searching for a better life and certainly better treatment. For Native people, a fresh "Indian leadership" emerged that rivaled that of traditional leaders on reservations. A different genre formed that one scholar called the "new Indians."[5]

John Kennedy's youthfulness influenced America. Unfortunately, his untimely death in 1963 caused grief and confusion for the entire nation. And Lyndon Johnson inherited a languishing country. In the end, most young Americans agreed that not enough happened to meet the great expectations of LBJ's "Great Society." Time has an impish way of manipulating things, and the timing proved right for Indians. The unpredictable 1960s produced a modern American Indian and a proud reclamation of Native identity. Some might call it an Indian renaissance; others would say they were lucky to have survived all of the things that happened during this turbulence.

Most important, relocation to cities presented opportunities for Indians to regain control over their own lives and make their own decisions while deflecting federal paternalism. Timing, relevant issues, and key persons were the pertinent factors for creating a 1960s experience that precipitated enormous transformations in American society and its history. As American Indian leaders took up issues in the 1960s under the guise of "Red Power," a backlash began to fester. In the larger context, the 1960s promised great expectations of social change, but for most of America this did not happen, and a public awareness of civil rights occurred at best.

The presidential election of John F. Kennedy in 1960 enlivened hope for Native people and the rest of the country as Cold War activities took center stage at a global level. Society began to emphasize the freshness of youth and the questioning of social values. Television produced CBS Nightly News and a national awareness. Americans became the television generation as many of us stared in grief watching Kennedy's funeral procession and events surrounding his assassination. November 22, 1963, immortalized President Kennedy and placed all of the anticipated changes on the square shoulders of a nearly 6 foot, 4 inch tall Texan, Lyndon B. Johnson, who assumed the presidency. If you recall the Rolling Stones' hit song mentioned earlier at the top of the chart in 1964, then you likely also remember exactly where you were and how you learned the news that JFK had been shot.

At first, most people confused "Red Power" with Soviet communism and did not seriously associate it with Indians. Red Power came to symbolize the American Indian struggle for political justice, fair treatment, and the honoring of treaty rights. Some Indians preferred "Indian Power" as the slogan for what was happening. In the beginning, Indian activism floundered as a feckless imitation of other activist groups. Indians used word arrows to attack a paternalistic government that had suppressed them since long before Wounded Knee in 1890. In this persistence for sovereignty and respect, various Native leaders exuded anger. These young Native men and women represented a new prototype warrior. Skilled in oratory like many of their ancestors, they possessed an intrepid desire to speak out for Indian rights no matter what the consequence. Standing up for past wrongs against their people, these warrior leaders became the modern Indian leaders of the twentieth century on a national scale. Their time had arrived.

In the Pacific Northwest, Indians had been struggling to protect their fishing rights. Frank's Landing on the Nisqually River in the state of Washington became a focal point of tension, protests, and fighting between Native fishermen and local whites in 1964. Bill Frank and other Nisqually Indians led the effort to net salmon in local rivers off reservations. The newly formed NIYC sent members to support the Native fishermen as both sides realized that a court of law would have to settle the dispute. State officers responded to fights breaking out, and they arrested Indians on regular occasions. The Native fishermen and supporting Indians made the decision to march on the state capitol at Olympia on December 23, 1963. In early 1964, some of the protestors and other Indians established the Survival of the American Indian Association. Using their education and cultural navigation, members of the association realized that their leaders needed to know the complete history of Indian treaties and federal law. Boarding school education now paid off as this protest group became the organized effort to fight for Native fishing rights.

Environmentalists joined the Indians, as well as hippies, Black Panthers, the NAACP, and Students for a Democratic Society. The continual protests for Indian fishing rights was joined by celebrities like Marlon Brando and the African American comedian Dick Gregory, who was arrested with the protesting Indians. When asked by a news reporter if he had become a member of one of the tribes, he replied "No thanks, I've got enough problems."[6]

In 1968 war veteran Richard Sohappy, a Yakama, and his nephew David were arrested for net fishing by local authorities. The Sohappys obtained a grant from the NAACP to pay for legal assistance, and a lawsuit known as *Sohappy v. Smith* was filed on their behalf with twelve other Indians in the district court in Portland. The case was joined with a similar one, *United States v. Oregon*, and they went to trial as one case in 1969. Judge Robert C. Belloni ruled in favor of the Indians that the treaties were valid in guaranteeing Native net-fishing rights and that the indigenous had a right to an allocation of salmon.[7]

The *Belloni* Decision was soon followed by a similar court case that became a landmark ruling known as the *Boldt* Decision that influenced all Indian fishing rights cases thereafter. The prolific author and legal scholar Charles Wilkinson wrote, "The 203 page opinion [Boldt] was rich with history, as it should have been: after all, the Supreme Court had said in [*United States v.*] *Winans*, back at the turn of the century, that treaties should be construed as the Indians themselves would have understood them."[8] Importantly, the 50–50 allocation of the division of salmon and steelhead between Indian and non-Indian fishermen was a grand victory for Native people.

Indian activism soon broke out in other parts of Indian Country. The American Indian Movement (AIM) began in the streets of the Twin Cities in Minnesota during the civil rights protests. Initially the movement started as a reaction to bring peace and protection to the Indian neighborhood, known as the "reservation" in Minneapolis. Fourth Avenue, Dennis Banks (Ojibwa) said, was "the center of Indian life in Minneapolis" where many Native people lived.[9] AIM would soon step forward as the national Indian voice of the late 1960s and 1970s, denouncing the federal government's mistreatment of Indian people while inspiring the next change in federal Indian policy, a shift toward Indian self-determination in the post-termination years.

AIM's origin possessed deep historical roots in Indian mistreatment and in the bigger picture of the civil rights protest era; Indian activism hit the national scene like a tsunami. From a deep well of frustration, in large part stemming from unwanted cultural transition from rural life to urbanization during the 1950s and 1960s, indigenous people began to push back. Inside of Native communities, the proliferation of an indigenous generation living in cities, plus the influence Indian youth gained from a college education, created cultural and generational gaps among Native peoples. The outcome fostered two kinds of leadership, tribal leaders and new Indian leaders on a national stage promoted by the media and sensationalist newspapers competing for the latest headlines. This storm backlashed against the previous Eisenhower era of termination and relocation. Because of political activism among American Indians and the national attention that this garnered, tribal leadership played a lesser role compared with the emergence of young Indian leaders in urban areas who demanded federal retribution.

Relocation had promised an "American Indian Dream" to Native peoples much like the "rags to riches" Horatio Alger hope for all Americans. The Indian community in Minneapolis burgeoned to become the third largest urban Indian population in the United States.[10] By the end of relocation in 1973 and in the 1980s, nearly 100,000 Indians had become urbanized in all major metropolitan areas.

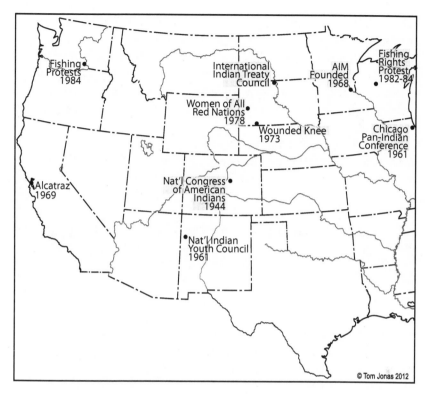

Map 3. Indian activist sites.

The urbanization of Indians via the relocation program created angst for Native people and a paradox of problems for them and the federal government. An "urban Indian problem" developed much like the old Indian problem on reservations during the late nineteenth century. Myopic bureaucrats in Washington could not understand why Indians had such a hard time assimilating into the urban mainstream. Decades of working with Native people only insulated bureaucrats who were so steeped in their conservative ways that they had a greater effect on Indian affairs than their liberal colleagues, and they cared even less. They either ignored tribal ways or believed that Indians should immediately conform to mainstream norms. Incoming bureaucrats working in Indian affairs also knew little about Native cultures. They failed to entertain the idea that the real problem might be the racist urban white mainstream rejecting Indian relocatees. For example, employers first laid off urban Indians from jobs for their lack of seniority and lack of training, and most of the time they did not give Indian workers a second chance. Physically, Indians looked different and did not act like whites. For example, brown-faced Indians did not fit in the public schools in Minneapolis and St. Paul. No Indians sat as members on the elected school boards for the Minneapolis public schools to represent Indian concerns.[11] In short, Indian people were powerless without influence and lacked a meaningful presence in a hegemonic situation.

Government bureaucrats exercised a federal paternalism that told Indians what to do; hence the other meaning of "BIA"—"Boss Indians Around." On his reservation in the 1960s, Floyd Taylor, a Hunkpapa Lakota, said, "I don't think in the past [one] hundred years or so that the Indian was allowed to make a mistake. He was never given an opportunity to make a mistake. I think that at the present he is being given the opportunity to make a mistake, and he is learning from that." The government paralyzed reservation communities and their leaders. "They made the Indians as such totally dependent on the federal government," said Taylor. "There were hand-outs, there were doles, and there still is, and now you got a president, probably starting with President Kennedy, that stated that, the Indian more or less should be self-sufficient type person, creating his own opportunities and more or less governing himself. There was a circle that was complete gone around. The Indian stands in the midst of it completely confused, where you have the old Indian and the young Indian, and this confusion creates this bitterness between the age groups, and the bitterness between the full-bloods."[12] Relocation and urbanization expanded Indian Country to include Indian populated cities, yet one has to realize that the mobility of Indians traveling back and forth from the reservation to city created more problems for Native people.

After sixteen years of relocation, it became evident that conditions were not going to get any better for indigenous people. Something had to change. As his presidency approached its end, on March 6, 1968, a weary-looking President Johnson delivered a special message to Congress, "The Forgotten American." Johnson assessed the situation of U.S.-Indian affairs at a time when the civil rights protests and Vietnam War controversy denigrated his administration. He articulated a new future for Indians and the government. The President said, "I propose a new goal for our Indian programs: A goal that ends the old debate about 'termination' of Indian programs and stresses self-determination; a goal that erases old attitudes of paternalism and promotes partnership self-help."[13] It would be interesting, in retrospect, if LBJ had mentioned the 43,000 Indian men who served patriotically in the Vietnam, the war that discredited his presidency.[14]

The census for 1970 recorded that the average Indian family had an income only slightly more than half that of the population average. About 35 percent of Native families lived below the poverty level. Some 15 percent of Indian children suffered from poor nutrition, and 90 percent more than fourteen years old had periodontal disease. Half of the adult population was chemically dependent, and the average age of death among Minnesota Indians was twenty-five years less than that for whites.[15] Apartment managers refused to rent to Indians based on racial stereotypes and viewed them with biased eyes. As a result, Indians had no choice but to seek out the worst housing in impoverished neighborhoods. Indian ghettoes began to emerge,[16] known by such names as the "Reservation" for Franklin Avenue in the Twin Cities, the "Little Reservation" in the mission district of San Francisco, and "Uptown" for the Indian neighborhood in the Near North Side of Chicago.[17]

Feeling impuissant, many Native people turned to alcohol to forget their problems temporarily. A new urban Indian problem of alcoholism added to the frustrations and anger that Native people felt. In a 1968 article published in the *Journal of Nervous and Mental Disease*, Dr. Joseph Westermeyer wrote, "In the drinking histories of the Chippewa [Ojibwa] patients, there were possible reasons for the earlier age of Chippewa [Ojibwa] women: they began alcohol usage early (mean age 14.0 years)."[18] In the same year another medical doctor noted that not all tribes drank excessively. Dr. Maurice L. Sievers observed that "especially noteworthy is the significantly lower frequency of heavy drinking for the Hopi than for the other tribes. Their rate approximates that of Caucasians."[19] In Minnesota, however, alcoholism occurred six and a half times more frequently among American Indians than for the rest of the state's population.[20]

Sievers' observation failed to influence the growing popular opinion that Native people had a drinking problem both in urban areas and on reservations. In one case study, a scholar who studied the Potawatomi noted, "There is desperation about the desire for alcohol which sometimes pushes the characteristic mode of indirect expression to the extreme. For example, [one] informant . . . felt no qualm about using a ritualized request for money to purchase beer and wine."[21] Drinking amplified urban stress and focused on underemployment and other problems. Simultaneously, excessive drinking unleashed such repercussions as domestic violence in the home life of Native people and led to other related concerns.

Alcoholism caused critical problems for Indians. Ojibwa author Gerald Vizenor noted that "alcohol related deaths for American Indians are four to five times higher than for the general public. Two-thirds of those deaths are caused by cirrhosis of the liver. Alcohol is also related to higher arrest rates, accidents, homicide, suicide, child abuse."[22] Many Indians spiraled downward, encountering many personal problems at work and home. There seemed to be no way out. They were trapped in the city until enough money could be scraped together or borrowed for gas or borrowed for a bus ticket to take them back to the reservation. This first generation of urban Indians could only comfort each other.

As alcoholism permeated many tribes, some Natives attempted to solve the problem, at least in their area. In the Southwest the All Pueblo Council passed a resolution stating that alcoholism "has developed as a social alternative. . . . There are however, five accepted statements which define the reasons for the use of alcohol among the American Indians." The council listed the concerns:

1. To relieve psychological and social stress produced by their own tribal culture. 2. To facilitate the release of repressed hostility and aggression. 3. To help attain a state of harmony with nature. 4. To make for more pleasant social interaction with friends. 5. To relieve psychological pain caused by pressures from acculturation and lack of employment opportunities. . . . [The] All Indian Pueblo Council proposes to implement and maintain an extensive program in treatment, rehabilitation and control of alcoholism and alcoholic related problems for members of New Mexico's Indian community.[23]

Alcoholism persisted as a problem even after the forming of AIM, and a concerned chapter of the organization strove to help its local members. In October 1972, Herb Powless, Green Bay AIM director, said, "Green Bay AIM has been working in the field of alcoholism for the past year. They have organized, sensitized and brought awareness to Fox Valley and to the Oneida Reservation. [There are] approximately 4,000 Indians in this area. The Green Bay American Indian Movement Chapter has as its 1st priority, the battle against alcoholism."[24] During the late 1960s and 1970s, alcoholism claimed the lives of 35 percent of all American Indians, according to the Department of Health and Human Services.[25] For the remaining decades of the twentieth century, alcoholism had the same effect, but with drug abuse added as another serious problem.

In the San Francisco Bay area, Indian people suffered the same frustration and felt alienated from the urban mainstream. Warren's Bar in the

Mission District became a popular meeting place. A local newspaper described one Native woman at

> Warren's Bar in the Mission District. Her hand shakes so badly she can barely bring the bottle to her lips. . . . The woman is an American Indian who came from a rural reservation to San Francisco eight years ago to learn a vocation through the Bureau of Indian Affairs Relocation Program. She has a job picking up glasses and bottles in Warren's Bar. She is 26 years old. . . . The general complaint is that police who appear on 16th street are disrespectful to the Indian and use greater numbers and force than are necessary to deal with problems.[26]

Such conditions in the Mission District helped to spark the Indian occupation of Alcatraz on November 20, 1969, a little over a year after the founding of AIM in the Twin Cities. Meanwhile, other Native people moved to the Bay Area at this time.

Georgia Lowman, a Pomo Indian and a counselor at the Oakland American Indian Association, summed up the feelings of the group: "We're all drunken Indians—whether you drink or not. Or dumb Indians." Capt. Philip G. Kiely, in charge of the Mission District police station, says, "We're in the police business—we're not sociologists. . . . They're their own worst enemy. They just can't drink." Unlike the police brutality in the Twin Cities that caused AIM to be founded, Kiely referred to the California Indians as children. He said, "We take them in as kindly as we can. I feel sorry for them. We know they're not violent. They're just children, really. Just grown up children. . . . Warren's Bar, [is] dark, dirty and rough . . . mixing poverty, frustration and loneliness with alcohol."[27] Frustrated and lonely, Indians turned to each other for comfort. An American Indian nurse described a familiar situation in the Bay Area. She said, "I'm Mary Grey Cloud. I'm a nurse and I work here in San Francisco. . . . They [Indians] go to a bar and drink with the white people, and what do they get? They get drunk; and if anything starts, they get a little belligerent because the white guy walks in and says he's no good."[28] This would provoke anyone to respond, but it often resulted in physical confrontations. Too much drinking in public led to confrontations between Indians and non-Indians. Fights broke out and even among Indians themselves.

The continual nonacceptance from the mainstream created anger, frustration, and self-doubt among Indian people. Such oppression became a psychological maze of trying to find one's true identity in an urban labyrinth. In addition, urban Indians began to form a subculture of downtrodden conditions that became a way of life for many Native people in the cities. One anthropologist observed that "internally, the group emphasizes Indian identity and a rejection of the dominant society they perceive as an oppressive colonizer. . . . Amongst themselves, community members are often warm, supportive, and positive, but this social solidarity is also used to enforce a high degree of conformity to apparently typical Skid Row behaviors."[29]

Certain parts of Minneapolis perpetuated enmity toward American Indians. The Indians were viewed as intruders who brought unkempt habits with them. A petulant storeowner of a north-side grocery and liquor store denigrated Indians. "Put them in a newly painted place and in a month it is wrecked," he said. "Rent to one and you have 20 living there. They live like pigs. Windows are broken. The place is unbelievably dirty."[30] Such attitudes had a negative impact on all urban Indians and did irreparable harm to their social and psychological state.

Indian stereotypes remain embedded in the minds of many non-Indians in Minneapolis and St. Paul. Minnesota's troubled racial history dates back to U.S.-Indian wars in the mid-nineteenth century. Much of the negative feelings toward Native people derived from a hostile past between Indians and whites. The U.S. military constructed Fort Snelling in 1825 at the confluence of the Minnesota and Mississippi rivers as an early post to keep peace between Indians and whites. Settlers encroached on Indian land and had to be forced out by soldiers. During the Civil War, the Little Crow War occurred in 1862 when starvation forced the Dakota people to leave their reservations to find food. They had agreed to accept a reservation, according to a treaty, but did not receive the promised annuities and food supplies because the Union diverted practically all supplies to the fighting front against the Confederacy. Dakota men raided the chicken coops and farms of mostly German settlers and provoked several skirmishes that resulted in what has also been called the Minnesota War of 1862. Little Crow led his warriors against the local militia and military in early victories. In the end, the military forced the Dakota from the reservation as many fled westward and then into Canada. Military officials captured a total of 303 Dakota men and blamed them for the war and the death of settlers. The list of individuals to be executed was reduced to a little over a hundred names. President Abraham Lincoln assiduously studied the list, crossing out some Dakota names based on advice from Bishop Henry Whipple. The reduced list included 39 culprits. Local officials constructed new gallows, 39 of them for the mass hanging. In the final hour, one Dakota received a reprieve from execution. The day after Christmas in 1862, a large crowd of 3,000 settlers and

curious onlookers gathered at Mankato, Minnesota, and watched 38 Dakota Indians being hanged at once, the largest mass execution in the history of the United States.[31]

The Indians of Minnesota never forgot this mass execution. They never
will. Broken treaties added to Indian resentment of the federal government and whites. As a reminder of the historic hostilities between Indians
and whites, in April 1968, Fort Snelling was rejuvenated when the state of
Minnesota announced a ten-year program of $4.5 million to restore the
old fort and to create Fort Snelling State Park for a total expansion of 4,460
acres.[32] Two months later AIM would be born to confront the present and
the past.

Later in the year, San Francisco State College started the first American Indian studies program as a result of the African Americans and Hispanic Americans gaining approval for black studies and Hispanic American
studies programs. The Black Student Union, Third World Liberation
Front, and Students for a Democratic Society led protests, marches, and
teach-ins attacking college policies and the Vietnam War. A year later, the
University of California at Berkeley, University of Minnesota in Minneapolis, and Trent University in Canada started Native studies programs for
similar reasons and goals.

Minneapolis became embroiled in student protests over civil rights and
Vietnam along with Kent State University, Columbia University, and the
University of California at Berkeley. Native students joined these protests,
too, but in the Twin Cities the urban Indian community became involved
in protesting due to their particular grievances of wanting improved relations with the mainstream and stopping police brutality. "Every Saturday
night at nine o'clock, the police arrived to conduct their manhunt," said
Dennis Banks.

> You could set your watch by the arrival of the paddy wagons. The cops
> concentrated on the Indian bars. They would bring their paddy wagons
> behind a bar and open the back doors. Then they would go around to
> the front and chase everybody toward the rear. As soon as you went
> through the back door, you were in the paddy wagon. The cops' favorite
> targets were Bud's bar on Franklin Avenue and the Corral, which was
> less than a hundred yards away. They rounded us up like cattle and
> booked us on 'drunk and disorderly' charges, even if we were neither.[33]

In describing his own experiences, Banks related those of many other
Indians living in the Twin Cities. The continuous police mistreatment

provoked the Indian community. Minneapolis became the focal point of resistance when local urban Indians came under brutal police attacks and public degradation. Along with Banks, a main Indian leader responsible for the founding of AIM was Clyde Bellecourt, an Ojibwa from White Earth reservation in northern Minnesota. Clyde was one of eleven children whose father was totally disabled during World War I. Clyde lived a reckless young life that led from a boarding school to a reformatory when police arrested him for the first time at age eleven. A court sent Clyde to the infamous Minnesota Training School for Boys at Red Wing and then to St. Cloud Reformatory. Petty crimes led to stealing cars, and a judge sentenced Bellecourt to Minnesota's Stillwater State Penitentiary. Prison life took its toll, and he entered a deep depression. "I was convinced," Bellecourt said, "that I was an ignorant, dirty savage—so I just gave up." He cursed his Indianness, blamed himself, and resolved that he would never eat again. Disgusted with himself, he hated his life, and contemplated self-destruction.[34]

Eddie Benton Benai befriended Bellecourt in prison, and through much patience, he became Bellecourt's trusted friend. Benai was a prison trustee; he visited Bellecourt frequently, and they had long talks. They discussed Bellecourt's outlook on life, and Benai told him about the proud history of the Ojibwa. Reflecting on the Indian's place in American society, Benai said, "The system beats Indian people down. It robs them of their self-respect. It demoralizes and discards them, and too often leads to resignation and defeat." Bellecourt's attitude changed noticeably, and he began taking pride in himself. "I realized that I wasn't a savage," he said. "I wasn't filthy and I wasn't ignorant. I was smart and capable." Rebounding to put his life back together, Bellecourt founded the Native American Folklore Group at Stillwater Prison in 1964. While Bellecourt was at Stillwater he met Dennis Banks, who was serving three and one-half years for forgery and burglary.[35]

In Stillwater Prison authorities locked Dennis Banks in maximum security. He refused to be a part of the general inmate community, and prison officials put him in solitary confinement. He said, "I started to educate myself while in solitary and found that there was a lot of social and political unrest happening on the outside. I began to follow the anti-war movement, the marches and protests, the Students for a Democratic Society . . . , the Weathermen, and the Black Panthers. Inside Stillwater, I made a commitment to myself that there would be an Indian movement."[36] Banks dreamed about an Indian movement different from the other protest movements. White activists formed the core of Students for a Democratic Society and the Weathermen. They were the children of the educated upper class echelon of mainstream America.[37] In contrast, Banks envisioned a movement led by and consisting of Indians themselves, similar to Black Panthers. "Red Power" was first introduced publicly on February 5, 1967, in a report of the Frank McGee television newscast. The National Congress of American Indians met in Denver and apparently used the term in its protests to protect Indian rights. The protest movements wanted political power to be equal to the white American status quo, and "Black Power" and "Brown Power" became equated with Black Americans and Hispanic Americans.[38] Whites were the power, and Indians were the powerless. Native people held practically no positions of authority in the mainstream. Throughout the colonized history of Indian-white relations, white power in the persona of teachers, police, BIA officials, priests, and nuns contrived to oppress Native people.[39]

Dennis Banks said, "When I got out of prison in May of 1968, I no longer had a family. . . . I called up my old friend George Mitchell, who had been at the boarding school with me, and said, 'George, I want to get a movement going, and I would like you to help me.'"[40] They immediately began to make plans and wanted to seize the moment to get something done for Indian people. They were tired of things getting done to Indian people.

Upon his release, Clyde Bellecourt returned to Minneapolis where AIM would be born. The "reservation" contained a few square blocks whose central street was Franklin Avenue. Minneapolis' Indian population of approximately 8,000 lived in this neighborhood, which was poor and dilapidated, with tenant apartments. During the early summer nights of 1968, the city police patrolled the area heavily and frequently arrested Indians. Rampant fights broke out between the police and Indians. An urban Indian protest group began to form under the name the Concerned Indian Citizens Coalition, but it was changed to the Concerned Indian Americans.

The momentum for action began to grow among the Minneapolis Indians. The Indian protestors contacted their friends, relatives, and anyone interested in trying to improve the Indian slums in the city. The Indians went house to house and apartment to apartment, handing out more than five hundred leaflets. The first meeting was "set for eight o'clock on the evening of July 28, 1968, in the basement of a rundown church," Dennis Banks recalled.

> By eight o'clock the place was packed. Almost two hundred people had gathered to listen and to begin making their voices heard. I opened the

meeting. I told these people that I had called them together because I felt that we needed to talk as a group about issues that concerned us all. . . . As the meeting went on, people began to speak up. One man spoke of the police brutality and said, "When do you propose to go down there to Franklin Avenue, to all those Indian bars where the cops inflict abuse on our people every night?" I told him, "We could go down there tomorrow night." He said, "Hell No, let's go down there right now, tonight!" People started to get excited and speak up. I knew that this excitement was going somewhere. The man in a hurry to get things done was Clyde Bellecourt, a Loon clan member from the White Earth reservation. During that first meeting, he spoke with such intensity that his enthusiasm swept over us like a storm.[41]

Some people say Indian women renamed the organization the American Indian Movement (AIM). Vernon Bellecourt stated that the members were going to call the organization the Concerned Indian Americans. " 'They couldn't use that!' So a couple of older, respected women said, 'Well you keep saying that you *aim* to do this, you *aim* to do that. Why don't you call it AIM, the American Indian Movement?' That's how we got our name."[42] "We start right now, this evening," said Banks. "And that is what we did . . . We immediately made Clyde the first chairman of AIM. I became the first field director. Together with George Mitchell, Harold Goodsky, and a number of determined women—among them Francis (*sic*) Fairbanks and 'Girlie' Brown—we formed AIM."[43]

In late July 1968, in response to police brutality, Clyde Bellecourt, Dennis Banks, and other concerned Indians met with attorney Gus Hall at 1111 Plymouth Avenue in Minneapolis. Several noted individuals also added to the early organization of AIM, including Eddie Benton Benai and Mary Jane Wilson, both Ojibwa. Hall helped AIM to understand its members' legal rights.

The Native people organized patrols to scrutinize police and started to locate drunken Indians before the police found them. The patrols carried citizen band radios to intercept police calls so that they could witness arrests and make sure that the arrested Indians were not abused. Some carried Polaroid cameras. Patrol members began wearing red jackets. Later a black thunderbird emblem was added, and the other members referred to the patrols as "shock troops." At this time, the coalition became a structured organization with an Indian board and staff. The primary purpose of AIM focused on the spiritual uplift of revitalizing pride among Indian Americans. In the process, protecting their brethren and the general welfare of their communities were immediate concerns. AIM activities increased and involved gaining a nonprofit corporate status. AIM started a school solely for Indian youths at the Little Red Schoolhouse in St. Paul. Little Red Schoolhouse was a survival school with an alternative curriculum to help Indian children meet both their cultural needs and their academic needs for grades K through 12. Later AIM opened another survival school, Heart of the Earth, near the University of Minnesota campus. At the junior high level, Ojibwa youths had a dropout rate of 65 percent in public schools. Not too long afterward, AIM started an elders' program. AIM assisted new arrivals from reservations and provided the unemployed with temporary shelter and meals.

In 1969 Dennis Banks and Russell Means met. Means had worked as an accountant, computer operator, rodeo hand, ballroom dance instructor, janitor, and farmhand. He grew up in California and was an intelligent, rebellious youth, always challenging his teachers. Participating in the marijuana and drug scene, he was a "low rider without a ride."[44] In his initial encounter with AIM, Means opposed the organization and its radical ideas. He was instrumental at the time in the operation of the Cleveland American Indian Center. Banks called Means on the phone and asked for his support in a planned protest against the National Council of Churches triennial convention in Detroit. When he asked why AIM wanted him, Banks told Means, "Because you're a good speaker and we need your help." Means caught a plane to Detroit and met AIM members Dennis Banks and Clyde Bellecourt. They looked very "Indian," wearing beads and moccasins.[45] Later that day Means asked Banks, "How do I join AIM?" Banks replied, "You just did."[46] He soon became one of the principal spokespersons for AIM.

AIM appealed to many young Indian men and women. AIM leader Dino Butler described the early years: "In the beginning of AIM, a lot of us brothers and sisters came together, and we formed a solid bond. We learned how to pick up that pipe, and we learned how to pray again, and dance together and sing together. And we grew spiritually. . . . We progressed to a point where we became Sun Dancers, pipe carriers, sweat lodge people."[47] As AIM pushed forward politically and proliferated, their members wanted spiritual fulfillment. This was the Indian way, possessing spirituality for safety, security, and empowerment. These were trying times that required spiritual strength.

On the West Coast, Indian protests for fishing rights in the Northwest and on the campuses of San Francisco State University, University of California at Berkeley, and UCLA for correcting the wrongful treatment of indigenous people led to attempts to take over Alcatraz Island. The government closed the penitentiary in March 1963, and Indian activists wanted to claim the island. Bay Area Indians organized Indians of All Tribes, which included Richard Oakes, LaNada Means, Adam Fortunate Eagle, and others who wanted to take the island based on the 1868 Treaty of Fort Laramie with the Lakota, which included returning unused federal land.[48]

The idea to take over Alcatraz was a topic of discussion among Bay Area Indian activists. In fact, two previous attempts had been recently made. On October 6, a mysterious fire burned down the San Francisco Indian Center, which added to the agitation that something important was going to happen. The Bay Area Indians had been in a turf war with Samoans in the Missions District. In the early hours of November 20, 1969, the third attempt to take the island succeeded when seventy-nine Indians landed on the island.[49] The island's one caretaker, Glen Dodson, saw the commotion of the activists coming onto the island. He ran out of his run-down building yelling, "Mayday! Mayday! Mayday! The Indians have landed!"[50] This was the beginning of the Alcatraz takeover, and Native activists held the island for nineteen months.

Alcatraz became a beacon in the West for Indian activism. A charismatic Mohawk, Richard Oakes became well known for his oratory, and his flamboyant leadership added to the excitement as more Indians from across the nation rushed to be a part of the Alcatraz occupation. AIM members joined the occupation, including John Trudell (Lakota), who became known as the "Voice of Alcatraz" in his radio broadcasts from the island. As a community began to form, plans included establishing a spiritual center, an ecology center, and a museum. The media focused on the takeover, and the Bay Area Indians saw themselves on television and in the headlines of newspapers. For certain, the Indians had gotten the rest of the country to listen to them. People donated food, clothes, and supplies to the island occupiers.[51]

As failed attempts of negotiations between the federal government and the activists were interrupted, government officials even tried to blockade the island, but this did not work. In May 1970, officials cut off the electricity to the island's buildings. The FBI and reporters followed the activities at Alcatraz very closely, and the latter wrote stories as the occupation became old news. At the same time, President Richard Nixon realized that definite action had to be taken. He ordered Special Counsel Leonard Garment to take over the negotiations. By this time, the activists were out of fresh water, and many began to leave the island. While many of the islanders were

Figure 5.1. American Indian Movement takeover of the Bureau of Indian Affairs. Courtesy of Battman/Corbis.

away in San Francisco, a force of federal marshals, agents, and government officers invaded Alcatraz and removed the remaining fifteen Indians on June 11, 1970.[52]

On November 3, Indian activists jumped the fence of a set of abandoned military communications buildings near Davis, California. Jack Forbes (Powhattan) and Dave Risling (Hupa) filed paperwork with the government and proposed a joint Indian-Chicano university on the site. With much effort, Deganawidah-Quetzalcoatl University (DQU) was founded via Native activism. On April 2, 1971, the federal government turned the land title over to the trustees of the DQU with the message that this action was in response to the Alcatraz demands for an Indian university.[53] Indian activism seemed to be everywhere at the same time.

In the fall of 1970, AIM held its first national organizational meeting in St. Paul. Indians from other parts of the country heard about the meeting and drove there to see what AIM was about. Reuben Snake, a Ho-Chunk, had been reading the newspapers about Dennis Banks, Clyde Bellecourt, and Russell Means, but he only knew George Mitchell at the time. He and Mitchell had been classmates at Haskell Indian School many years earlier. Reuben and his family decided to drive to the AIM meeting in St. Paul. On the second day of the meeting, AIM members voted Russell Means as chairman. AIM surprised Reuben Snake by electing him Vice chairman.[54] In two years after AIM's birth, its members increased to an estimated 5,000. In five years after its founding, AIM had established seventy-nine chapters, with eight of them in Canada. AIM had legal assistance from the Legal Aid Society, which met weekly with AIM leaders to help any Native person. AIM established a housing improvement program and rented a trailer to help move people to better places to live. It also had its own radio program on station KUXL to broadcast Indian concerns and raise issues.[55]

Over the next four years, AIM proliferated throughout Indian Country, forming chapters in cities and on reservations. Russell Means organized the first chapter outside of the Twin Cities in Cleveland; taking the initials from the city and adding AIM, CLAIM was established.[56] Ultimately, chapters developed in Canada as well as in U.S. cities, such as San Francisco, Los Angeles, Denver, Milwaukee, and other urban areas.

A new generation of Indian activist leaders became well known—Clyde's brother, Vernon Bellecourt; Richard Oakes, Mohawk; and Lehman Brightman, Lakota, who became the director of Native American studies at the University of California at Berkeley. Other leaders included John Trudell, Santee Dakota, who served as AIM national chairperson from 1974 to

Figure 5.2. Oren Lyons (center) and AIM members at Wounded Knee takeover. Courtesy of Carol Sullivan and New Mexico Digital Collection, University of New Mexico.

1979; Leonard Peltier, Métis; Anna Mae Aquash, Micmac; and Carter Camp, Ponca. AIM activism resulted in demonstrations at the nineteen-month occupation of Alcatraz that began in 1969; at Mt. Rushmore in September 1970; and at the *Mayflower* replica at Plymouth, Massachusetts, on Thanksgiving 1971. Ubiquitous protests occurred in the early 1970s. In 1970 Dennis Banks, John Trudell, Lehman Brightman, and Russell Means led an Indian protest and three-month occupation at Mt. Rushmore involving AIM and members of United Indians of America from northern California. Most of the protestors were Lakota who were responding to the threat that their traditional lands might be seized. They wanted to assert that the Black Hills belonged to their tribe according to the Fort Laramie Treaty of 1868. Russell Means recalled, "We had no weapons, no food or water, no camping gear, no flashlights, but everyone caught the spirit." It began to get dark and the Indians argued with the Forest Service rangers. John Trudell finally said, "Screw it, let's take over the mountain." Trudell and Means started up Mt. Rushmore in the dark. The rangers yelled at the Indians to stop. Trudell yelled back, "Arrest us." The Indians wanted to be arrested to make the local news, perhaps even the national news. The rangers threatened to shoot the Indians. Trudell retorted, "Go ahead, shoot! You can't get all three of us." Means agreed, then thought quickly to yell, "Wait a minute! Don't shoot!" He knew if anyone got shot, it would be him. One ranger kept asking, "Are you coming down?" The Indians refused. "Nope," said Means. In December, state police broke up the demonstration and arrested the remaining protesting Indians.[57]

During 1971, AIM members dared to seize an abandoned building, startling sailors at Fort Snelling Naval Base in Minnesota. AIM members then established a convincing security perimeter with plans to start a survival school for Indians. AIM entered into negotiations with Minnesota senators Hubert Humphrey and Walter Mondale, who sympathized with them but could do very little for the Indians. The U.S. Military tolerated the situation at Fort Snelling for only a week. On a Sunday in April 1971, the occupation began. On the following Friday, Mondale was to meet with Dennis Banks, but at five o'clock on that very morning, a heavily armed SWAT unit swept the base and arrested all the Indians. When Mondale showed up there was nothing left to discuss.

On August 19, 1971, the Milwaukee AIM chapter seized an abandoned Coast Guard base. Led by Herb Powless, the Indians set up a halfway house and detoxification center for Indian alcoholics, as well as a community school for Indian children. Both state senators, the governor of Wisconsin, and the city mayor supported the self-help site. The Indians also established a program for the elderly, job training, day care, tribal language classes, and craft workshops.

In February 1972, the brutal murder of Raymond Yellow Thunder provoked AIM members to converge on the small town of Gordon, Nebraska. Yellow Thunder was fifty-one years old and from Pine Ridge. Two brothers, Melvin and Leslie Hare, along with Bernard Ludder and Robert Bayless, who all were white, stripped the clothes from Yellow Thunder and pushed him around at a dance held at the American Legion Post no. 34 in Gordon that night. Five days later Yellow Thunder's body was found slumped over the steering wheel of his pickup parked in a used car lot. Local police questioned the culprits and released them. The Yellow Thunder family called AIM for help. AIM arrived in a large caravan and pressured local officials into charging the two brothers with Yellow Thunder's murder.[58]

On the night of January 28, 1973, at 10:45 p.m., six AIM members waving guns and carrying shoulder-held weapons entered the Public Health

Service Hospital in Gallup, New Mexico. The FBI reported that AIM members led by Victor Cutnose threatened the doctors and nurses that they better provide better medical care to Indians. They held everyone hostage until surrendering to the senior president agent at Gallup and the McKinley County district attorney on the following morning.[59]

Operating at full scale, AIM sponsored the First International Indian Treaty Council for nine days. The Standing Rock Sioux hosted the council at the Chief Gall Inn. The American Indian Press Association announced that 3,000 persons attended the event. In the preamble of the Declaration of Continuing Independence, the following words described the overall objective of this gathering:

> The United States of America has continually violated the independent Native peoples of this continent by executive action, legislative fiat and judicial decisions. By its actions, the U.S. has denied all Native people their international treaty rights, treaty lands, and basic human rights of freedom and sovereignty. This same U.S. government which fought to throw off the yoke of oppression and gain its own independence, has now reversed its role and become the oppressor of sovereign Native people.[60]

In 1972, AIM coordinated what became known as the Trail of Broken Treaties March. The nationwide trek ended in Washington, DC, with the takeover of the BIA building. The AIM occupiers renamed it the Native American Embassy. Much damage was done inside the building as the Indians barricaded themselves against officials. They held out for several days; negotiations with federal officials finally ended with a compromise that no arrests would be made if everyone went home.

Following the BIA takeover in Washington, another situation called for AIM's intervention. Two cowboys confronted Wesley Badheart Bull, an Oglala Lakota, outside of Bill's Bar in Buffalo Gap, South Dakota, on January 22, 1973. One of them held Badheart Bull while the other stabbed him several times with a knife in the chest. Badheart Bull died shortly afterward, on the way to a hospital in the next town. The murderer, Darald Schmitz, a white man who worked as a gas station attendant, was charged with second-degree manslaughter. An all-white jury acquitted Schmitz of the murder in Custer, South Dakota. On February 6, AIM mobilized toward Custer, making local authorities uneasy. They arrived with about two hundred Indians in a snowstorm. Custer armed itself with state troopers and deputized locals. AIM leaders wanted Schmitz charged with first-degree murder and the county attorney, Hobart Gates, refused, calling the incident a barroom brawl. In the snowstorm, a riot between AIM members, local Indians, and officials broke out at the Custer courthouse. In the end, officials arrested about twenty Indians, including Russell Means, Dennis Banks, and Sarah Badheart Bull, the mother of Wesley Badheart Bull. Many people on both sides were hurt from the confrontation, but the Indians received the worst of it as they had been beaten with police batons. Sarah Badheart Bull served five months in jail for the riot. Darald Schmitz served one day in jail for arrest and questioning.[61]

About the same time, AIM was summoned by some concerned members of the Oglala Sioux at Pine Ridge in South Dakota. The Oglalas requested AIM assistance to protect them while tribal chairperson Richard Wilson held office. Faced with allegations of the misuse of tribal funds and abuse of authority, Wilson hired a "goon squad" he called Guardians of the Oglala Nation for his own protection. His squad, however, physically abused tribal members. During the morning prelude to the occupation of Wounded Knee, Wilson's police assaulted Russell Means and his lawyer at a local shopping center.

From all parts of the country, AIM and other Indians gathered in South Dakota and were to meet at Porcupine community hall. Because of the burgeoning numbers arriving, the desultory group drove to Calico, a small town nearby with a large meeting hall. In the process, the Indians stopped at Wounded Knee to pay respect to the people of Big Foot's Lakota band killed during the Wounded Knee Massacre in 1890. Disconsolate emotions engulfed the people whose indignant anger compelled them to seize the small hamlet of Wounded Knee, South Dakota, on February 27, 1973.

The Indians occupied the town for seventy-one days and armed themselves with hunting rifles when they learned that state authorities requested the National Guard to restore order by returning the town back over to its inhabitants. The federal government in Washington ordered more than three hundred U.S. marshals to Wounded Knee, including a Special Operations Group. Over one hundred FBI agents set up roadblocks on two of the highways going to the takeover site. The Central Intelligence Agency was involved as well.

U.S. Senator James Abourezk of South Dakota tried to call anyone in Wounded Knee to investigate what was going on. The Senator recalled,

> Then, . . . using a Pine Ridge telephone book, I called the first number
> I found listed in Wounded Knee Village, which belonged to someone
> named Wilbur Riegert. It was an amazing coincidence. Riegert's house

was being used by the Indians as their headquarters. Russ Means, whom I had met years before, answered the phone. When I asked him what was happening, he told me that the Indians were holding eleven hostages. "They would not be released," he said, "until Henry Kissinger, Bill Fulbright, Ted Kennedy, and I came to Wounded Knee to listen to the Indians spell out their grievances."[62]

On the second day AIM leaders issued a formal call for then-Senator J. William Fullbright, chairman of the Senate Foreign Relations Committee, to start hearings in order to examine treaties that had been signed by the Sioux Nation with the United States. This did not happen, and Senator Abourezk and Senator George McGovern worked jointly to talk to the AIM members holding the Knee.

Senator Abourezk later recalled the aberrant drive with Senator McGovern into Wounded Knee to negotiate with AIM leaders on the second day of the occupation: "Just like actors in a western, we tied a white cloth to a tree branch and hung it out of the car window." Abourezk, McGovern, and their driver, John Terronez, the Justice Department's community relations representative, drove slowly toward the hamlet of Wounded Knee. They passed the government perimeter, moved slowly into the demilitarized zone, and finally reached the first AIM checkpoint. There was no turning back. Abourezk said, "My nerves began to shatter. . . . we found ourselves staring directly into the barrels of an assortment of weapons—shotguns, rifles, automatic weapons—all aimed directly at our heads by the meanest-looking bunch of Indians I had ever seen. The tension inside the car increased . . . as our car crept deeper and deeper into Indian territory. Suddenly McGovern leaned over to me and said, 'Jim, why did you have to be so fucking courageous?' "[63] Abourezk and McGovern got out of the car and told all of the hostages that they were free to go. After all of this, they learned that all of the hostages lived in Wounded Knee and did not want to leave.

Dennis Banks was the primary negotiator for the Wounded Knee occupants. Banks estimated that the feds had as many as five hundred personnel on their side, including ranchers and vigilantes who wanted to "bag themselves one of them red savages." Banks recalled,

Almost as soon as we occupied the Knee, army advisors and observers from the Pentagon made plans to drive us out of the village. They supplied the federal agents at Wounded Knee with an unbelievable amount of military hardware, enough to kill the whole Oglala tribe. Ready for action were fifteen armored cars—APCs—one hundred thousand rounds of M-16, eleven hundred parachute illumination flares, twenty sniper rifles with night-vision scopes, powerful searchlights, submachine guns, bulletproof vests, gas masks, C rations, ponchos, blankets, and helmets. Low-flying army planes performed photo reconnaissance missions, which frightened some of the older women. They thought we were about to be bombed.[64]

During the seventy-one-day occupation, supporters airlifted food and supplies to the AIM camp inside the war zone. The FBI harassed local Indian families outside of the area, and their homes were fired upon.

Finally the negotiations began. Both sides agreed to an investigation into charges against Dick Wilson and treaty meetings with the Oglalas in order to review the Fort Laramie Treaty of 1868. On Friday, May 8, 146 Indian men and women laid down their arms, including fifteen inoperable rifles, and surrendered to the government authorities. Government law enforcement lowered the AIM flag over Wounded Knee and raised the American flag. A military helicopter hovered overhead as one of the marshals made a victory speech. Banks described the tense situation, saying,

> The marshals and FBI were in full camouflage battle dress, looking for booby traps and hidden enemy holdouts. We had been promised that no goons would be let in, but they were there all right, robbing and destroying whatever they found. Carter Camp and Leonard Crow Dog, in handcuffs, chains and leg-irons, were put in a helicopter and taken to the jail in Rapid City. All of the others were lined up, searched, and fingerprinted. Wallace Black Elk was mishandled and robbed of his medicine pouch and sacred pipe. Over the loudspeaker a voice proclaimed, "Gentlemen, the village of Wounded Knee is secured."[65]

During the entire occupation, two Indians were killed.

Dennis Banks and Russell Means faced charges of conspiracy. In all, officials filed more than one hundred indictments against Indians involved at Wounded Knee. On January 8, 1974, the trial of Dennis Banks and Russell Means began in what the Indians would call the "trial of the century." If convicted for the variety of crimes that both leaders were charged with, they could have been sentenced to eighty-five years in prison. Means was charged with forty crimes and was exonerated on thirty-nine of these claims. His single conviction stemmed from his courtroom performance during the harassment-type trials. In St. Paul the trial dragged on for more than eight months before a judge dropped all charges against Means and Banks due to grounds of government misconduct. Banks was still charged for the deaths of the two FBI men in 1975, and after being given protection against extradition in California and in New York State, he surrendered to begin serving a prison sentence. Leonard Peltier was also charged with the deaths of the two FBI agents, and he continues to serve two consecutive life sentences at the U.S. penitentiary in Leavenworth, Kansas.

In March 1975, Greg Zeiphier and Fred Zephier led members of the Eagle Warriors Society and seized the Yankton Sioux Industries Park in Wagner, South Dakota. With rifles and shotguns, the warriors and AIM members entered the business park at 8:00 a.m. as it opened with fifteen to twenty people inside, making sixteen demands. Frustration with low wages and poor working conditions were the reasons for the takeover. The Warriors wanted better pay for the workers and safer working conditions. Three days later the occupation ended with both the warriors and Yankton officials agreeing to renegotiate the contract with the workers and the plant's owner.[66]

In the three years following the Wounded Knee occupation, federal officials made 562 arrests, which resulted in only fifteen convictions, five of which were for "interfering with federal officers" as people tried to pass through an FBI roadblock to bring food to those inside the occupation. Judge Fred Nichol dismissed the charges, stating, "The waters of justice have been polluted." It was his belief that the misconduct by the government and FBI "in this case is so aggravated that a dismissal must be entered in the interests of justice." Members of the jury, finding the tactics employed by the FBI and government attorneys repulsive, agreed with the judge.

AIM's militant actions did not always have full support from Indian Country. Some Indians rejected AIM's aggressiveness. Nez Perce Cathy Wilson said,

> I will say how I feel [about AIM]. I don't particularly agree with their methods of getting things done, but I do know that there are a lot of people who are behind them and supporting them, a lot of Indians, and that's just how one group of Indians feels about things. And I would say I think that probably most of the AIM followers are people who really have been treated rawly, very poorly, all their life and really show it. And that might be one reason why I'm not so sympathetic with AIM, 'cause I've never really had any big problems with being an Indian, like, say

people on the reservation who live near communities which really are prejudiced against them.[67]

The more militant that AIM became, the more rejection that it received from Native people who were not involved. "Well, a lot of people, they consider AIM as being so vicious, you know, tearing everything down, and guns and the whole works," said Janice Nack, a Shoshone-Navajo. "Well, a lot of my friends are AIMs and they're not like that. They've got their beliefs and they're proud to be Indian. . . . I guess it just depends on the people who are in AIM. There are some people who don't protest . . . they've got a lot of good opinions and there's just, I guess, a way of going about it that gives them a bad name."[68]

The Red Power years were aided by the sympathetic administration of Lyndon B. Johnson, who advocated Indian civil rights. In the eyes of the indigenous population, Indian rights were more important than civil rights. They wished to coexist with the mainstream without being discriminated against for any reason. Although cultural pluralism has continued to persist in America, a nation made up of many diverse and multiple layers of ethnicity and different races, the federal government continued to act on the plan to assimilate Native people during most of the twentieth century, until the 1970s. The 1960s were a defining moment that suspended government thinking of desegregating Indians and making them forgo their Native ways. Yet this volatile time marked the genesis of rebuilding Indian nations that the government had tried to terminate less than ten years earlier.

AIM remained an organization to take up the Indian cause and lend support to minority issues. Red Power became the voice of Indian protest. The Indian community at large was not represented in the Red Power movement, although it acted for all Indian concerns. In essence members of the Red Power movement were the warriors of the community. In a pan-Indian militaristic manner, they sought to fight for their people like warriors of the 1800s. They were, indeed, warriors in the twentieth century. They were warriors who did not fit into mainstream America. Many Indians dropped out of school, feeling like outcasts. Rural Indian students dropped out at a 35 percent rate before the ninth grade. As an individual, the Indian student entered an alien school environment and had to learn how to navigate the educational system with often little from relatives who lacked a formal education to supply sound advice.[69] The Red Power movement offered an alternative and hope.

Several factors interacted to provoke the Indian outcry that led to Red Power. This Indian initiative was a revitalization of community within urban settings. Native people redefined home space in urban Indian communities as leaders began to organize. One time during lunch with Clyde Bellecourt, I asked what was the key to AIM's success and leadership. He replied with one word, "organization." The movement created a new spirituality in an attempt to defend Indian communities in cities and on reservations. Organization was the key to all of the activities of the AIM chapters. This included a new educational influence of Indian youth that produced a new leadership, which advanced a new identity of Indianness. Dino Butler recalled, "Then we [activists] came to a point [in our lives] where I feel like we began to not learn any more. Because we do carry hate [inside us] and refuse to let it go, then it still controls us and determines our actions. . . . Until we are able to release these things we carry inside of us, we are not going to be able to grow. When AIM was growing spiritually as a movement, it had credibility with the people."[70]

Related to AIM, other radical Native American organizations formed such as the Menominee Warrior Society in Milwaukee, Wisconsin, and the Montana Survival of American Indians Association. By the late 1970s, AIM no longer occupied national headlines, although it served an important purpose in altering federal Indian policy. The last national protest made by AIM was the Longest Walk in 1978 as a protest and reminder to the country of Indian mistreatment and the injustice done to them. Although AIM was known for its militant position, another side of AIM involved helping native communities, such as the Navajo. Melvin McKenzie said, "The [AIM] group, up here, they did quite a few things for us. In major events they helped us in the parking situation, and in a very large dance they helped with the security department, maintain security on the grounds."[71]

Marcus Sekayouma, Hopi, said, "I think that one of the spinoffs from the AIM, one of the greatest things they've done, is the fact that there has been a greater awareness by the Indian people of what they can do if they have a concerted effort, rather than saying, 'I can't do it because the superintendent says I can't.'"[72] By capturing national attention while other minority groups were protesting too, AIM made the American public aware of the issues concerning indigenous Americans.

In the 1990s AIM divided into two organizations. This status became official in 1993. The AIM Grand Governing Council was led by Vernon Bellecourt. This part of AIM continued to confront white oppression throughout Indian Country by coming to the assistance of Native people. Russell Means and others led the AIM-International Confederation of Autonomous Chapters that took up indigenous issues in South America. Means spoke out against the Sandinistas in Nicaragua in an effort to protect the Miskito Indians.[73] In the twenty-first century, Dennis Banks and other leaders continue to speak out about the international mistreatment of indigenous people. Following the first decade of the twenty-first century, AIM continues to focus on issues affecting Indian people such as the mascot controversy of sports teams berating Native people, and updates on Leonard Peltier's imprisonment at Leavenworth for the deaths of two FBI men. Since the founding of AIM and before in the mid-1960s, Indian activism involved pan-Indianism, fighting for treaty rights, forging new leadership, and producing a new Indian identity.

This new proactive identity of Indian leadership emerged with the Chicago pan-Indian conference, the National Indian Youth Council, the fishing rights protests in the Pacific Northwest, the Alcatraz takeover, and AIM. As political activists, these new Indian leaders were articulate and used the white man's language with oratorical skills. Their knowledge acquired in boarding schools and assiduous awareness of U.S.-Indian law assisted them in decolonizing the white society's hegemonic framework forced upon them and all Indians. Their new day represented a defining historical moment of fresh political leadership across Indian Country that would begin to rebuild Native nations and spearhead Indian organizations. Indians began to take control of Indian Country from the federal government.

All of this occurred with the right timing when other ethnic and political interest groups gained support, the media provided national coverage, and AIM struck the conscience of Americans who acknowledged the historical mistreatment of Native people. If anything, AIM and the Indian protest groups that preceded it unshackled the stigma that the government "bossed Indians around." In a violent climate of protests exacerbated by uncertainty and a possible oncoming social revolution, Indians borrowed the tool of protesting from other groups, adapted to conflict within society, and moved forward with uncertain plans to rebuild their nations. The 1960s protest years had provided the right timing to take action, and an indigenous leadership responded and got some satisfaction.

CHAPTER SIX

Political Economy and Tribal Natural Resources

Resource Management

I decided to organize several tribes into a coalition I liked to call the Native American OPEC. . . . Following our first meeting with the president's special assistant in the Department of Energy, we were told to organize ourselves in order to gain White House backing. This we did in a room assigned to us in the D.O.E. We discussed our concerns, trying to come up with a name for our group. . . . It was after midnight, we were tired, and the name continued to elude us. Fighting hunger and exhaustion, I reached into my pocket and removed a package of Certs breath mints. I glanced at the wrapper just before slipping one of the mints into my mouth. Then, joking, I said, "Why don't we call ourselves CERT?" No one realized I was referring to the mints in my hand, so they asked me what the initials stood for. Thinking for a moment, I replied, "Council of Energy Resource Tribes." We adopted the name. We were finally able to adjourn and get some sleep. I was grateful that I had not been carrying Tic-Tacs or Life Savers, for had I been, we might have spent more hours trying to find a name.

PETER MACDONALD, NAVAJO, 1975

"Some people have a deep abiding respect for the natural beauty that was once this country and some people don't. People start pollution. People can stop it," said the public service announcement in a deep resonating voice. Simultaneously, an American Indian dressed in buckskin gets out of a canoe; he stands tall as trash is thrown at his feet from a passing car. He turns his bronze chiseled face slightly as a single tear rolls down the curve of his cheek. This cause célèbre is an unforgettable scene etched in the minds of many older Americans. This commercial aired regularly during the early 1970s, a sign of the times that introduced the environmental movement.[1] Even though Iron Eyes Cody in the commercial was actually Italian, the American people got the message: "Take care of the Earth! Don't screw up!" Everyone was responsible for the natural environment.

The plethora of natural resources on reservation lands in the modern West provoked another epochal struggle between Indians and whites, which has continued into the twenty-first century. Power and control determined who would end up with the final say about tribal finite natural resources remaining on tribal lands. Ironically, for a long time white settlers, ranchers, miners, and railroad industrialists did not desire these seemingly worthless lands. Who would have guessed that rich natural resources would rest under these worthless Indian lands? More important was anticipating the potential of mining tribal resources, and what the consequences were for the tribes. Native leaders, especially those of what would become known as the energy tribes, learned an invaluable lesson from previous generations of Indians that were bilked out of their lands and royalties. These history lessons included gold and silver on Indian lands, then oil, coal, gas, timber, uranium, and water were at risk. And it has been said, experience is the best teacher. But the tribes have learned much more than this. Resource management became a vital tool for tribes in planning, developing programs, and rebuilding their nation with a political economy approach.

Political economy here is used as an approach of analyzing the progress of a community in history, economics, law, political science, and sociology. Essentially, by examining how tribal communities have utilized their natural resources in these five areas, one can see their progress over time as their state of economy improved while operating legally under trust relations with the federal government. In addition, by studying the social relations within the community, the political context indicates varying degrees of improvement in the economy. In the case of Native groups, their longtime relationship also with the earth is an ingrained one in their various cultures. By examining the changes within a tribal community over time, we can understand the economic progress and relationships sustained by the people.

At the close of the nineteenth century, Wooden Leg of the Cheyenne described his view toward conflicting human-earth relations. His words still hold importance today as they have throughout the western Indians' struggle to defend their tribal natural resources. He recalled,

Another thing the white people appear not to understand: The old Indian teaching was that it is wrong to tear loose from its place on the earth anything that may be growing there. It may be cut off, but it should not be uprooted. The trees and the grass have spirits. Whenever one of such growths may be destroyed by some good Indian, his act is done in sadness and with prayer for forgiveness because of his necessities, the same as we were taught to do in killing animals for food and skins. We revere especially the places where our old camp circles used to be set up and where we had our old places of worship.[2]

Wooden Leg's view of the human relationship with the earth reflects that of other Native groups whose philosophies and worldviews are connected to the earth. In fact, all things are related in this general worldview.

Oil followed gold as the immediate natural resource on Indian lands that brought national attention, including international interests, to Indian Country. Deep black oil pools in Oklahoma in the early 1920s made the state the top oil producer in the entire United States as the country retooled itself following the Great War with a gluttony for crude oil. Other states like Texas soon vied for the claim of oil capital. Oil magnate John D. Rockefeller would monopolize petroleum to unimaginable wealth that made him, alone, almost as rich as the entire United States. At the same time, Blackfeet forebodings voiced concern for protecting oil on their land. In 1923 John Galbraith explained to the tribal council that his personal experience with oil companies taught him to operate their own wells and the tribe would control its own natural resources. George Starr said to his tribesmen, "The oil is here, it is all around us. . . . You half breeds are just as smart as any white man and some are smarter and we can do our own drilling, form a company and do our own work and you can do it if you just get it into your neck that you can do it."[3] In response, the Blackfeet tribal council formed a new oil committee to investigate innovative ways that it could develop its resources. When the oil rush declined, coal became the next concern on tribal lands in the Native West.

The Blackfeet tribal council was forced to learn "resource management" in trying to provide a better livelihood for their communities. Resource management simply meant how a tribal council like the Blackfeet learned to practice capitalism while negotiating the leasing and development of their natural resources like oil. In these years, they found themselves still very dependent upon the government, and they realized that they needed to change the situation. Their desire for more control over their oil also compelled them to forgo their old moral economy of making sure that everyone was taken care of. They also realized, as many other tribes did, that they were entering a new area, perhaps a kind of third space where they dealt with the mainstream business world. This in-between third space would become permanent and full of negotiations for tribal resources. What is important to note is the irony of wanting to respect the traditional relationships with the earth, but communal needs to help tribal members via programs like health and education outweighed the past. The following is a specific tribal example.

Peabody Coal Company of St. Louis, Missouri, a subsidiary of Kennecott Copper Company, mined coal on the Hopi and Navajo reservations to send it to the Navajo Generating Station at Page, Arizona. Using a dragline bucketlike shovel, Peabody could mine to a depth of 300 feet in the Mesa Verde sandstone that contained veins of coal nearly 65 feet deep. A dragline can tower up to nearly twenty stories tall, and it cuts deeper into the 150- to 300-foot Mancos shale lying under the sandstone, containing small seams of coal. Below the shale of Dakota sandstone of 20 to 300 feet in thickness are rich veins of coal.[4] Peabody is the world's largest privately owned coal company. The overall result is the largest privately owned coal company mining on the largest reservation and yielding the largest strip-mining operation in the world. An important question to ask is, how did this happen?

The United States continues to depend on fossil fuels to run an automobile culture; thus, energy companies pressure tribes with natural resources according to the demand of the American market economy. This consumption spiraled upward in the 1970s, and little has changed since then. With many of the needed natural resources like timber, coal, uranium, oil, and others on Indian lands, tribes still face the enormous question of whether or not to mine their resources to benefit their peoples and for their fossil fuels to go to the rest of America.

Attempting to understand this serious dilemma requires an exploration of tribal communities and cultures. This dilemma posits the question of what kind of new culture will manifest due to the forceful catalyst of energy demand acting as an agent for permanent change among these tribes. Most of all, people should try to understand the earth as Indian people do, like the Iron Eyes Cody commercial, and the way in which mining natural resources contradicts fundamental traditional beliefs.

Sacred acknowledgment of rain connects rainbows and ceremonies. For example, a desert needs rain for its inhabitants to live, and they adjust to survive. The Navajos say that praying under a rainbow gives a person "strength and force," and the individual will be fortunate and strong.[5] The vastness of their part of the West compels Native people like the Navajo and other tribes to drive considerable distances even to obtain water in large vats. Many prefer trucks to cars. Ford, Toyota, Chevy, and Dodge pickups are popular. The terrain dictates a changing culture among Indian people who have quickly adopted the automobile and pickup, especially after World War II. Such adaptation, like acquiring the horse, improved life and altered culture, including reinventing identity in a less traditional direction, always with the environment in mind. Nature rules.

Leslie Silko described the war years and what happened to the Native world in the Pueblo West as it confronted increasing contact with the outside world. Such change might be said to represent modernization. The land endures all change; the Pueblo people use only what they need from the modern world. Referring to the aunt of one of her characters, Silko tells the way things used to be and what they became:

> An old sensitivity had descended in her [the aunt], surviving thousands of years from the oldest times, when the people shared a single clan name and they told each other who they were; they recounted the actions and words each of their clan had taken, and would take; from before they were born and long after they died, the people shared the same consciousness. The people had known, with the simple certainty of the world they saw, how everything should be. But the fifth world had become entangled with European names: the names of the rivers, the hills, the names of the animals and plants—all creation suddenly had two names: an Indian name and a white name.[6]

Friends and foes shared the water and earth.

Long before this time, Hopi prophecy foretold the day when Indians would share the earth with the white race. In his eighties at the time, Dan Katchongva repeated this prophecy in his words:

> In ancient times it was prophesied by our forefathers that this land would be occupied by the Indian people and then from somewhere a White Man would come. . . . We knew that this land beneath us was composed of many things that we might want to use later such as mineral resources. We knew that this is the wealthiest part of this continent, because it is here the Great Spirit lives. We knew that the White Man will search for the things that look good to him, that he will use many good ideas in order to obtain his heart's desire, and we knew that if he had strayed from the Great Spirit he would use any means to get what he wants. These things we were warned to watch, and we today know that those prophecies were true because we can see how many

new and selfish ideas and plans are being put before us. We know that if we accept these things we will lose our land and give up our very lives.[7]

Making choices on the basis of one's free will is inherent sovereignty, autonomy, and self-determination. This perspective, however, has been continually challenged by the federal government, and even when bureaucrats support self-determination, it is a determination that must operate under delineated constraints.

The prevailing Indian policy favors Indian self-determination; Richard Nixon introduced this incarnation of Indian policy in the early 1970s. This policy was reaffirmed with the American Indian Self-Determination and Education Assistance Act of 1975 that President Gerald Ford signed into law.[8] During this decade the average income for all families in the United States, according to the U.S. Census for 1980, was $19,917. For American Indians, the average income was $13,724. The unemployment rate for Indians stood at 13.2 percent, compared with 6.5 percent for the rest of the country. While many Native people seemed to be enjoying the same privileges of the mainstream middle class, a significant portion of Indians lived in poverty. Only 55 percent of American Indians twenty-five years and older had graduated from high school, compared with 66.5 percent of all Americans, according to the U.S. Census for 1983. Five years later, the Census reported that 23.7 percent of Indian families lived below the poverty line.[9] To make matters worse, other groups of color seemed to make better wages and obtain more education as American Indians slipped down the economic ladder. As the government spent money on various programs, at least one Native person believed that Indians were being left out. In 1971 Oliver Eastman, Sioux-Wahpeton, admonished, "We hear all the time about government funding for birds that are going to be extinct, or turtles that are gong to be extinct; they spend thousands and thousands of dollars. In that same time they will take our culture away, assimilate, try to assimilate us into the white race, so that now we are struggling to save our culture and save our race. If we don't do something about saving our race, there will be no more Indian race on this earth."[10] With the minority activism of the early 1970s, the government began to respond to the exigencies of Native people.

In 1975 tribes with significant amounts of oil, uranium, water, coal, timber, and other natural resources on their reservations began to organize as a group. Their collective concerns brought about the establishment of the Council of Energy Resource Tribes (CERT), with twenty-five member tribes.[11] Two years later CERT opened its new office, in Denver, Colorado and the Bureau of Indian Affairs aided in starting a mineral technical assistance center in Denver. Limited federal spending, unfortunately, allowed only five of twelve positions to be filled.[12] Immediately facing growing pressure, CERT found itself surrounded by energy companies wanting tribal oil due to an oil embargo and long gasoline lines throughout the country, rationing at gasoline stations in 1979, and a second gasoline shortage within the next five years. In some states, stations sold gasoline according to whether one's license plate ended in an even or odd number, which determined which days gas could be bought. One photographer in San Francisco snapped a picture of a gas station attendant standing by a gas pump with the effrontery to display a handgun strapped to his hip. America had to ration its supply of gasoline and other uses of oil, coal, and other resources. This lionized action of strict control pressured tribes with energy resources on their lands.

CERT organized under the guidance of Peter MacDonald, then chairman of the Navajo Nation. He described the early effort to recognize their potential resources and the comical way that their organization received the name CERT. At the new Department of Energy's invitation, several tribes visited Washington to form a coalition. MacDonald said:

> We discussed our concerns, trying to come up with a name for our group. We agreed on all the issues we were facing except this one. It was after midnight, we were tired, and the name continued to elude us. Fighting hunger and exhaustion, I reached into my pocket and removed a package of Certs breath mints. I glanced at the wrapper just before slipping one of the mints into my mouth. Then, joking, I said, "Why don't we call ourselves CERT?" No one realized I was referring to the mints in my hand, so they asked me what the initials stood for. Thinking for a moment, I replied, "Council of Energy Resource Tribes." We adopted the name.[13]

The newly formed CERT started with an executive board of eight tribal leaders, plus a chairman. The executive director, Peter MacDonald of the Navajo, a vice-chairman, secretary, and treasurer made up the rest of the nine tribal chairmen. Within four years, CERT employed sixty-five people on staff in 1980, with twenty-three of this number in the Washington office and forty-two people in the Denver office. In 1981 CERT entertained its highest budget of $3.9 million, with 74 percent of this amount coming from the federal government and 26 percent from the energy tribes.

Roughly half of the budget paid salaries and provided CERT with offices at $181,000 a year.[14]

Under the newly announced federal Indian self-determination policy in the mid-1970s, natural resources, especially oil, were closely scrutinized by the U.S. government internally and externally. The spiraling upward demand on oil and other natural resources affected both America's domestic policy and foreign policy in the Middle East, where much of the country's oil supply came from. Wanting to get back to business as usual, Americans elected a southern, religious Democrat—Jimmy Carter—as president in 1976 in the midst of an energy crisis. It seemed best to elect someone not associated with Washington politics following the Watergate scandal that made Richard Nixon the first U.S. president to resign from office. The Organization of the Petroleum Exporting Countries (OPEC) of the Middle East had Carter over a barrel. As the country's demand for natural resources turned inward, Indian tribes who had been under government leases for their resources for years began to respond. Simultaneously, the Carter administration passed four important laws, the Energy Conservation and Production Act (1976),[15] Surface Mining Control and Reclamation Act (1977),[16] Natural Gas Policy Act (1978),[17] and the National Energy Conservation Policy Act (1978).[18] The Energy Conservation and Production Act encouraged and facilitated the practices of energy conservation and renewable energy measures in old and new buildings. The Surface Mining Control and Reclamation Act was passed "to provide for the cooperation between the Secretary of the Interior and the States with respect to the regulation of surface coal mining operations, and the acquisition and reclamation of abandoned mines, and other purposes." The Natural Gas Policy Act empowered the Federal Energy Regulatory Commission to oversee intrastate natural gas production. The National Energy Conservation Policy Act authorized the Department of Energy to set minimum energy performance standards on vehicles. The law also empowered states to ensure that residential energy conservation plans were carried out.

The Four Corners area continued as the largest strip mining operation in the world, and it remains so large that astronauts claim to have seen it from outer space. The Hopi and especially the Navajo have been vulnerable in this strip mining operation. As early as July 26, 1957, the Navajo Nation had a lease negotiated for them by the Bureau of Indian Affairs with Utah International. The lease paid the Navajo Nation between $0.15 and $0.20 per ton of coal. And for the same coal, Arizona Public Service paid Utah International $6 per ton. The more dangerous threat proved to be Peabody, which held one-third of all tribal mining leases in 1989. On January 12, 1982, Congress passed the Federal Oil and Gas Royalty Management Act. The measure permitted the interior secretary to negotiate agreements with any state or tribe to share oil and gas royalty management information. The law also called for government inspection, auditing, investigation, and enforcement, if necessary, under this act in cooperation with the interior secretary.[19] The energy tribes could feel the firm hand of paternalism controlling the business of their resources, and they responded with the support of CERT. Under the law, CERT and the energy tribes worked in collaboration with the best possible experts in geology, engineering, and other related fields to provide them with information.

At the end of the year, Congress passed a significant measure, the Indian Mineral Development Act. This law allowed tribes to enter into agreements for the disposition of tribal mineral resources.[20] CERT helped its member energy tribes by arming them with the latest scientific and business research data. With the best estimations of how much coal, oil, gas, or uranium was under tribal lands, for example, the energy tribal leaders could negotiate more effectively by using wise resource management.

Obtaining specific information about natural resources remained at best an expert's guess, as reported by Jim Pierce, CERT chief administrative officer, in *CERT First Decade Report for 1985*. The Hopi possessed coal, uranium, oil, and natural gas. The Hualapai had uranium, oil, natural gas, and hydroelectric sources. The Navajo Nation had coal, oil, natural gas, uranium, and geothermal sources. The White Mountain Apache had timber. More than half of the coal in the United States was found in the West, with one-third of the coal fields on the reservations of twenty-two tribes.[21] In total, 25–40 percent of the uranium, one-third of the coal, and roughly 5 percent of all oil and gas remained on Indian reservations west of the Mississippi River.[22]

At the time, fifty-three members belonged to CERT, including another four member tribes in Canada. CERT and its member tribes felt an urgency to increase its membership as it had doubled its number since the original twenty-five founding tribes in 1975. In each case, the big question loomed over each critical decision of whether or not to harvest the resources of Mother Earth. Furthermore, the energy tribes continued to face the vital decision of how much to develop their mining programs for finite supplies of natural resources on their reservations. The big decision for each tribe has been influenced by the fact that there were only certain quantities of energy resources, and they cannot be replenished. And, what did this do to their homeland? Native leaders and their business councils faced a grim decision of resource management. "It does create problems within local areas where people don't like to see their land torn up and that sort of thing, but the Navajo tribal council will have to make a decision, because that's the income of the Navajo tribe," said Annie Wauneka. She added, "So they'll have to kind of abide by the decision that's made by the tribal council. Many tribes they don't like the decision, but it works in another way, that resources [timber, uranium, oil] has [*sic*] to be managed, and has to be developed and so forth."[23]

Various tribes of the West believe that their people came from the earth. Their ancestors lived in stone dwellings in the sides of mountains and in pit houses dug into the earth. They were of the earth. Even the traditional eight-sided hogan of the Navajo is designed with an earthen floor to remind the people where they come from. In "Starlore," a short story published in *Blue Horses Rush In*, Navajo poet and writer Luci Tapahonso describes the connection of the geometric cultural paragon to her people and the earth:

> On this June night, we gather at our parents' home and leave in a caravan of nine cars, a string of headlights across the flat desert to the home of the man who will listen and help us. It is almost midnight when we park outside his hooghan, the round ceremonial house. We enter slowly, clockwise, then sit on the smooth, cool ground. Above the flickering fire in the center of the hooghan, we see clouds rushing by through the chimney hole. The wind whistles through the opening. It makes us hope for rain. The family has filled the hooghan. We whisper among ourselves until he arrives—the one who knows the precise songs, the long, rhythmic prayers that will restore the world for us.[24]

The Diné (Navajo) believe in a supreme Earth Mother called Changing Woman, who created their people, according to Diné mythology. Changing Woman created the four original clans, and she was the first to be honored with Kinaalda, a girl's puberty ceremony. Changing Woman was the mother of "hero twins" who saved the world from monsters. She symbolized the four seasons of the year by representing the young girl changing from youth to age and returning to youth. Called the Earth Mother, Changing Woman represented the gift of life and its phases.[25] Changing Woman gave other important things to the Diné. To women, the Earth Mother gave the responsibility of protecting the Earth Bundle. Soil from four or six sacred mountains and the power of renewal was contained in the bundle. The power of rendering life came from within the

Earth Bundle, and the Diné used the bundle in their most important ceremony, called the Blessingway.[26] The Diné believe the earth to be a
female deity that serves as a host to other metaphysical powers.

In the beginning, the Diné say their ancestors passed through four
worlds. Like hemispheres, they were piled on top of each other, and they
were pillars of precious stone of striking colors—red, blue, yellow, and
black and white. In his autobiography, George Lee wrote,

> We came to the surface of the land from several levels far beneath the
> earth's surface. Just thinking of the earth caused me to watch the deft
> hand strokes of the medicine man as he made sand images upon the
> earthen floor. The bright array of colors connected in my conscious
> thought. Black, red, blue, and now this world, yellow, representing the
> levels Diné, my people, had passed through to arrive upon the earth's
> surface. My father's interpretation of the legend was that the five-
> fingered people (earth people) came from beneath the earth through
> much water. The medicine man was using three promising colors in
> the sand painting on the floor. This sacred sing was for me, for some-
> thing in the outside world had brought a terrible sickness upon me.
> This was the way of my people. And I believed it.[27]

One must believe if good things are to happen. The Navajo believe that
it is the earth that holds power, not human beings. Even medicine makers
like Annie Kahn acknowledged, "We really don't have any power at all to
heal anybody. It's the natural power that the Earth has that heals."[28] Native people have studied the earth for centuries. According to the creation
myth of the Muscogee Creeks, their ancestors once emerged from the
earth. The world was dark and unknown to them for they could not see.
They emerged from the earth, and a dark mist shrouded everything for
they could not even see each other. Hearing strange sounds, they were
afraid. At the next moment, a wind blew the mist away so that they could
now see the different animals and plants, and they observed and studied
them to learn.[29]

Other tribes have their sacred sites, like the Choctaw's mound called
Nana Wayah, and perhaps they emerged from there. The Kiowa tell the
myth of crawling from a hollow log, again the emergence from the earth.
The Hopi have an account of coming from a hole in the ground and
becoming a part of the present world.

The sacred mountains upheld the universe of the Diné, and the people
held the role of women's responsibility for life in high regard. The Diné

have Mt. Blanca to the East, and Mt. Taylor stands in the South. To the West, the San Francisco Peaks tower upward. To the North, the La Plata Mountains rise skyward.[30] Facing the four cardinal directions, the mountains stand as sentinel guardians of Navajo land.

For other Indian groups, special places of the landscape were empowered, and these sites protected the people. Throughout Indian country, hundreds of sacred and empowered places exist. Some of the renowned ones—Taos Blue Lake among the Pueblo people of New Mexico, San Francisco Peaks in Arizona for the Navajo, Devil's Tower in Wyoming for the Kiowa, Pyramid Lake for the Paiute in Nevada, Mt. Adams in Washington for the Yakama, and other spiritual sites dot the landscape. Others exist that only Native people know about. Ironically, sacred Indian land has not always been protected, and it has a long history of exploitation, outside control, and restricted access for Native peoples.

"Walking in Beauty" is walking with the earth, feeling it against your skin, and feeling that it is a part of you. In this way Native people humanize animals and everything else. Native people talk to things and try to understand responses from things. In other words, they humanize nonhuman entities, calling them by name in their tribal languages. All things can be humanlike. Tapahonso wrote, "Before the world existed, the holy people made themselves visible by becoming the clouds, sun, moon, trees, bodies of water, thunder, rain, snow, and other aspects of this world we live in. That way, they said, we would never be alone. So it is possible to talk to them and pray, no matter where we are and how we feel. *Biyazhi daniidli,* we are their little ones."[31]

The Hopi have lived for centuries in the Southwest. From their Uto-Aztecan language, the Hopi call themselves *Hopituh,* which means "peaceful ones." Still today, they cultivate fields of corn, squash, beans, and melons, using a planting stick that is a method used by their ancestors as long ago as 300 B.C. Orayvi remains as the oldest continuing community north of the Rio Grande River. Some believe that Acoma Pueblo is the oldest community. Located on the Third Mesa, Old Oraibi dates back to A.D. 1100. The majority of the Hopi people live in the twelve villages atop the three mesas on the reservation.[32]

The Hopi Indians maintain that in the beginning there was only Tokpela, endless space. Somehow in this endless space a spark of consciousness was struck. The Hopi named this Tawa, the Sun Spirit. Tawa created the first world. It was a cavern with nothing but insects in it. The insects disappointed him. Tawa sent Spider Grandmother down to them as a messenger. She said, "Tawa, the Sun Spirit who made you, is unhappy because you do not understand the meaning of life. Therefore he has commanded me to lead you from this first world to a second one." The journey upward to the second world proved very arduous and long. Tawa sent Spider Grandmother to lead the animals upward until they reached a third world, which was somewhat lighter and less forbidding. On that new and extremely difficult journey, some of the animals became people. The story continues, "Then Spider Grandmother taught the people how to weave cloth to keep their bodies warm and how to make pots for storing food and water. Men and women began to have some glimmering, after a time, of the meaning of life. But certain *powaka*, or sorcerers, distorted this intuitive knowledge. People began to feel that they had created themselves."[33]

The instinct for human beings is to search for something that is valued thus, driving the human spirit to locate or seek these valued things. The above myths speak to the issue of finding a homeland. The search for an environment that would furnish food, shelter, and security seems endless. In the Hopi oral tradition, "if surviving myths and legends are listened to with care they may tell us that these restless ancestors were also in search for places of spiritual harmony with nature."[34] Such a sincere quest is always based on the exigencies of the people, compelling human beings to migrate to new home areas. Constructing stone houses in clusters among cliffs, the ancestors of the Hopi were likely driven to their current homeland by drought. One migration led to the Rio Grande Valley along the river, enabling pueblo communities to thrive.[35] The Hopi found their new home on the land below and three mesas above in northwest Arizona.

The land is the home to various tribes and each possesses a distinct viewpoint of it. The region is demanding, and its inhabitants have learned this lesson. They have learned that one cannot permanently control the land, for its climate and terrain are too powerful. One Navajo person, Freddy Big Bead, stated, "You don't own the land. You just use it. Some people have a small patch. They plant melons and corn. If the crop fails, they go hungry. They live the best they know how."[36] The secret to living in the Southwest is to learn about the environment and adapt to it, learning to be flexible. This is Native logic.

In the outside world, Native people deal with the white man, and this long Indian-white history of enmity must change for the better. It is one of politics for the control of the land, the homeland of Native peoples long before the Spanish arrived in the Southwest in 1541. This economic contest for control has especially involved those tribes with large natural resources. The harvesting of natural resources and even the decision to mine them has tormented Native people. Harming Mother Earth has taken its toll on the indigenous, plaguing the homeland with illnesses and huge empty cavities. Leslie Silko describes the impact of mining on her main character, Tayo, in *Ceremony*:

> Waves of the heat caught him [Tayo], and his legs and lungs were vapor without sensation; only his memory or running and breathing kept him moving and alive. He stumbled and ran behind the sun, not following, but dragged with it across arroyos, over mesas and hills. At sundown he was lying on the sand at the bottom of the long mesa, feeling the heart recede from the air and from his body into the earth. The wind came up and he shivered. He crawled through the strands of barbed wire. Twilight was giving way to darkness. He scooped water off the top of thick green moss that clogged the steel water trough under the windmill. The water was still warm from the sun and it tasted bitter. He sat on the edge of the trough and looked across the wide canyon at the dark mine shaft. Maybe the uranium made the water taste that way.[37]

According to their traditional beliefs, Native people contend themselves with the earth before deciding what is best for their people. Mining the natural resources has grave consequences. Whereas previously federal paternalism had excluded tribal leaders from much of the negotiations with energy company officials, now the tribes are involved in almost all of the decisions to be made. The great shift of decision making falling to the tribal leaders came about during the mid-1980s. On October 27, 1986, Congress passed the Indian Civil Rights Act. This measure amended the earlier Indian Civil Rights Act and allowed the tribal courts to impose fines of $5,000 and one year in jail for criminal offenses.[38] This civil law indicated that the tribes could exercise more autonomy not only over their resources but also in the governing of their own communities. More tribal authority meant greater control over resource management and control of the economy for each Indian nation. The Indian Housing Act of 1988 established a separate program to provide housing assistance to Indians and Alaska Natives under the secretary of housing and urban development.[39] Improved housing with assistance from the government enabled tribal leaders to assert their leadership in other areas to help their people. An act called Indian Law Enforcement Reform, passed by Congress in 1990, clarified and strengthened the authority of law enforcement and officers in Indian Country.[40] Another measure, the Environmental Regulatory

Enhancement Act, was passed by Congress that same year. This law authorized federal grants to improve the capability of tribal governments to regulate environmental quality on their reservations.[41] Specifically, the law empowered tribes to develop their resources. However, the government viewed itself as rendering a policy not just of self-determination but of partnership with Indian nations to help them. Almost two months later, Congress passed the National Indian Forest Resources Management Act. This law allowed the interior secretary to participate in the management of forests on tribal lands. The law also took into account forests on individual Indians' lands as a responsibility of the federal-Indian trust relationship.[42]

From the 1980s to the end of the century represented a time of positive relationships between tribes and the federal government as the latter assisted with legislative measures. At the same time, the tribes had to work within Reaganomics, which meant cuts in federal funding to Indian programs. President Reagan strove to end the energy crisis of 1970 and to return to the free enterprise system. In this light, Reagan's domestic policies

Figure 6.1. Navajo uranium miners. Courtesy of Cline Library Special Collections, Northern Arizona University.

challenged the tribes while trying to get states more involved in Indian affairs. Smart resource management and careful planning of harvesting tribal natural resources became the concerns of tribal leaders as they worked to rebuild their economies at a modern political level. In essence, they were forging a tribal modern political economy in working with the federal government and CERT as an ally. For certain, the new so-called energy tribes understood the importance of alliances that their people had practiced for centuries. Furthermore, energy development became a part of the new tribal cultures and thinking of Native leaders as they headed into the twenty-first century.

In August 2005, President George W. Bush signed into law the Energy Policy Act.[43] Title V of this law is known as the Indian Tribal Energy and Self-Determination Act. After being delayed several times, Congress passed this timely legislation. The United States imports 54 percent of the crude oil that it uses. Tribes possess a little over 2 percent of the entire land in the United States, yet approximately 30 percent of the fossil fuels consumed in the country come from this small percentage of Indian lands. The Indian Tribal Energy and Self-Determination Act focuses on improving relations between tribes and the federal government. A new political forum occurred, with the government working with energy tribes as equal partners. Basically, the legislation gives more control over tribal lands to tribal governments to develop them. Energy resource management via tribal leadership is essential to the tribes in an accelerating political climate for developing all energy resources on the continent. Energy tribes are seeking new ways to advance their developing energy programs. In this rebuilding of nations, the tribes seek self-sufficiency by producing enough electricity and monitoring water supplies, as well as micromanaging other resources to meet their people's needs. In effect, the tribes have and continue to develop their own energy policies in accepting responsibility for the treatment of the environment.

This important act will have a major impact on all 566 federally recognized tribes, as 64 of them on 326 reserved land areas possess energy resources that the nation needs. An important part of the self-determination development includes water, especially in the West and Southwest. Finally, the act will profoundly affect the development of Indian sovereignty and tribal governance. With all of this said, what have we learned from the earth, and what do we understand? Are we able to comprehend possible global consequences while viewing life from a capitalistic mindset? George Lee's wise Navajo father said to him, "Our people began to covet what the white man had. The white man is learned, but his knowledge has not brought him to understand the Mother Earth. He may own the land and be in control, but only we have the power to understand the spirits within the land. So, on a higher level, it is yet ours. Only an Indian has the power to understand the spirits within Mother Earth and all creations."[44]

In 1992 Hopi elder Thomas Banyacya gave this testimony to a World Uranium Hearing in Salzberg. He used a map, describing his homeland of the Four Corners. He shared the Hopi prophecy with these insightful words:

> This white part is on the rock near my home in Oraibi. The Great Spirit laid this path for us to follow. There's no end to this work, none to the circle, there's no end to that as long as we follow instructions. The white brother came. Instead of bringing this circle he brought this cross. And we let him go on up the road. We refer to that materialistic path, inventing of many things, powerful things that are supposed to help. They go side by side—First, Second, Third World, First World War, Second World War and this . . . on the upper line, to the Hopi, is beginning a Third World War, the Persian Gulf, but it stopped. So it gave us people to correct, to change, to stop this thing we were talking about. Uranium mining is a dangerous thing—we know that now. Are we going to continue to develop that? Are we going to continue to mine them? We know it's dangerous and we test out many things like the Nevada testing area—some day, we're going to burn ourselves up. So many things known to the Hopi tell the world not to do that any more. Stop uranium mining, testing. Stop everything. . . . We are brothers and sisters, and we are going to help to protect this Mother Earth for the next generations, and then we will have a good life again.[45]

What is the response to the prophecy? What precautions will be taken? Who will make the right decision? Perhaps the answers to such questions are in the earth itself. Annie Kahn, a Navajo medicine woman, said to ask the earth. She said, "Everything one wants to know is in these [sacred] mountains. To test our beliefs, they remain quiet. They're so old. They've witnessed so much."[46] In this way, all people must be patient and alert to hear the earth. Tribal ways are of wisdom, but such wisdom derives from the source called earth.

Native people know the past through stories passed from one generation to the next one. These stories contain knowledge that helps us understand the world around us. Peterson Zah, former tribal chairman of the Navajo and former special adviser to President Michael Crow of Arizona

State University, wrote, "Our stories teach us where we come from and who we are. They say we arrive here in this, the Fifth World, after dwelling in four lower worlds below. . . . We are called the Earth-Surface people because of our ancestral resistance in other worlds."[47] It is on the earth's surface that the politics are waged over what is below. This story of energy demands for tribal lands will become a part of the stories told about the white man. The story will involve the perceptions of how Native people like the Navajo and Hopi participate in this shared experience involving developing natural resources with white-owned energy companies. This is not a new story of Indians and whites fighting for the earth. It will not be the last one as Native people strive for a better livelihood.

Possessing natural resources and monetary resources makes a difference. For example, in Arizona the average family income in 2000 was $40,558. Nationwide the average family income for American Indians and Alaska Natives was $30,599. The average Indian family income of all the twenty-one recognized tribes in Arizona, according to the U.S. Census for 2000, was $26,083. The average U.S. family income had risen in the first few years of the twenty-first century: in 2002 it stood at $41,994, and by 2005 it was $46,326; the average for Native families lagged by about $10,000.

As the United States concluded the first decade of the twenty-first century, Americans continued to luxuriate in their automobile culture. Most families own a car, and in the West some have two and three automobiles, perhaps more. This indulgence of a new car, often costing $18,000 to $28,000, reflects America's consumer economy. Luxury cars and trucks cost even more. In the last decade, Americans have exhibited a desire for SUVs and Hummers with little thought to the energy consumption such iron beasts require. Someone must pay as the nation's economy has slumped, and hard decisions have to be made concerning resource management.

The top ten energy tribes possess about one-third of the coal in the West on reservation lands, as well as large amounts of oil, especially in Wyoming and Oklahoma. Timber-rich areas exist in Wisconsin, Oregon, and Washington. Navajo in particular is the largest coal-producing tribe. The Navajo is followed by the Crow as the second largest coal tribe. From 2005 to 2010, the Blackfeet of Montana annually produced 50 million barrels of oil. The Ute of Utah and Southern Ute of Colorado accounted for nearly 36 percent of oil sold from Indian leases in 2004, and the Shoshone and Arapaho in Wyoming accounted for 21.5 percent. The Oklahoma Osage have continued to hold impressive amounts of oil under their lands. The Colville Confederated Tribes have maximized timber resources and are one of the top tribes for timber harvesting. The Warm Springs Indians of Oregon own Warm Springs Power Enterprise, which operates the largest hydropower producer within the state of Oregon, and the Flathead Tribes of Montana (Confederated Salish and Kootenai Tribes) have timber industry sales.

The situation for energy tribes has not changed significantly in regard to the demand for their natural resources. As Americans remain captivated by their consumer culture with an increasing driving population, the demand on the energy tribes increases as well. In 2005 Americans drove 13,657 miles on the average, burning an estimated total of 141.6 billion gallons of gasoline.[48] To compound this critical situation, the rate of inflation adds fuel to the fire, forcing more pressure on tribal leaders to decide whether or not to mine and develop their tribal resources. Added to this dilemma, energy tribes have mined much of their resources since the mid-1970s. Although cultures change and go through various transitions as communities are in control, traditionalists in the energy tribes find themselves in a smaller minority than before. Finally, this is not an assessment, but rather stating the situation for tribes with abundant natural resources and the pressures of change that they face. Of utmost importance, to understand the earth, one must "see" this dilemma of whether or not to mine from the perspective of the tribal leaders involved.[49] From this Native ethos, precious insight is revealed with regard to Indian attempts to deal with this issue. Indians must make the changes; change cannot be carried out by non-Indians on behalf of Indians. This was the case in the early decades of the twentieth century when Native people were deemed "incompetent" to make their own decisions. Federal paternalism and energy monopolies are under scrutiny as modern tribal leaders use all sophisticated tools at hand, including resource management, to shape their tribal political economies with the remaining natural resources on their reservations. Stabilizing tribal political economies remained a sine qua non in the rebuilding of Indian nations during the uneasy American economy of the first decade in the twenty-first century. The decision of whether to mine tribal resources is in the hands of Indian leaders, and they have learned much about resource management.

CHAPTER SEVEN

Indian Gaming in the West

Indian Entrepreneurship and Modern Political Economy

When I see kids, come to a small rural school with $100 bills in their pockets [from tribal casinos] . . . believe me, it creates some problems in the community. We need to make sure our kids don't lose their way with the greenbacks.

SENATOR BEN NIGHTHORSE CAMPBELL, NORTHERN CHEYENNE, 1992

I have observed the same thing happening twice, and I think that it is worth mentioning here for the symbolic importance and to reinforce my argument that Indians are rebuilding their nations. I recall the first time I sat among twenty Native faculty and administrators in a meeting on the Gila River reservation in Arizona. On this delightful fall day early in the semester, a welcome relief from the desert's late summer heat, one of the walls of the meeting room was mostly glass. As the meeting slogged along with sporadic inspiring moments, I gazed outside like several of the committee members sitting near me. Every now and then, a car would go by. Not too far away stood the tribe's casino. In one of my countless gazes, I saw an armored truck leaving the reservation. If you will imagine this scenario and put it in a comparative historical context, it becomes quite remarkable. Over a hundred years ago, Indians on a reservation waited for days, weeks, for a wagon of supplies that had been promised via treaties. When it arrived, they lined up to receive their rations distributed by the Indian agent. A hundred years later, the tribal casino makes hundreds of thousands of dollars in a week to be hauled away in an armored truck—an experiential doppelganger-like irony.

Indian gaming has introduced a new era of American Indian history and tribal relations with other peoples. It would seem that the tables have turned 180 degrees from the time of a hundred years ago when most Americans presumed that Native peoples would vanish with the close of the nineteenth century. Well, this has not happened, and Indians are still here and thriving in many communities. In fact, a new reality developed that is grudgingly changing how the mainstream views Indians. This is because the most difficult thing to change in the world is the attitude of a people.

Prior to modernity, Native nations practiced what might be called moral economy. In such an economy, communities functioned to take care of their members with food supplies and whatever was needed that could be acquired through trade.[1] For example, Plains Indians practiced a hunting and raiding economy that was in the best interest of the group, which shared food and supplies with its members. In a sense, the group was more important than the individuals. The moral economies of tribes centered on sharing wealth and distributing goods to make sure everyone had enough to eat, were comfortable, and were secure.

As tribal moral economies came in constant contact with American capitalism, tribes readapted their communities to practice a political economy as Native leaders learned to negotiate with traders and government officials. With each decade passing, tribal leaders readapted again to modern political economy as they worked within the American capitalistic system. Modern political economy theory involves the practice and progress of a nation in five key areas: history, economics, law, political science, and sociology. It is suggested here that during the last hundred years and more tribes have adapted a modern political economy and Indianized according to a Native way of doing things via cross-cultural borrowing.[2] Tribes are rebuilding their nations. Having survived the early decades of the twentieth century through their resilience, the postmodern era provided them with the opportunity to rebuild their communities and governments. The impressive result is a tribal modern political economy that accounts for the tremendous economic progress that many tribes have achieved under Indian self-determination. But there is something disturbing about this kind of progress.

"Gambling"—should people make their living by it? Is it okay and legitimate? What is the legality for Indians? Is there a moral issue involved? What is the government's role? Should Indian tribes benefit from others'—including other Indians'—gambling addictions? These are some of the questions raised involving Native people and gambling. Everyone seems to have a view on the subject. Yet most people do not understand all that is involved. Because of its controversial nature, the subject of Indian gaming has provoked the mainstream American public and Indian opinions across the United States and into Canada. Most important are what Native people think about the gaming situation and how they see it. This direction of Native leaders developing indigenous capitalism adds fuel to the discussion and criticism voiced against Indian gaming from outsiders.

Legally, the Native nations have interpreted the U.S. government's trust responsibility to American Indians to serve their gaming operations. Indians' legal rights derive from the 374 ratified treaties and agreements signed between them and the U.S. government. In order to begin a gaming operation, an Indian tribe needs a land base, which also requires "trust" status, meaning the government has the final authority over it. One common Native view is the law has limited the sovereignty of tribes in their necessary political negotiations at the state and local levels. Whereas in the historic past Indian legal relations existed only on a level with the federal government, the whole situation has changed so that state governments are also involved in compact negotiations with tribes. Indians have had to accept this limitation of tribal sovereignty due to the plenary power of Congress and more federal laws passed that pertain to Indian Country.

Locally, for the most part, communities are upset with American Indian groups for wanting to build casinos too close to them. The response has been largely due to the gambling clientele that would frequent Indian bingos and casinos. Most non-Indians do not want Indian casinos in their neighborhoods, but many will go to them to gamble and eat. Furthermore, Indian gambling has proven to compete too well with local church-operated bingos. Yet Indian gaming has brought more jobs and improved local economies affecting Indians and non-Indians.

Morally, religious organizations and Christian individuals have been divided over Indian gambling from the beginning. Catholics do not oppose Indian gaming, nor do the majority of Protestant denominations. Yet in the eyes of critics, gambling is a sin, and promoting it is morally wrong. At the same time, some Christian Indians agree and oppose Indian gaming. These people and organizations believe that American Indians should pursue other avenues to better their communities. They also claim that promoting such Indian gaming operations promotes gambling addicts who frequent Indian bingos and casinos.

Economically, bingos and casinos have been a financial windfall for many, but not all tribal nations, and many have tried other industrial ventures in the past involving tourism, small factories, and assembling parts for companies. Their gaming financial success amounts to over $2 billion on the whole per year. If there is a sustained future for Indian gaming, how can it be made to serve Native values and needs? How long will it last? During the 1990s, Indian gaming was a success and even challenged Atlantic City, Reno, and to some extent Las Vegas. The business tycoon Donald Trump even filed a lawsuit against one Indian gaming operation. What is the future of Indian gaming in the twenty-first century now that Indian gaming is more than twenty-five years old?

Trump's lawsuit against Indian tribes in 1993 claiming that they discriminated against him demonstrates that Indian gaming has become a part of American life.[3] Usually what happens in Indian Country is not newsworthy to the rest of the nation, but such large Indian gambling operations as Foxwoods, owned by the Mashantucket Pequot tribe of Connecticut, cannot be ignored. When television commercials refer to Foxwoods, Indian reality has intersected with public reality in the same space. In essence, Indian gambling has made an impact on the American public and caused people to turn their heads toward Indian Country and take notice.

This modern entrepreneurship is a dynamic force that is changing the economics of Indian Country and other communities located nearby. In the new world of indigenous capitalism, Indian leaders and their nations are independently altering the course of their history and that of the United States. As a spin-off from Indian self-determination of the 1970s, Indian gaming has resulted from the initiative and imaginative thinking of tribal leaders to emulate the casino owners in Las Vegas, Reno, and Atlantic City. They learned how gambling operates in the mainstream, although games and gambling were much a part of their multiple pasts. Adopting white values and presenting gambling opportunities in attractive packages of resort surroundings have enticed people to board the bingo bus to the reservation, each smiling inside themselves that they might get lucky.

Historically among the many Indian nations, communities played various games of sport and chance. Some games dated back to prehistoric years. The Cherokee played a marble game, and archeological evidence dates this gamesmanship to A.D. 800. This evidence suggests that a field about a hundred feet long contained five holes approximately ten to twelve yards apart in an L-shape. Players tossed billiard-size balls at the holes in order, and the first team to complete the course was the winning side. Each side had two to four players, and tournaments were held with many teams.[4] Other Indian games of chance included the Crow plum pit game: five pits were painted on each side; players tossed the pits up in the air in a bowl, and the painted sides showing up counted as points, with the winner having accumulated the most.

Native peoples enjoy playing games for the pleasure of socialization and solidifying friendships and communities. Indians of the West were great horsemen, and horse racing has been one of the social ways that Plains peoples loved to bet. One epic story began with the Comanche and soldiers at Fort Chadbourne on the Texas Plains challenging each other to a horserace during the 1850s. The soldiers laughed at the small mustang that the Comanche leader rode, calling the Indian's horse a sheep. The soldiers ridiculed the horse and rider, saying they would race their third fastest horse as they offered flour, sugar, and coffee against buffalo robes and other Native items. The "sheep" mustang won the 400-yard race, barely. In disbelief, the soldiers trotted out their second fastest horse and added more goods to the bet—double or nothing. The Comanche horse won again, just by a nose. The incensed soldiers quickly brought out their prized horse, well over fifteen hands high, and they doubled the bet. The Comanche laughed as the soldiers added more goods to the large pile on the ground. The signal was given and the race began! And, it was quickly over. Bolting forward even faster, the "sheep" horse sped so far ahead that the Comanche leader quickly turned around riding backward and taunted the soldier rider as he raced toward the finish line.[5] Although the Comanche commanded royal attention for their equestrianism, it remains an unsafe bet to say which were the fastest horsemen among the Indians of the West. The Nez Perce of the Pacific Northwest were well known for breeding Appaloosa horses to race. And the Lakota, Crow, Cheyenne, and others of the twenty-eight Plains tribes were known for their expert equestrianism.

Aside from horse racing, Indians have applauded games of skill based on an individual's talents. Victory in most cases was celebrated by ubiquitous exhilaration. A survey of the traditional games of chance among American Indians indicates that an estimated 130 tribes played a form of the dice game. Roughly eighty tribes played the hand game, an estimated sixty played some version of the stick game, and about thirty played the moccasin game.[6] With this historical background, a new game would be introduced, Indianized, and flourish among many Native communities.

The idea of bingo dates back several centuries. Bingo originated in Venice, Italy, about 1530 as a common game with several versions. Europeans associated more than one name with bingo, and different communities called it Loo, housey-housey, or lotto. As a game, the playing began with a square playing sheet of letters across the top and rows of numbers.

An American or perhaps a European who had traveled in Germany whose name is lost in history carried some cards and a bag of beans with him to the small town of Jacksonville, Georgia, just south of Atlanta. He referred to the game as "beano" because players used coffee beans to mark the designated squares. The caller picked small numbered-lettered wooden disks from a cigar box and called out the numbers. The players placed a bean on the correct number, if they had it on their card. The game's objective called for completing a line of numbers in a diagonal, horizontal, or vertical direction. At the same time, the winner had to be the first success-ful person to call out "beano!" The prizes consisted of inexpensive items—typically, the winner won a small Kewpie doll. The players paid a nickel, and the beano caller supervised a game of twelve players. The Kewpie doll was worth about a nickel, enabling the beano manager to earn a profit of fifty-five cents, a good sum for Georgia during the Great Depression years.[7] For the players, the thrill of winning became the pursuit of the hunt, and an exhilarating desire was fulfilled in a single moment of yelling "beano."

Edwin Lowe, a nineteen-year-old toy salesman from New York, ob-served beano being played at a county fair. The son of a Polish Orthodox rabbi who came to America, Lowe was a born salesman pursuing his dream of success in the United States. But his story starts at a low point. Lowe was bored at a fair in Jacksonville, and began walking toward his Nash automobile to drive north. As he looked back one more time, he noticed a long line of people waiting to go into a tent. He heard laughter and excitement. What was going on inside? Lowe went inside the crowded tent and watched all of the excitement until he got his chance to play. He spent several nickels, despite not winning one game. Beano captured his imagination.

Lowe bought a handful of cards from the game supervisor and drove back to New York with them. After studying the cards, Lowe created his own game cards, bought some dried beans, and invited some friends over to play the mystery game. He proceeded to call out numbers from a cigar box. One of the players, a young enthusiastic woman, caught onto the game. She got five beans in a row as the first player, but in her excitement she forgot the name of the game. In the thrill of the moment, she yelled out "bingo!" Lowe recalled later that at that moment, he decided he would call this game Bingo. He traveled to the patent office to register the Bingo trademark but was unsuccessful. Lowe still believed that there was interest in the game. At some point, Lowe showed his game to a parish priest of a Catholic church in Wilkes-Barre, Pennsylvania, who saw the game's promising potential to fill up his church's social hall. The Catholic Church became the first big customer of Lowe's idea: in 1934 it bought bingo cards from his 226 presses, with 1,000 employees printing cards around the clock. By 1934 roughly 10,000 bingo games were played each week throughout the United States. Lowe's hunch proved correct about bingo appealing to people as they played it in various regions, including Florida.[8]

The first noted Indian bingo began in Florida with the Seminole Indians.[9] The Seminoles' successful business venture started with a cigarette shop opened along U.S. Highway 441 in 1975. Soon cars from Ft. Lauderdale and Boca Raton transported customers to purchase tax-free cigarettes for $5.50 a carton. The state of Florida lost $2.10 on each carton, amounting to $2,456,769 from April 1977 to February 1978. The public criticized the Seminoles for earning money from people's addiction to smoking, but untaxed cigarettes were also obtained in Florida from military installations and veterans' hospitals. And people could mail order them from North Carolina.[10]

With the cigarette business succeeding, the Florida Seminole Nation began contemplating bingo as another enterprise. Tribal representatives approached the Bureau of Indian Affairs for funding for a bingo hall, and government officials refused them. Then banks refused the Seminoles based on the fact that they could not foreclose on tribal cigarette shops held in trust status as federal property. Seminole representatives then contacted Eugene "Butch" Weisman and George Simon in 1977. Weisman and Simon, white businessmen, had been successful previously in raising $2.5 million for the Seminole Nation to build a new drive-in facility for the tribe's cigarette business.[11] But the Indian bingo story has another, little-known component.

In the extreme opposite part of the country, members of the Puyallup tribe in Washington approved a proposal for casino-type gambling on their reservation. In an unofficial vote of 134 to 89, voters passed the referendum. The Puyallups had more than 400 eligible voting members. By early March 1979, the tribe submitted its gaming code to the Department of the Interior for review and approval. Assistant U.S. Attorney Chris McKenna commented that should the Interior Department approve the Puyallup proposal, a precedent would be set for nationwide gambling operations on trust lands throughout Indian Country. Although tribal members had set up individually owned casinos against federal authority, resulting in raids, fines, and convictions, this time the tribe sought federal support and approval. Silas Cross Jr., chairman of the tribe's gambling commission, believed that gambling could begin later in the summer of 1979.[12]

During the coming months the Puyallup tribe moved their plans for a bingo into action. As soon as news about the Puyallup's gambling proposal became public, the mayor of Tacoma and other officials expressed their opposition. They asserted that gambling was not going to happen in the area. Mayor Mike Parker said that he opposed any casino in Tacoma "because the city would have no control over it."[13]

In the following weeks Interior Secretary Cecil Andrus responded to Senator Henry "Scoop" Jackson and his supporters' efforts to halt Puyallup gaming. The secretary stated that the assistant secretary of Indian affairs had met with the Puyallup tribal council on March 27 and that the tribe had "rescinded the gambling code it had earlier prepared, and that the Tribe will not be entering into any type of casino gambling." The Puyallup cited that they did not want to violate federal law, even in regard to card games permitted under Washington state law. Furthermore, the secretary iterated that the gaming move conflicted with tribal laws and the Puyallup constitution and with federal law.[14] Puyallup efforts remained in abeyance.

Back in Florida, the Seminole Nation pushed forward with their plan to open a bingo operation. The Seminoles negotiated an agreement with Weisman and Simon to locate financial backers for opening a bingo hall on the Hollywood Reservation, located north of Miami. The agreement called for a split of 45 percent to the financial backers and 55 percent to the Seminoles. Plans called for a bingo hall to accommodate 1,500 players, complete with valet parking, security guards, closed-circuit television, a large announcement board, and climate control. All of this was to be established at Stirling Road and Highway 441 on the 480-acre Hollywood Reservation. The Seminoles planned to open doors for business in December 1979. Seminole leaders put the price of admission at $15, but a person could also purchase chances to win from $10,000 to $110,000. Soon bingo players came by the busloads from as far north as Jacksonville and as far west as St. Petersburg to play bingo.[15]

The Florida Seminoles anticipated correctly that their investment would succeed, as about 1,200 people frequented their bingo hall. The tribe learned what bingo players wanted and created a gaming client subculture of valet parking, drink services, and other amenities, including armed escorts to walk winning players to their cars. Gambling proved to be addictive and successful for the Seminole. Clients spent $35 per night and more on certain nights when the super jackpot went up to $19,000.

Chief James E. Billie had his accountants at work and he surmised that the tribe would earn $1.5 million after the first year, after paying 45 percent of the earnings to Weisman, who retained a business partnership with the Seminoles. Billie had assiduously done his homework and knew who his potential clients were. "I looked at the white man's weaknesses," said Billie.[16]

Since the 1980s, American Indian nations' success in the gambling industry has provoked considerable controversy and sporadic support. And it is fair to say that not all gaming tribes have caused such controversy. In fact, only about 20 percent of the Indian gaming tribes succeed at breaking even or earning a profit. Yet American society has wanted to believe rhetoric and illusions rather than facts and reality. When the Florida Seminoles opened up the first bingo hall in 1979, an important precedent occurred to launch a new era of American Indian capitalism and tribal political economies. Other Indian nations soon followed. These developments led some optimists to believe that the metaphorical buffalo had returned to replenish Native people with hope.

Undoubtedly, Indian gambling is complex and problematic. Indian gambling involves many people and attracts many interests. Governmental interests are involved at the federal, state, tribal, and local levels. Religious and other gambling organizations, even state lotteries, have a stake in the matter. American Indian economies are directly affected, but the sudden impact of the success of Indian gaming also affected local and state economies and has conflicted with local ordinances and state laws. As the holder of trust responsibilities to tribal governments, the federal government is legally mandated to protect the Indian interest. And within the Indian communities, people are divided over the morality of the gambling operations, how they are run, who is actually benefiting, and a host of other concerns.

The first Indian bingo test case involved the Seminoles of Florida in *Seminole Tribe of Florida v. Butterworth* in 1981.[17] In this case the state of Florida challenged the right of the Florida Seminoles to operate a bingo operation. The Seminoles' bingo operation had become highly profitable. Florida claimed that it must conform to bingo operations according to a Florida statute that "authorized bingo games operated by certain religious, charitable, and civic groups so long as the entire proceeds from the game were used by the organizations for charity."[18] The federal court ruled in favor of the Seminoles that the state of Florida had no authority to regulate the Indian bingo operation. Having lost three wars (1817–1818, 1835–1842 and 1855–1858) against the United States, this Seminole victory proved to be significant as Indian gaming proliferated throughout Indian Country.

In the following years, federal action continued. Congress passed the Indian Tribal Governmental Tax Status Act in early 1983. This measure changed the tax status of tribal governments. It granted some of the federal taxing authority to tribal governments similar to that enjoyed by state governments. This included allowing the tribes to issue tax-exempt bonds to finance governmental projects on reservations.[19] By generating tax-collected revenue, the tribal governments gained more control over their economy and financial infrastructures, thus helping to stabilize operational budgets.

On March 3, 1983, an incident on the other side of the country involved a small tribal community in southern California. In Riverside County, the Cabazon tribe of twenty-five enrolled members opened the Cabazon Bingo Palace. The Cabazon band operated a bingo room according to a management agreement with an outside firm. The Morongo band of about 730 enrolled members had a similar agreement, called the Morongo Band of Mission Indians Tribal Bingo Enterprise Management Agreement, in running its bingo operation. Over a hundred years earlier, an executive order of President Ulysses S. Grant had created the Cabazon Reservation in 1876, and he had previously established nine small reservations, including the Morongo Band of Mission Indian Reservation in 1865.[20]

In California the local and county governments regulated card games since they were legal. On May 6, 1983, the Riverside County Sheriff Ben Clark closed down the Cabazon gambling establishment, and Judge Laughlin E. Waters issued a preliminary injunction against the county. The Cabazon received some bad publicity when a takeover of the band was attempted by outside businessmen Wayne Reeder, Peter Zokosky, John Patrick McGuire, and Jimmy Hughes, and the conflict was reported on Geraldo Rivera's *20/20* show in 1985. On February 25, 1987, the U.S. Supreme Court ruled that state and local governments could not regulate high-stakes bingo and other gaming on Indian reservations if state law allowed such forms of gaming by anyone.[21] However, the state of California argued that the Criminal and Civil Jurisdiction Act, passed in 1953, had included it as one of the original five states. This law gave these states the right of criminal and civil jurisdiction over Indian reservations within their boundaries,[22] and California argued this included Indian gaming. States had tried to insert themselves into the legally locked federal-Indian relationship, and the Criminal and Civil Jurisdiction Act allowed this

Figure 7.1. Cabazon Indian casino and hotel. Courtesy of the author.

intervention to occur in a limited way. They argued that the involvement of state governments in Indian gaming was necessary to protect state interests.

In 1987 unregulated "high-stakes" bingo faced a serious test in *California v. Cabazon.*[23] In this case, two Indian groups or communities, the Cabazon and Morongo bands of Mission Indians, had opened successful bingo operations in Riverside County, California. The state of California contested the bingo operations when the Cabazon band opened a card club, offering draw poker and other card games to the public, predominantly non-Indians. The Cabazon operated the site for about three years. The state of California sought to apply two state ordinances, although the statute did not prohibit the playing of bingo.

After a four-year labyrinth of legal processes, the most important Indian gaming court case to date was resolved. On February 25, 1987, the U.S. Supreme Court handed down a major decision in favor of Indian gaming tribes, although it was divided. In brief, Riverside County had no legal authority to enter the reservations and close the card playing; thus, the small Cabazon and Morongo groups could reopen their gaming operations. Justice Byron White stated the ruling of the court, with Chief Justice William Rehnquist and justices William J. Brennan, Jr., Thurgood Marshall, Harry Blackmun, and Lewis F. Powell, Jr., in agreement. Opposed opinions included justices John Paul Stevens, Sandra Day O'Connor, and Antonin Scalia.[24]

As the landmark court case meandered through the courts, what would become the largest gaming resort in the world was being created—Foxwoods in Connecticut. Richard "Skip" Hayward was the principal individual behind what would become the Pequot gaming empire. He was one of nine children and one-sixteenth Indian. His mother, Theresa Plouffe, married a Navy man, Richard Hayward. With her husband often away at sea, Theresa took her many children to visit their grandmother on the reservation. These visits made the grandmother's small house crowded. It dated back to 1865 and had cold floors, no hot water, and no electricity. Skip's father wanted him to enter the U.S. Naval Academy, but the likelihood of going to Vietnam convinced Skip to go to work after high school graduation. Skip worked as a pipe fitter and welder at Electric Boat, a submarine manufacturer in Groton, Connecticut, for $229 a week. Skip spent a lot of time on the reservation with his grandmother until she died on June 6, 1973.[25]

In late 1983, President Ronald Reagan signed a bill federally recognizing the Pequot as a tribe that was previously a state recognized tribe by Connecticut. Influenced by the Penobscot operating a bingo hall in Maine, Skip Hayward and a cousin visited James Billie and the Seminoles in Florida. Exiting a Florida turnpike and finally reaching the reservation, the Seminole operation as large as four football fields astounded Hayward. He asked Billie, "how did you do this?" Billie responded, "It was like somebody handed me a loaded gun and said if you want it, pull the trigger. I pulled it."[26] On July 5, 1986, the Pequot opened the doors of its bingo parlor for gaming. Congressman Sam Gejdenson cut the red ribbon to officially allow a thronging crowd to come in and enjoy closed-circuit television, electronic scoreboards, and fried-chicken dinners. Lavishly designed, the parlor welcomed thousands to gamble, and the crowds did not stop coming to Foxwoods.[27] In a year and a half, the Pequot bingo parlor grossed $20 million a year, with 25 percent as pure profit. A windfall had occurred for the small tribe with only about a hundred members. Per capita payments to each member were $60,000 annually for every man, woman, and child on the reservation.[28]

The proliferation of the Indian gaming industry provoked the federal government to try to harness this wild buffalo herd of operations called unregulated Indian gaming. Possibly two events helped to bring about a final act of Congress to settle the polarizing differences between states and tribes. The Democrats regained control of the Senate in 1986. This victory permitted Senator Daniel Inouye of Hawaii to replace Mark Andrews of North Dakota as chairman of the Select Committee on Indian Affairs. During October 1986 Senator Andrews introduced an amendment to a House resolution that introduced regulation of Indian gaming. Andrews claimed that his amendment gave states more control over class III gaming. Inouye, in contrast, strongly advocated the protection of Indian sovereignty.[29]

The second event involved the declining health of Representative Morris Udall. He informed his staff that he did not believe that he could effectively be a part of the Select Committee on Indian Affairs. Udall had become an influential congressman with his knowledge about Indian affairs in his home state of Arizona and the rest of the Southwest. As a result, he also believed that some control was needed for Indian gaming, and he chose to go along with the new legislation regulating Indian gaming.[30]

On February 19, 1987, Senator Daniel Inouye, the Japanese American hero of the "go for broke" infantry in World War II and champion of Indian issues in Congress, introduced a Senate bill for regulated Indian gaming, six days before the Supreme Court decided the landmark *Cabazon* case. On the floor of the Senate Inouye stated,

> The issue has never really been one of crime control, morality, or economic fairness. . . . At issue is economics. At present Indian tribes may have a competitive economic advantage. . . . Ironically, the strongest opponents of tribal authority over gaming on Indian lands are from States whose liberal gaming politics would allow them to compete on an equal basis with the tribes. . . . We must not impose greater moral restraints on Indians than we do on the rest of our citizenry.[31]

On September 15, 1988, the Senate called for a voice vote and passed the bill. Eleven days later, the House of Representatives voted on the bill. Representative Udall called the bill a "delicately balanced compromise" and insisted that he understood the frustration of Indians, but "felt that this bill is probably the most acceptable legislation that could be obtained given the circumstances." On September 27, the House passed the bill by a vote of 323 to 84, and President Ronald Reagan signed the Indian Gaming Regulatory Act into law on October 17, 1988.[32]

The new law undermined tribal sovereignty, yet it also established a procedure that protected potential gaming tribes against intermingling from state governments. At the time, the Indian gaming industry increased so fast that the regulatory act provided some stability for both tribes and states. The act defined three kinds of gambling: Class I gaming included traditional forms of Indian gambling usually a part of tribal celebrations and social games for minimal prizes. Class II involved bingo and card games for prizes. Class III included casino gambling, especially baccarat, blackjack, and slot machines. The National Indian Gaming Commission was set up to supervise class II and III gaming.[33]

This important measure outlines the regulation of Indian gaming. It is an act "to establish federal standards and regulations for the conduct of gaming activities within Indian country" [and] "as a means of promoting tribal economic development, self-sufficiency, and strong tribal governments," "to shield it [Indian gaming] from organized crime and other corrupting influences, . . . to assure that gaming is conducted fairly and honestly by both the operator and players," and "to establish a National Indian Gaming Commission."[34]

Following the passage of the Indian Gaming Regulatory Act, seventy casinos began operations in sixteen different states. Ten years later, 260 casinos existed in thirty-one states.[35] This burgeoning situation placed growing responsibility on the legal partnership between the federal government and casino tribes. Furthermore, the act introduced a third important player: state governments. With state compacts or agreements specified by the act, the daily operations stood between the states and tribes, not the federal government and tribes. By law, the tribes and states had to reach an agreement for the tribe to build a casino, and the state government received a small portion, such as 2 percent, of the slot machine yearly revenue.

As Indians made more money, more admonishing people hurled criticism at them. Relentless adversaries attacked gaming tribes throughout Indian Country. The threat of organized crime entering the Indian gaming industry has been the biggest innuendo. Mainstream critics argued that organized crime had infiltrated Indian gambling, that Indians have fed off of gambling addicts, and that the tribes themselves were in trouble due to mismanagement and infighting. In response, the tribes charged that state governments and the federal government were out to usurp Indian sovereignty and legally limit the Indian gaming industry.

The passage of the Indian Gaming Regulatory Act did not immediately regulate gaming throughout Indian Country, however. Before the creation of the National Indian Gaming Commission mandated in the new act, many reservations continued to ignore government threats to close their operations, and they offered bettors computerized games that looked like and played like slot machines. Such computerized games in Florida, Arizona, California, and other states put Indian gaming tribes in opposition to state and federal officials. In particular, California officials seized hundreds of machines from California tribes. In November 1991, California seized a hundred machines from the Table Mountain Reservation. "The state of California has been opposed to all forms of Indian gaming from the outset," said Howard Dickstein, attorney for the reservation. He continued, "The state continues to treat Indian people and Indian tribes like children. It's an outmoded and racist approach."[36]

On March 18, 1992, a report from the Department of Justice to the Senate Select Committee on Indian Affairs concluded that organized crime had not infiltrated gaming operations run by tribes. Based on several years of investigation by the FBI, no substantial evidence of organized crime existed in Indian gaming.[37] Yet the FBI's report did not erase the suggestion of organized crime linked to the casino tribes. This overall situation has proved not to be a serious problem, although the perception of organized crime has been an issue for casino tribes.

Then Indian gaming operations exploded at an astounding rate in the 1990s. Gaming tribes earned $1.5 to $2.5 billion annually. By the end of the decade, the tribes took in over $7 billion a year. In 2000, an estimated 212 of 562 federally recognized tribes either invested in or operated Indian gaming sites in twenty-four states. As the twenty-first century witnessed an unparalleled influx of 340 Indian gaming operations in twenty-nine states, casino revenue soared to $13 billion by the end of 2001.[38]

Senator Ben Nighthorse Campbell of Colorado offered one Native perspective. In regard to Indian gaming and the future, Campbell expressed serious concern about Indian values at risk and about a white backlash unhappy with the fact that Indians did not have to work because of casino money made available to them. "When I see kids, come to a small rural school with $100 bills in their pockets . . . believe me, it creates some problems in the community," Campbell said. "We need to make sure our kids don't lose their way with the greenbacks." He worried that some Indian children did not care about furthering their education or decided against going to college because of per capita payments distributed to them by their tribe.[39]

Gambling is legal in forty-eight states; Hawaii and Utah are the exceptions. In 1994 nearly 100 million Americans gambled $400 billion. Now Las Vegas, Reno, and Atlantic City have to contend with state-authorized casinos and lotteries, where a lucky person can win as much as $100 million. But to win the Mega Millions lottery in the United States, the odds are 1 in 175,711,536; this means a person has a considerably better chance of being struck by lighting, at 1 to 576,000 odds. In 2010 Mega Millions and Powerball joined in allowing each operation to sell the other's lottery tickets.

In Arizona, the Gila River Indian Community has benefited tremendously from the gaming industry. In an all afternoon and evening affair on January 7, 2012, the tribe inaugurated a new administration, with Governor Gregory Mendoza and Lt. Governor Stephen Roe Lewis leading their people into a "new era of prosperity." In the celebration ceremony at the Sheraton Wild Horse Pass Resort on a Saturday, Lewis proclaimed that "the opportunities are reality" for the Gila River Indian Community. Governor Mendoza pledged that the "greatest resource is the people," and as he ended his inaugural address, he looked at Lt. Governor Lewis with a wide grin and said, "Are you ready to go to work?" "I'm ready!" quipped Lewis with no hesitation.[40] This partnership of leadership for the Gila River community represented the synergy in the community to advance the tribe by using gaming revenue to expand the tribal economy.

Like 20 percent of the gaming tribes that are successful in the gaming industry, Gila River Indian Community has made giant strides. Their capitalistic entrepreneurship represents a modern political economy that invests in its people and communities. With considerable business experience and assiduous planning, Gila River has built a resort hotel, a profit-making casino, and the Whirlwind Golf Course. The tribe has accomplished this through a sustainable and self-sufficient economic model that provides per capita payments to its members. The tribe has invested to improve its peoples' medical care with the Komatke Health Center, Ak Chin Health Clinic, and Hu Hu Kam Memorial Hospital. The tribe is moving forward with plans to construct an upscale outlet shopping center of ninety stores off of the I-10 Freeway near the Wild Horse Casino and hotel.[41]

On the same January 7, the Muscogee Creek Nation in Oklahoma inaugurated Principle Chief George Tiger and his new administration. "We are on the cusp of being an ever great Nation but that future will only be realized through unity, endurance and ultimately, change," asserted Tiger. The new principle chief also stressed preserving the highest priorities for the Muscogee Nation citizens: "Better health care, educational opportunities for our youth, jobs, housing, and to bring this Nation back to the prominence it once held as a leader and innovator among all sovereign tribal nations."[42]

Since opening their first bingo operation, the Muscogees have built on their initial success. Starting with a new government under Principle

Figure 7.2. Gila River tribal casino and hotel, Gila River, Arizona. Courtesy of the author.

Chief Claude Cox in 1971, the Creeks used gaming revenue to add to its capitol complex, as well to establish community center buildings through the Creek Nation in eight Oklahoma counties. From its gaming enterprises, the Creeks provide dental and medical care to their 72,740 enrolled citizens, as well as scholarships for college-bound students and grants to communities. The Creek Nation offers language classes by certified instructors and holds an annual fair as a means to help preserve its Native culture. It has four community health centers, the Creek Nation Community Hospital, Elderly Nutrition Program, WIC Program, Community Health Representative Program, Contract Health Representative Program, Contract Health Service Program, Diabetes Program, Tobacco Prevention Program, and Caregiver Program. In addition, the Creeks have started the College of the Creek Nation, and the tribe is expanding to construct a new museum, cultural center, and archives.[43] While the Muscogee Creek and Gila River Nations have invested in their people's welfare and businesses, they are continuously rebuilding, with much of their revenue coming from gaming.

One serious problem has been addiction. Gambling addiction affects all groups, and many addicts visit tribal bingos and casinos. Ed Looney, the executive director of the New Jersey Council on Compulsive Gambling, stated that "about 70 to 75 percent of people who go into a casino do so socially—they have fun, lose some, and it's OK." Unfortunately, an estimated 20 percent have some form of gambling addiction. "That group will steal, embezzle or borrow to gamble," said Looney. He explained that compulsive gamblers go through three stages: "A big winning phase when the action is intoxicating, followed by a losing phase when they borrow money and can't stop until finally desperation sets in with even larger betting to recoup losses." In the last phase Looney said that 90 percent of the compulsive gamblers will commit crimes "to feed their habit."[44] In a meeting on regulating gambling casinos held in Detroit on November 25, 1996, Michigan State Racing Commissioner Nelson Westrin, also named interim executive director of the Michigan Gaming Board, said, "There are hidden social costs. It's hard to tell children that hard work pays off when we're all involved in gambling."[45]

Rena Comeslast, a seventy-eight-year-old woman who has raised dozens of foster children in Poplar, Montana, said that "there'll be a lot of food stamps for sale this week," as she referred to the first of the month when welfare and child aid checks are issued on the reservation.[46] The idea of instantly getting rich by hitting the jackpot has infected tribal communities where there are tribal casinos. In this ironic twist, the tribes are getting rich off of their own people, especially those who cannot afford to gamble.

John Pipe, a member of the Fort Peck tribal council, did not support Indian gaming. Like Ben Nighthorse Campbell, he was concerned about the youth. He remarked, "Parents are already selling food stamps to go to bingo. And who suffers? The children."[47] Pipe observed this happening on his reservation. Located in the northeast corner of Montana, Pipe's reservation contains bands of two tribes, Lakota and Assiniboine, and is the ninth largest reservation in the United States. In the first decade of the twenty-first century, Fort Peck operated six gaming sites located at Poplar, Brockton, and Wolf Point.

Economically, bingos and casinos have been a financial windfall for the tribal nations, bolstering their political economies. Their potential success of making millions of dollars per year is now in the billions. With the expansion of the Indian gaming industry, more jobs have been created on tribal lands. This proliferating contagion employed scores of Native people and non-Native people. Another plaguing question for the tribes is what are the tribal benefits? The obvious response is decreased unemployment. Whereas some reports show that unemployment on reservations averages 40 to 60 percent, and as high as 80 percent during the winter, bingo has decreased unemployment on some reservations. Among the Seminoles in Florida, the unemployment rate decreased by as much as 50 percent in the 1980s as the tribe enjoyed considerable prosperity from the leadership of James Billie.[48]

Even with the plenary power of Congress to regulate Indian gaming, a number of gaming tribes have done well—perhaps the water gourd was more than half full at the time. The Indian Gaming Regulatory Act introduced something new that the tribes had not previously had to contend with before. This wrinkle allowed state governments to become players in the Indian gaming business. State compacts made with gaming tribes, on the average, have led to 8 percent of tribal slot machine profits going into state coffers and 2 percent going to local government treasuries. Feeling threatened by the increasing economic power of gaming tribes, state interests sought to intrude into the legal status of American Indian nations. As of 1996, ninety-seven tribes had compacts with twenty-two states for casinos with class III gaming.[49] By the end of the twentieth century, Indian gaming had become a part of a new Indian culture in state-tribal relationships.

To put it mildly, the Indian gambling industry has changed Indian Country remarkably. The direct impact has been that tribal economies have been uplifted by the tribes themselves. Their leaders have exercised fecund imagination in their meticulous planning of the development of their business practices that has changed their histories, improved tribal economics, involved an intricate knowledge of the law, expanded political relations, and improved Native societies—all of the areas of an Indian modern political economy. The obvious impact is the evidence of financial windfalls, with some distribution to all tribal members in some successful Indian tribes. Gambling profits have enabled tribes to fund needed programs to help all of their people such as health care, educational scholarships for college, agricultural assistance programs, and care for the elderly and youth. In the process, the tribes have become less dependent on the federal government for program assistance. Importantly, this era of Indian gaming has advanced Indian sovereignty and reinforced tribal self-determination.

The success of Indian gambling operations has also attracted outside interests such as the public coming onto reservations. This is a major change since most people never had a reason to visit Native reservations. Overall, Indian Country is transforming, and more change is forthcoming. Additional construction of Indian bingos and casinos is evident, and the values of Indians and whites are on the line. On a daily basis, Indians and the general public are becoming increasingly optimistic about winning the lottery or hitting the jackpot in casinos. Upon hearing about someone winning the lottery or hitting a huge jackpot, other people want to believe that they could be the next winner. Since the late 1970s, Indian gaming cut across economics, society, tribal communities, and the law as the sine qua non that proved essential for healthy tribal political economies in order to rebuild Indian nations. Success for gaming tribes continued into the twenty-first century, but large profits began to dwindle when a recession started with the home loans industry in 2006. As mortgage companies and banks overqualified many people applying for loans, the housing market dropped, and southern California and urban Arizona especially felt the drop in the economy. As the recession grew worse, casino tribes made less money, causing tribal leaders to scale down growth and expansion as Americans in general had less money to spend and many lost their homes. Interestingly, tribal economies fared better than the national economy as the country headed into 2013.

At this date the history of Indian gaming is by no means over. Perhaps it has not reached its zenith, but it is time for an overall assessment and an introduction to how this whole story began and how the legal entanglements resulted from attempts of various actors to regulate this great change that is reshaping tribal communities. The challenge is that tribes have had to envision tomorrow's needs and have reinvested their earnings into expanding their gaming operations and funding programs that help their people as a whole. This is moral economy thinking like it once was. This would seem like a cycle of traditional tribal moral economies becoming modern political economies and back again to moral ones. If this is a contradiction, then Indians have learned how to live with opposites. Such internal growth within Native communities has helped tribes in the rebuilding process of making stronger indigenous nations, although the improbable occurred when the Pequot tribe went bankrupt in 2009.

One real issue to outsiders is per capita payments paid to tribal members from tribal gaming earnings. In fact, only a small percentage of tribes are able to make per capita payments to their enrolled members, as only 20 percent of the more than 200 Indian gaming operations succeed in turning a profit. This raises the next question for many tribes: "Who is a tribal member?" People on the outside are asking, "How can I prove my membership in a tribe, especially one successful in gaming?" The quick answers are that the tribes themselves determine who their tribal members are and who can become an enrolled member. Second, documented evidence of relatives who are already members is pertinent to any case involving desired tribal membership. In short, it is the burden of the outsider to prove his or her heritage to possibly become a tribal member.

For example, it is not difficult to find parallels between Annie Lowe, the Kansas City prostitute who married the oil-rich Creek Jackson Barnett in the early 1920s, and Jack A. Abramoff, a businessman and former lobbyist convicted in 2006 of mail fraud and conspiracy to bilk the Mississippi Band of Choctaw Indians, Agua Caliente Band of Cahuilla Indians, Coushatta Tribe of Louisiana, and Saginaw Chippewa Indian Tribe out of tens of millions dollars from 1999 to 2003. Ultimately, Abramoff pled guilty on January 3, 2006, to three felony counts of defrauding American Indian tribes and corruption of pubic officials in a federal court. From a wealthy Jewish family in Atlantic City, New Jersey, "Casino Jack" served almost six years in prison and was released on December 3, 2010. A lengthy investigation led to the conviction of Casino Jack's partner, Michael Scalon, who conspired with Abramoff to cheat tribes out of $85 million. The federal court also convicted White House officials J. Steven Griles and David Safavian, U.S. Representative Bob Ney, and nine other lobbyists and Congressional aides.[50] Sometimes justice catches up with greed, especially when people want Indian money.

Although poor conditions still exist on many reservations, which are far below the level of modern standards, tribal governments continue to make progress to improve the livelihood for all of their people. In spite of high unemployment, substandard health, alcoholism, insufficient education, and discrimination from the mainstream, American Indians have made substantial progress. Tribal governments—Mississippi Choctaw, North Carolina Cherokee, Florida Seminole, Arizona Fort McDowell, and Oklahoma Chickasaw, to name just a few—now resemble business corporations whose leadership is acutely sophisticated. American Indians have always learned to adapt to circumstances for survival as an enduring people possessing resilience. Whether they are content is a relevant question to them, but according to outside values of the mainstream it will always appear that Native peoples are not doing as well as they could because of many negative stereotypes about the indigenous. For example, outsiders would perceive the water gourd as half empty, but it does depend on perspective and whose eyes hold the view. A part of this presumption derives from the stereotype of the "poor Indian," which has changed to the "casino Indian." The truth is the overall Indian effort to thwart more than five hundred years of stereotypes such as the plight of the Indian. The 20 percent of successful gaming tribes prove otherwise, that the water gourd is half full.

As the Indian gaming industry moved into the twentieth-first century, this Native venture is now more than twenty-five years old. The so-called "new buffalo" has already lived a healthy life despite ill wishes from some critical non-Indians who would like to be included. As of 2010, 240 tribes operated 474 Indian gaming operations.[51] On an annual basis, the sum of the operations reached $18.5 billion, and the next five years seem just as promising. Through Indian eyes, the water gourd is half full with optimism for the future, while the rebuilding of Indian nations continues. Native leaders want more than just satisfaction; they want prosperity, security, and respect for their communities.

Many Native people hope that gaming does not lead to the downfall of their nations and communities. Thus, the pressure increases on tribal leadership and business managers to continue to navigate their people in the white man's business world as Indian capitalists. The long-term success of the Indian gaming industry relies on the American human desire to become rich with little effort. Yet in a larger sense it is about Indian people developing a respectable Indian entrepreneurship that provides for families and communities in a non-Indian business world. In the view of tribal leaders, gaming is a means for providing efficient services for their people that the federal government could not achieve alone. For tribal leaders it is the combination of operating within a two-value system, making smart business decisions, and following through to make successful deals. Indians have learned to think like white businessmen and imaginative Indian entrepreneurship is driving modern tribal political economies.

CHAPTER EIGHT

Sacred Land Returns and Repatriation

Power of Federal Indian Law

As the nation looked to the West for more land, this agency [BIA] partici- pated in the ethnic cleansing that befell the western tribes. War necessar- ily begets tragedy; the war for the West was no exception. Yet in these more enlightened times, it must be acknowledged that the deliberate spread of disease, the decimation of the mighty bison herds, the use of the poison alcohol to destroy mind and body, and the cowardly killing of women and children made for tragedy on a scale so ghastly that it cannot be dismissed as merely the inevitable consequence of the clash of compet- ing ways of life. This agency and the good people in it failed in the mis- sion to prevent the devastation. And so great nations of patriot warriors fell. We will never push aside the memory of unnecessary and violent death at places such as Sand Creek, the banks of the Washita River, and Wounded Knee.

KEVIN GOVER, PAWNEE, 2000

Within a frequency range of 200 to 700 Hz, sounds occur when air pres- sure from lungs hits vocal folds (also called vocal cords) housed in the larynx, an organ that regulates pitch and volume of the sounds. The tongue, lips, mouth, and pharynx refine such sounds, which produce conversation, singing, snoring, screaming, crying, and other humanoid howls. All of this involves and constitutes the human voice. Men and women speak as many as 16,000 words every twenty-four hours. For Indians, "finding voice" and being heard by the mainstream have been some of their biggest challenges in overcoming American conversational narcissism. Even in the long his- tory of U.S.-Indian relations, the Native voice has been ignored in most of the court decisions, lawmaking, and policy developments. In America, where individuality is stressed and the squeakiest wheel gets the grease, Indians as the subaltern have learned to make themselves heard.

On September 8, 2000, Kevin Gover of the Pawnee tribe in Oklahoma, Princeton graduate and lawyer, headed the Bureau of Indian Affairs (BIA)— the U.S. institution that represented the oppression of tribal sovereignty and Native freedom. Gover made the conscious decision to make a public apology on behalf of the BIA in addressing the U.S. Congress. One might say it was ironic, illogical, and actually wrong for an Indian to make an apology to all Indians, something that someone else should have done, like the president. Also ironic, that day was the 175th anniversary of the founding of the BIA, another important reason for Gover to make this historical apology.

Perception has been one of the key differentials that have divided Indians and non-Indians, positioning them in a binary of "us" versus "them." Cultural differences and different ways of perceiving their surroundings have led to ill relations. One of the most explosive issues in Indian Country in the late twentieth century has involved the struggle by Indian people for the protection and return of their sacred sites. This important issue relates to the repatriation of Indian artifacts and burial remains that has occurred for most of the last quarter century. The repatriation movement has created much debate in Indian Country, and it is a response to the unfortunate crime of stealing artifacts and human remains, as well as desecrating sacred sites that are a part of Native people.

American Indians were at a loss as their concerns went unheard until the late 1960s and the rise of Indian activism and the Red Power movement. Red Power meant asserting Indian legal and cultural rights. President Richard Nixon listened and put words into action following his special message to Congress concerning American Indians in 1970. During these years, the public heard Indian views on the news and read them in newspapers across the nation. Finding voice happened for Indians when the American mainstream heard Indian protests and read about Indian activism in newspapers. With television becoming a part of American culture in the early 1960s, more people witnessed Indian issues being debated every day.

In their quest to ensure the return of artifacts, burial remains, and sacred sites, Indians regularly encountered obstacles due to the complexity of federal Indian law. The controversy raised significant questions, especially for Native people in the West. The dialogue addressed the fundamental interpretation of the Constitution as the document pertaining to Americans, but not American Indians, although Native people became U.S. citizens. For example, what are the cultural rights and ethics involved?

What is sacred to American Indians? What are the laws protecting Indian historic and recent burials? Why has collecting and preserving Indian artifacts and burials become so controversial?

Understanding the historical background is essential to begin addressing these questions. The collection of Indian artifacts and burial remains began with deliberate actions during the mid-nineteenth century. The founding of the Army Medical Museum in 1862 called for the study of human craniums, and Indian skulls were easier to gather. The study of the human brain and craniums began officially with the influential publication by Samuel G. Morton, a physician of Philadelphia, titled *Crania America* in 1839. Morton argued for a racial hierarchy based on the capacity for brain size of different racial groups. This study became a part of the scientific movement in the study of the human body and brain as more museums opened their doors prior to the Civil War. The federal government established the Smithsonian Institution in 1846 after receiving a monetary gift from British scientist James Smithson. Harvard's Museum of Comparative Zoology opened in 1859. The American Museum of Natural History in New York opened in 1891, and the Field Museum in Chicago followed about ten years later. All of this institutional action meant that more craniums had to be collected, and a plethoric source was the heads of dead Indians from wars.[1]

Surgeon General William A. Hammond, who created the Army Medical Museum, ordered all medical officers to collect and send Indian skulls to the museum in Washington, DC. Following battles, officers ordered their men to cut off the heads of warriors, women, and children. Other soldiers dug up ancient and more recent Indian graves to comply with Hammond's directive.

On the night of November 28, 1864, the Colorado militia raised by Colonel John M. Chivington drank heavily and boasted about killing Indians the next day. The next morning of November 29, 1864, Chivington led the attack on Black Kettle and the Cheyenne and Arapaho, who had signed a peace treaty. Black Kettle waved an American flag, and another leader held a white flag of truce. Following the massacre at Sand Creek in southwest Colorado, Chivington, a former Methodist minister, had his men behead Indians and sent the skulls to Washington.[2] Such heinous action added more psychological pain to the Cheyenne, Arapaho, and other Native people.

Another request followed in 1868 with the Army "urging upon the medical officers the importance of collecting for the Army Medical Museum specimens of Indian crania." Two years later the Army released the results of its study, stating that "the American Indian must be assigned a lower position in the human scale than has been believed heretofore."[3] Five years earlier zoologist Louis Agassiz of Harvard University wrote to Secretary of War Edwin Stanton to "let me have the bodies of some Indians; if any should die at this time . . . all that would be necessary . . . would be to forward the body express in a box. . . . In case the weather was not very cold . . . direct the surgeon in charge to inject through the carotids a solution of arsenate of soda. . . . I should like one or two fellows entire and the heads of two or three more."[4] Franz Boas, a highly regarded authority of cultural anthropology, supported the collection of Indian bodies. Although Boas studied the early cultures of Northwest Coast Indians and knew the importance of the afterlife to these people, this did not deter his own studies. He stated, "It is most unpleasant to steal bones from a grave, but what is the use, someone has to do it."[5]

Samuel Morse, called by some the "father" of American physical anthropology, examined 147 skulls. He concluded that Caucasians had an average brain capacity of 87 cubic inches, while Indians had an average of 82 cubic inches. For the white scientific community, Native people and African Americans were deemed inferior.[6] The federal government only furthered the desecration of Indian remains when President Theodore Roosevelt signed the Antiquities Act in 1906.[7] Congress designed the law to prevent the commercial looting and selling of Indian skeletons and artifacts but defined Indian bones as "archeological resources." Under the law, archaeological resources were regarded as federal property. The act called for the issuance of federal licenses to certain individuals for excavating Indian gravesites. Furthermore, the act prohibited the reburial of Indian bones. No one listened to Indians at this time, rendering Native people powerless to stop these barbaric actions sanctioned by the U.S. Congress.

The collecting of Indian bones did not disconnect the tribes. Survivors of battles told accounts of fallen comrades. Their stories expressed a strong sense of place, emphasizing the location of the battles where their warriors died. As a result, tribes are associated with certain places of their past. Such places were and are known through the telling of the oral tradition in the form of stories. Stories are shared and passed onto the next generation; the places in the stories become points of references for tribal communities. For every important place, a story accompanies it. One can imagine that each important tribal place has a host of stories like an oral library in the memories of elders who share this information. Stories when shared perpetuate the knowledge of why certain places are so historically important to Native communities. Such important places have been empowered by the

Creator, and people sought Divine assistance from them. They found strength imbued in them like the mainstream churches, yet all were the natural setting created by the Great Spirit. Such sites connected the people with the other side of spiritual life.

Many places that are sacred Indian sites exist throughout the United States, Canada, and Mexico. In the United States alone, such well-known places include the Serpent Mound in southern Ohio for the Shawnee, Taos Blue Lake in New Mexico for the Taos Pueblo, Mackinac Island in northern Michigan for the Ojibwa, Minnewakan Chantay (Devil's Lake) in Minnesota for the Dakotas, and Spirit Cave in Montana for the Crow Indians. In all, a minimum of sixty-three recognized sacred sites exist, with as many as another two hundred or more such places possible. Interestingly, federal officials recognized Devil's Tower in Wyoming as the first national monument.[8]

The Kiowa tell of a story long ago when seven sisters and their brother played and he chased them. As the boy ran after them, he turned into a bear and frightened his sisters. The sisters prayed for help as they ran, and the earth shot up suddenly into the sky, becoming Devil's Tower. The bear clawed the rock, leaving his claw marks to this day. The seven sisters kept going up and became the stars of the Big Dipper.

To the Cheyenne, Devil's Tower is a holy place and is central to many ancient stories. Wooden Leg, a Cheyenne warrior in the nineteenth century, described this important place: "I have seen many times the long upright marks of the bear's claws on this great column [tower] of stone. They are deep seams or furrows. It must have been a monster of a bear. As far back as I can remember, all of the Indians called this stone Bear Tepee or Bear Lodge." Wooden Leg retold a story about the Bear Tepee that he heard when he was young:

> He [an old Cheyenne man] said that a long time ago—nobody knew how long—an Indian man journeying along chose to sleep at the base of this tall stone. A buffalo head was lying near him. He slept four nights. During that time the Great Medicine gently took him down again to his leaf bed on the ground. The buffalo hat was left at the top, near the edge. . . . The Bear Tepee is four or five hundred feet high, maybe higher, and its sides are straight up and down. How else could a buffalo head get up there except it be placed there by the Great Medicine?[9]

Among the Crow Indians of Montana, Spirit Cave is especially significant. Thomas Leforge described in his memoirs during the late 1800s that

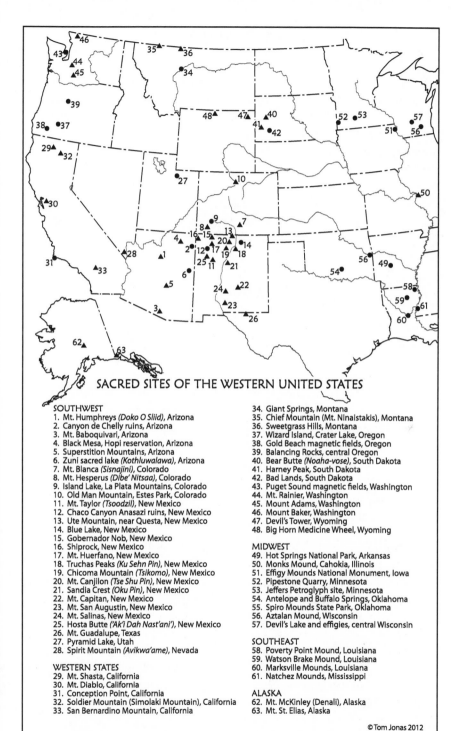

SACRED SITES OF THE WESTERN UNITED STATES

SOUTHWEST
1. Mt. Humphreys (Doko O Sliid), Arizona
2. Canyon de Chelly ruins, Arizona
3. Mt. Baboquivari, Arizona
4. Black Mesa, Hopi reservation, Arizona
5. Superstition Mountains, Arizona
6. Zuni sacred lake (Kothluwalawa), Arizona
7. Mt. Blanca (Sisnajini), Colorado
8. Mt. Hesperus (Dibe' Nitsaa), Colorado
9. Island Lake, La Plata Mountains, Colorado
10. Old Man Mountain, Estes Park, Colorado
11. Mt. Taylor (Tsoodzil), New Mexico
12. Chaco Canyon Anasazi ruins, New Mexico
13. Ute Mountain, near Questa, New Mexico
14. Blue Lake, New Mexico
15. Gobernador Nob, New Mexico
16. Shiprock, New Mexico
17. Mt. Huerfano, New Mexico
18. Truchas Peaks (Ku Sehn Pin), New Mexico
19. Chicoma Mountain (Tsikomo), New Mexico
20. Mt. Canjilon (Tse Shu Pin), New Mexico
21. Sandia Crest (Oku Pin), New Mexico
22. Mt. Capitan, New Mexico
23. Mt. San Augustin, New Mexico
24. Mt. Salinas, New Mexico
25. Hosta Butte ('Ak'i Dah Nast'ani'), New Mexico
26. Mt. Guadalupe, Texas
27. Pyramid Lake, Utah
28. Spirit Mountain (Avikwa'ame), Nevada

WESTERN STATES
29. Mt. Shasta, California
30. Mt. Diablo, California
31. Conception Point, California
32. Soldier Mountain (Simolaki Mountain), California
33. San Bernardino Mountain, California

34. Giant Springs, Montana
35. Chief Mountain (Mt. Ninaistakis), Montana
36. Sweetgrass Hills, Montana
37. Wizard Island, Crater Lake, Oregon
38. Gold Beach magnetic fields, Oregon
39. Balancing Rocks, central Oregon
40. Bear Butte (Noaha-vose), South Dakota
41. Harney Peak, South Dakota
42. Bad Lands, South Dakota
43. Puget Sound magnetic fields, Washington
44. Mt. Rainier, Washington
45. Mount Adams, Washington
46. Mount Baker, Washington
47. Devil's Tower, Wyoming
48. Big Horn Medicine Wheel, Wyoming

MIDWEST
49. Hot Springs National Park, Arkansas
50. Monks Mound, Cahokia, Illinois
51. Effigy Mounds National Monument, Iowa
52. Pipestone Quarry, Minnesota
53. Jeffers Petroglyph site, Minnesota
54. Antelope and Buffalo Springs, Oklahoma
55. Spiro Mounds State Park, Oklahoma
56. Aztalan Mound, Wisconsin
57. Devil's Lake and effigies, central Wisconsin

SOUTHEAST
58. Poverty Point Mound, Louisiana
59. Watson Brake Mound, Louisiana
60. Marksville Mounds, Louisiana
61. Natchez Mounds, Mississippi

ALASKA
62. Mt. McKinley (Denali), Alaska
63. Mt. St. Elias, Alaska

© Tom Jonas 2012

Map 4. Sacred Indian sites in the West.

"the Crows regarded [Spirit Cave] as a sacred place where dwelt mysterious and powerful spiritual forces." He added that Spirit Cave was "far up Pryor Creek" in Wyoming. Spirit Cave is part of Pryor Mountain, named after Nathaniel Pryor of the Lewis and Clark expedition. Pryor Mountain reaches 7,300 feet tall. As Leforge recalled,

> A favorite old-time place for the Crow Indians for devotional dreaming was on Pryor Mountain. . . . A wonderful eagle dwelt there. It screeched in terrifying manner as if human intrusion were resented. Lightning-storms came there frequently during the summer season. The mysteries of the environment were attractive rather than repellent to the Indians. A certain great cliff in this region was held in special awe. This cliff is far up toward the head of Pryor Creek, at the lower end and on the west side of a canyon.[10]

Wooden Leg retold the story of the origin of this special place's power:

> A legend belongs to this awe-inspiring place. Long ago, two lovers, a man and a woman, went up to Pryor Mountain for dreaming and prayer in expiation of sinful conduct. As they came down they stopped to sit and rest at the edge of the great cliff. Unappeased and angry, the Great Spirit kicked both of them over the precipice and they were killed. After that the Crows went there and left rings, ear-ornaments, jewelry of various kinds, and other sacrificial presents, varying in character, to appease the First Maker, who had revealed His presence there. Many Crows still go there annually for this sacrificial offering.[11]

Great feats are possible through the manifestation of power. Native people have tried to understand these deeds and they place considerable emphasis on powerful beings or mysterious places that are much greater than men and women. Like shrines, they hold them in great regard, singing, praying, and even dancing to them. They hope to benefit from the power of the sacred.

In the Southwest among the Pueblo communities, Alfonso Ortiz, a Tewa anthropologist, described the four shrines of the Tewa people. He explained that the spirits were the ancestral souls of his Tewa people and that they lived at the four shrines in each of the cardinal directions. "The supernatural 'Towa e,' who are counterparts of the Tewa political officials, dwell at earth navels which are located on top of four sacred hills and four sacred mountains, also of the cardinal directions," said Ortiz. The sacred mountains stand as four pillars of the Tewa world. According to Ortiz, "The spirits . . . who are the highest deities recognized by the Tewa, are believed to dwell within lakes which are located near the four sacred mountains. The Made People, who dedicate their lives to serving in the Tewa ritual join these high-level deities after death."[12] The sacred has spirits, and they live in both the past and present, for they have the power to do this.

Place is important to the sacred. Ortiz described and named the four sacred mountains of his people:

> Approximately sixty miles to the north of San Juan is "Tse Shu Pin" Hazy (or Shimmering Mountain); "Tsikomo" (Obsidian Covered Mountain) is about fifteen miles to the west; "Oku Pin" (Turtle Mountain) is about eighty miles to the south, and "Ku Sehn Pin" (Stone Man Mountain) is about twenty miles to the east. The northern mountain appears on topographic maps as Conjilon Peak; the second by its Tewa name, the third as Sandia Crest, just northeast of present day Albuquerque, and the last Truchas Peak.[13]

Power rests within such sacred places.

A spiritual existence is connected with sacred places. Native people and others who are close to the earth can sense this connection. At various times this sensation is easier to experience. Such happenings offer evidence of a connection between humans and the earth. Sacred sites are special places shrouded with respect and encompassing energy. People's experiences are identified with these places and are described in the oral tradition of tribes and told in stories. People describe how the energy of sacred places becomes active, emitting power into sound, feeling, or even sight. At some sacred places, people have seen aberrations. The site may have such power for more than one person to see the same thing.

One can ascertain that such energy in action is also beyond the senses of the human body, and only a certain percentage shows itself to human beings. In fact, we probably are not aware of most of the power of sacred sites. Not all people are witnesses to the manifestation of power and energy, and they may even see only parts of it or in different forms or colors. Released power occurs at specific times of the day or night or seasons of the year, or sometimes on a one-time basis. It has been said that sacred places become active at dusk when day and night meet or in the early morning when light and dark are almost the same. Metaphorical thresholds or portals occur at these times as two natural opposites like light and dark come close together, intersecting and momentarily creating a kind of third space as we might acknowledge it.[14] This is why Native people pray at these times or ask the Creator for blessings and guidance like in the scenario about Chitto Harjo facing the coming of dawn described in chapter 1.

To desecrate the sacred and the dead is dangerously disrespectful. One of the most contested issues has been burial remains. Native cemeteries have been the playground of looters, curious peoples, and grave robbers. Collectors want to possess treasures and looters have found commercial profits in selling Indian pottery, artifacts, and burial remains that they have dug up.

One infamous example in which a Native person's body was dug up for the purposes of outside interests is that of Osceola, a Seminole leader. From 1835 to 1842, the Seminoles of Florida engaged the U.S. military in many battles and firefights, the longest Indian war in history. Osceola of the Bird Clan emerged as the most renowned of several noted Seminole leaders. In late 1837, he became ill with pneumonia and requested to meet with General Thomas Jesup at Fort Marion in northern Florida. Under a white flag of truce, Jesup ordered Osceola to be captured, thinking that this would end the Seminole War. Instead, the fighting lingered for five more years.

On the morning of January 30, 1838, at the young age of thirty-four, Osceola died with his head resting in the lap of one of his two wives.[15] Army officials conducted a formal funeral to honor and show respect for Osceola, one of their greatest foes. Medical personnel, many white citizens, and many Indian leaders, warriors, women, and children followed the procession to the gravesite outside the entry of Fort Moultrie on Sullivan's Island in Charleston Harbor, South Carolina. With Osceola, all his weapons and personal belongings were put inside the coffin. As the coffin was lowered into the ground, the military detachment fired a salute in the air over the grave. Both Indians and whites joined together that day to honor Osceola.

In the following days, some unknown grave robbers dug up the body of Osceola and cut off the head. Fortunately, at least a cast of Osceola's head was made in preparing his body for the funeral, and a bust of the famed warrior is on display in the Smithsonian Museum in Washington. It was suspected that a local medical doctor assisted in the decapitation of Osceola. After years of inquiries, Charles Coe, author of *Red Patriots*, published in 1898, received a letter from G. M. Vincent of Braidestown, Florida, on March 24, 1898. Vincent claimed he had the skull of Osceola and replied to Coe, "In regard to [the] Osceola skull [I] will say I will dispose of it for one hundred dollars and the history of same that I have certified to before a J.P. Respectfully Yours, G.M. Vincent."[16]

Such atrocious disrespect is unabashedly unfathomable. Osceola is not the only case of such desecration. At the time of the death of Ishi, the last of his Yahi people, in California in 1916, his brain was removed from his head and sent to the Smithsonian Institute in Washington, DC, for study. It became lost there for many years and was finally found on January 27, 1999. The Cheyenne and Arapaho beheaded at Sand Creek also should not be forgotten for the heinous actions committed by Chivington and his soldiers.

Sacrilegious actions committed against Indian sacred sites and burial remains have provoked heated disagreements and cases brought to courts. As of 1991, the Smithsonian had as many as thirty requests for repatriation from tribal communities. In 2006 the estimated number of items repatriated under the Native American Graves Protection and Repatriation Act of 1990 had spiraled upward to some 30,000 remains and a half a million funerary objects that have been repatriated by tribes.[17]

Differences in cultural beliefs have caused misunderstandings and conflicts between American Indians and the United States. Their separate developments due to the separation by oceans enabled them to pursue their own belief systems for centuries. As a result, in instances of encounters, the two general belief sets have clashed, as one is based on Christianity and the other is founded on environmental relations and the supernatural. The Native spiritual world is inclusive, whereas the Christian tradition is exclusive and criticizes all non-Christian religions. Christian exclusivity led to Holy Wars and Christian denominations denouncing Native beliefs as heathenistic, thus the blatant disregard for Native sacred places and burial remains.

Native people believe in a Circle of Life that is inclusive and should not be broken. Yet the idea of a community as a circle is not a part of the American mainstream way of life and appears to be outside of the logic of Western thinking. The norm of the mainstream rejects inclusivity and prefers to be exclusive in regard to race, religion, and class, including gender. One young person said,

> The broken circle suggested to me what I felt in my heart and the feelings other people have in their hearts. Because the circle has been around for thousands of years, and now it's coming apart because people are forgetting about the ways of the spirit and the ways of kindness to people. They're greedy and money hungry and want power, and that won't do

much when they get to the spirit world. . . . that if people's visions vanish and our way of life isn't like a growing, healthy tree, then we will all vanish. . . . That's the philosophy of Indian life. It is centered around the spirits and around the Creator. All of it.[18]

In the context of this perspective, all things are included in a circular ethereal existence beyond the imagination of most people.

Circular philosophy is not a part of the ethos of the Western world. However, circular thought seems to be a universal part of some other indigenous cultures around the world. While Native people have made tremendous progress in understanding and thinking like the Western mind via adaptation, mainstream thinking has moved very little toward accepting circular philosophy. In linear thinking about life, the mainstream views death as the physical end of a person, with some religious denominations believing in a transformation into an afterlife such as residing in Heaven.

Death is one of the most important stages in life for American Indians. Their tribal cultures regard death as a continuation of a journey for the spirit. Each person that believes in his or her tribal ways has a spirit. Among many tribal beliefs, certain ceremonial rituals accompany the end of a person's life. Funeral ceremonies involve nonhuman forces and laws from the "other side of life." Thus, it is imperative that Native funeral ceremonies not be disrupted and that the body of the dead remain nonabused and intact. This restriction pertains also to the grave and the personal belongings of the dead, as well as tribal artifacts and markings that may accompany the ceremony. Different tribes have specific beliefs on life after death. The general view is that the spirit of life in a person leaves to begin its own journey to the other side of life, which involves going westward or going upward to the universe to live a spiritual existence.

During the 1970s, Leonard Crow Dog talked about the nature of life and its meaning. He was the spiritual leader of the American Indian Movement at the time. Crow Dog explained,

We live in a sacred cycle, the sacred hoop. We are born from Mother Earth and we return to Mother Earth. We feed on the deer who, in turn, feeds on the grass which, in turn, is fed by our bodies after we die. It's the story of the biological cycle you learn in school. Everything is harmony and unity, and we fit within that harmony. And when our bodies die, our spirits are freed and will be here. You see, it's not a religion in the white man's sense, but a philosophy of living, a way of living.[19]

This viewpoint demands a different understanding of human existence. A spiritual life in this manner is difficult in the Christian worldview that emphasizes faith in a certain religion. For Indians, another dimension exists for the soul similar to the Christian belief in a heaven after death, if the person has been good on earth.

With Native people, there is always an awareness of the power that lies beyond the human world. Unexplainable powers exist beyond the comprehension of human beings, and tribes have been studying them for generations. Like the powers of sacred sites, similar kinds of power are related to artifacts that have likely been produced from empowered places or individuals. Medicine making is a means of utilizing these powers to help cure people or even to hurt people, or perhaps to foretell the future. Power is bestowed upon certain individuals as gifts so that they can use them for the goodness of their communities. A concrete example is the life of Sanapia, a Comanche who was called to be an eagle doctor or else harm would come to her loved ones, if she refused the gift of medicine power.[20] Thus, it is the responsibility of gifted individuals to decide how to use power. At the same time, they are mindful that such gifts to exercise power can be taken away from them.

The natural world is full of powers, and so often the circle is a part of it. Circles are very much a part of life; it is up to Indians as people to learn this pattern and why it is so. The indigenous connection to the natural world has been challenged by the United States with its federal policies and programs. For example, the federal government has tried to forcibly assimilate Indians into the mainstream, forcing a round peg in a square hole of foreign values and blind American ethnocentrism. The frequent rejection of American Indians ironically became Native salvation to pursue their lives with resilience and rebuild their nations. Black Elk, an Oglala holy man, described the circularity all around us: "You have noticed that everything an Indian does is in a circle, and that is because the Power of the World always works in circles, and everything tries to be round." He continued saying,

> Everything the Power of the World does is done in a circle. The skies is [*sic*] round . . . and so are all the stars. The wind, in its greatest power whirls. Birds make their nests in circles, for theirs is the same religion as ours. The sun comes forth and goes down again in a circle. The moon does the same, and both are round. Even the seasons form a great circle in their changing, and always come back again to where they were. The life of a man is a circle from childhood to childhood and so it is in everything where power moves.[21]

In such circular philosophy, the cyclic existence is a continuum so that the past is often a presence in the present. In the same light, Native people have rebuilt their nations in cycles of history, starting with Indian removal, after the Civil War, and following the Dawes allotment policy through the Indian Reorganization Act.

In one of his visionary experiences in later life, Black Elk recalled being on top of Harney Point in the Black Hills at a height of 7,242 feet. He said,

> Then I was standing on the highest mountain of them all [Harney Peak], and round about beneath me was the whole hoop of the world. And while I stood there I saw more than I can tell and I understood more that I saw; for I was seeing in a sacred manner these shapes of all things in the spirit, and the shape of all shapes as they must live together like one being. And I saw that the sacred hoop of my people was one of many hoops that made one circle, wide as daylight and as starlight, and in the center grew one mighty flowering tree to shelter all the children of one mother and one father. And I saw that it was holy.[22]

At the same time, Black Elk experienced a oneness with the Natural World. All things are balanced in this natural democracy of respecting all things.

Since the turn of the twentieth century, Congress has paraded legislative measures into laws that have had limited effect on protecting Indian sacred sites and burial remains. For the next fifty years, federal legislation focused on policy making and reforming tribal governments under the Indian Reorganization Act of 1934 and then terminating the tribes' trust status in the 1950s. On July 12, 1960, Congress enacted the Indian Boundary Markers Act. This law made it unlawful to destroy, deface, or remove certain boundary markers on Indian reservations. The law also prohibited nontribal members "to trespass on Indian reservations to hunt, fish, or trap."[23] In 1966 Congress passed the National Historic Preservation Act. President Lyndon Johnson signed the act into law on October 15, 1966. This legislation became more effective for Native peoples with an amendment made by Congress in 1992. With support from tribes, Senator Daniel Inouye pushed this revised measure through Congress. The law called for "State and local governments, Indian tribes and Native Hawaiian organizations and the National Trust for Historic Preservation in the United States to expand and accelerate their historic preservation programs and activities."

The law strove to help Indian people and their communities to preserve their historic artifacts.[24]

The struggle for protecting Indian rights resulted in the founding of the Native American Rights Fund in 1970. Established as a nonprofit organization, the fund started with a grant from the Ford Foundation that was made to the California Indian legal services. After about a year, the fund came into its own when it opened its office in Boulder, Colorado, with David Gitches as the first director. Within five years, the Native American Rights Fund grew from a three-lawyer operation to an expanding organization of forty full-time staff workers that assisted fifteen attorneys to help Native individuals and tribes, especially protecting their legal and cultural rights.[25]

In the early 1970s, Native people also formed the American Indians Against Desecration organization to enable the reburial of Indian remains. In response, the American Committee for Preservation of Archaeological Collections lobbied against Indian efforts, arguing that significant information concerning the lifestyle, health, and diet of Native people would be lost if archeological work was stopped. But in 1971 the American Anthropological Association supported the Indian cause. The professional association produced a statement that read, in part: "In research, an anthropologist's paramount responsibility is to those studies. When there is a conflict of interest, these individuals must come first."[26]

In 1971, in the midst of civil rights and Vietnam protests, President Richard Nixon reversed the course of federal Indian policy and set two precedents in the history of U.S.-Indian relations. First, he halted the fearful policy of termination of Indian trust status, and second, his administration returned land to American Indians. After sixty-four years of fighting for their ceremonial lake, the Taos Pueblo people and allied interest groups succeeded on December 15, 1970, when Nixon signed the land-return bill into law. Taos Pueblo Governor John J. Reyna sent President Nixon a certificate of gratitude on August 14, 1971.[27]

Another battle was waged by the Yakama for the return of important lands. They found a strong ally in the National Congress of American Indians (NCAI). On September 28, 1971, NCAI lobbied President Nixon to return Mt. Adams to the Yakama tribe. The request involved 21,000 acres. The NCAI executive director wrote, "We would like to . . . strongly urge that the decision be made confirming the title of the Yakima land to the Yakima people for immediate occupancy and use."[28]

While the Nixon administrators were dealing with these two land return issues, the Menominee tribe of Wisconsin lobbied to have their ter-

Figure 8.1. Mt. Adams in Washington State. Credit: Mt. Adams from Sheep Lake/Ellis, General Subjects Photograph Collection, 1845–2005, Washington State Archives, Digital Archives, http://www.digitalarchives.wa.gov.

mination status reversed. Menominee activist Ada Deer pushed hard to organize a movement and worked harder to sustain it in her attempt to increase grassroots support and backing in Washington. Much of her effort was merely to educate congressmen about the termination policy and how important it was to restore her tribe to federal recognition. President James White of Determination of Rights and Unity for Menominee Shareholders, a grassroots organization on the former reservation, wrote all members of the Senate and House Committees on Interior and Insular Affairs on November 24, 1971. White stated, "We Menominee, an Indian tribe of Wisconsin, in 1954 became the first tribe upon whom the federal government imposed termination. This policy was forced on us completely against our planning process."[29] As a result of Deer's pushing for Menominee restoration, the government followed up with more than a dozen formerly terminated western tribes being restored to federal recognition.[30]

In the same year Congress passed the Alaska Native Claims Settlement Act, which called for the largest ever compensation to Native peoples: $962.5 million and a return of an estimated 40 million acres of land to Alaska Natives. In response, John Bordridge, Jr., president of the Central Council of Tlingit and Haida Indians of Alaska, wrote Congressman Sam Steiger of Arizona, stating, "It represents an effort by our country to do justice to the land rights asserted by the aboriginal inhabitants of Alaska since 'time immemorial.'"[31]

Nixon and Congress arranged for the return of Blue Lake to the Taos Pueblo people of New Mexico and the return of Mt. Adams to the Yakama in Washington State. His administration also returned the use of Pyramid Lake to Paiutes in Nevada for their ceremonial practices. No U.S. president had ever before returned sacred land to Indians. Natives had always been on the losing end, ceding enormous amounts of land to the United States. Sacred Indian sites were involved, and Indian legal land rights were at issue. The desecration of Indian burial remains has a long history that started with pioneers plowing the gravesites of Native people and building their own churches on top of American Indian sacred sites. In actuality, Indian sacred sites and burial remains meant nothing to white Americans, who held their own cemeteries and church sites to be sacred, but no one else's.

Toward the end of his presidency, Nixon summed up his Indian accomplishments in an annual address to Congress on the state of the union on January 30, 1974. His presidential career had been shaky, with the Watergate scandal becoming public in 1972 in the midst of efforts to end the Vietnam War. "The last five years have been historic steps in Federal Indian policy," stated Nixon.

In 1971, we worked closely with Indian leaders to achieve a settlement of Alaska Native claims, a settlement consistent with America's sense of fairness and also indispensable to the growth and development of Alaska. We also returned lands taken away long ago from the Taos Pueblo at Blue Lake. We returned lands taken wrongfully from the Yakima people. Because the Menominee people have seen their tribal states involuntarily terminated but had nevertheless kept their land and their tribal structure together, the Congress enacted and I signed the bill which restored the Menominee tribe to trust status.[32]

Nixon was not yet finished with Indians. A few months later on May 3, 1974, he announced his support for legislation to enlarge the Havasupai Reservation in Arizona. Senators Barry Goldwater and Paul Fannin introduced the legislation. "This addition [251,000 acres] would return historic and religious sites, ancient burial grounds, and life-sustaining springs to the Havasupai," said President Nixon. "In addition to its historic and religious claims, the tribe needs this land to relieve overcrowding on the reservation and to provide a better economic base."[33] In the eyes of American Indians,

Richard Nixon acted in the spiritual interests of the indigenous. He was the only president up to this time to return sacred land back to the Indians.

As mentioned, Indian life has often been described as a circle. All things are related, actually forming a communal sphere of human and nonhuman entities in Native reality. Unfortunately, mainstream influences have intervened in many tribal communities, thus disconnecting the circle. This disconnection is not healthy for Native people and all other people who realize the importance of maintaining firm, healthy relationships and understanding with all things, especially the earth. Mistreating the earth has disturbed Native people. One person concerned about the environment said,

> Yeah, ecology. Because white people are going whole hog with something that we've been knowin' right along. You know, preserve the land, live with it, appreciate it, and make it part of your total existence. But white people have to control it, manipulate it. . . . This has been the white man's attitude and its actions towards the United States, and that's why you see your polluted water when you guys came. Now you put your poop into it, your oil, name it! That's just a garbage disposal in some areas, you know, the streams, the lakes.[34]

The Circle of Life remains imperative to Indian people who are close to their traditions. They believe in an internal circle within each person and that everything outside of this internal circle belongs in the Circle of Life. When one considers the relationship among all things, he or she can easily see that all things exist within a spherical existence. The Muscogee Creeks call this *Ibofanga*, meaning the totality of everything within and its power.[35] This is a state of existence where the real and unreal blur in a borderland-like zone that connects the physical and metaphysical.

Oglala author Ed McGaa wrote, "Inside of us within this great Disk of Life that each and every one of us has been bestowed with; within that creation, therein lies our character, our record, our background, our reputation, our knowledge; this mysterious spirit that the dominant culture refers to as the soul. . . . You expand, alter and transform this disk, this circle of growing knowledge and related experience."[36] The circle is much a part of Native symbols and art designs.[37] To Indians it is the perfect form in the universe.

In the desecration of Indian sacred places and burial sites, the question of morality must be considered. While people respect their own cemeteries and cultural artifacts, Indian graveyards and artifacts have been grossly desecrated. They have been pillaged, looted, abused, and plowed up by farmers planting crops for their families' livelihoods. Even with knowledge of Native cemeteries, non-Indians have disrespected such graveyards in pursuing their own opportunities and personal gains.

Repatriation has been one of the most important issues of the *longue durée* Indian-white historical relations. But since the 1970s, John E. Echohawk and Walter Echohawk, both Pawnee and attorneys for the Native American Rights Fund, and others have led a proactive fight to restore artifacts and burial remains to tribes. As a part of the momentum to protect Indian cultural rights, Congress has direct access to the reports of the American Indian Task Force Commission established in 1977. In 1979 Congress passed the Archaeological Resources Protection Act.[38] The two-hundred year commemoration of the founding of the United States in 1976 had a ripple effect that all Americans' rights should be protected. Furthermore, President Jimmy Carter, who is devoted to his religious values, believed that Native beliefs should be respected as well.

On August 11, 1978, Congress passed the American Indian Religious Freedom Act.[39] While the act was the most important federal Indian law passed during the Carter administration, it had no provisions to actually enforce the guarantee of American Indian religious freedom. The Indians had a champion in Senator Daniel Inouye, who had been in Congress for a long time and strongly supported and introduced legislation for Native people. Additional legislation had to be passed in order to accomplish the protection of Indian artifacts, burial sites, and sacred places. In addition, Congress passed the Archaeological Resources Protection Act in 1979. This legislation provided for "the protection of important archaeological sites on public lands and on Indian lands and required special permits for people wanting to study or excavate them."[40] Despite such legislation, collectors' interests and commercial interests established an illegal market for Indian artifacts.

The Lakota protested when the Black Hills were taken away from them in the late 1800s, and they have not stopped. During the 1980s, pressure increased from all interested parties to resolve the Black Hills issue by either compensating the Lakota and other tribes claiming it or returning it to them. The latter was not likely to happen. With the Fort Laramie Treaty of 1868 and the Great Sioux Act of 1889, the Black Hills were not included in the creation of the Great Sioux Reservation. Since the late nineteenth century, the Sioux and other tribes like the Cheyenne and Arapaho have fought to regain their sacred Black Hills. The United States claimed the area via Congressional law and South Dakota Governor Carl Gunderson's signature into state law for the constructing of Mt. Rushmore. The work began to carve into the Black Hills four presidential profiles, with final completion occurring on October 31, 1941. Seven years later, several Lakota chiefs approached sculptor Korczak Ziolkowski to carve a monument of Crazy Horse into the Black Hills only eight miles from Rushmore. Ziolkowski, who had worked on Mt. Rushmore, accepted this invitation and began carving Crazy Horse Mountain into an enormous figure of the great Oglala warrior. At present, his family intends to complete this monumental project, which will be the largest sculpture in the world.

The Black Hills have always been sacred to the Lakota, Cheyenne, Arapaho, and other tribes in the area. According to former Lakota Chief Matthew King, eighty-four years old,

> Our religion was given to us by the Great Spirit, and our grandmothers and grandfathers have told us everything. Prayer is the most important thing for us. The earth gives us everything we need. White man tries to put fertilizer on the ground to make it grow better, but that is just because he is silly. He has no faith in what God has already given him. He burns up the ground, wastes it, puts poison on his food because he has forgotten. Our medicine comes also from the Black Hills, many plants and roots. We can cure anything; we can use a plant to make a gallstone just disintegrate. We have medicine for everything. But many of those medicines grow in the Black Hills; that is the only place, so we have to get it back. So, the Black Hills are our church, our hospital, our history, and even our bank, because we knew a long time ago about all the gold and minerals in the Black Hills.[41]

The battle for the Black Hills continued for the bones. In 1988 the American Association of Museums notified the Senate Select Committee of Indian Affairs that 163 of its member museums held 43,306 Indian remains. The Smithsonian possessed 18,600 Native remains, or 54.4 percent of the museum's entire collection of human species. It should be emphasized that American Indians at that time represented less than 1 percent of the nation's population.[42] About this time, the 2000 Census reported 1,959,254 American Indians and Alaska Natives. In 1989 the Smithsonian Institution decided after several years of negotiation to return skeletal remains and burial artifacts of hundreds of Indians to their modern relatives. One estimate projected that 300,000 to 600,000 Indian skeletal remains are held by museums around the country.[43]

During the 1980s, a movement began to reach closure for a national museum for American Indians. In 1989 Congress passed the National Museum of the American Indian Act. The law had three original purposes: to advance the study of Native people; to collect, preserve, and exhibit American Indian artifacts; and to provide for research and study programs of American Indians.[44] In 1990 Congress passed the Indian Environmental Regulatory Enhancement Act. This legislation was designed to "authorize grants to improve the capability of Indian tribal governments to regulate environmental quality."[45] The act amended the 1974 Native American Programs Act by introducing regulatory programs within their tribal governments. These new environmental programs were meant to enforce the monitoring and compliance of environmental quality laws, as well as to train and educate staff, and develop environmental policies.

In October of 1990, Congress passed the Native American Languages Act. This important measure was "an act to preserve, protect and promote the practice and development of Native American languages as deemed also by federal policy."[46] With each new generation, American Indian tribes lose many of their Native speakers. By the end of the twentieth century, it was estimated that less than 25 percent of tribal members could speak their tribal languages. This rapid decline in speakers provoked alarm and garnered attention to this crisis as tribes began to develop language revitalization programs.

In 1990 Zuni and museum officials reached an agreement for the return of rare wooden statues of Zuni war gods from museums around the country to their homelands in New Mexico so that Zuni ceremonial leaders could take care of them.[47] The carvings are two to three feet tall. Throughout the country, there are more than fifty war gods in various museums and five private collections. The tribal council of the Zuni tribe began making requests in 1978. Friendly negotiations by the Zuni have since resulted in sixty-five war gods being returned from thirty-four museums and private collections from 1978 to 1991.[48]

The repatriation movement became official with the passage of the Native American Graves Protection and Repatriation Act on November 16, 1990, as a result of Indian lobbying and support from non-Indians, along with intense lobbying by national and local Indian organizations. The act sought "to provide for the protection of Native American graves, human remains, and sacred objects."[49]

Due to the same momentum, on November 29, 1990, additional congressional action occurred. As the value of artwork and jewelry increased, tribal artists have faced competition from non-Indian, machine-manufactured artwork, and Indian rights had to be protected. Congress passed the Indian Arts and Crafts Act of 1990 to replace the 1935 Indian Arts and Crafts Act regarding cultural rights. The new law expanded court authority to bring civil and criminal jurisdiction over counterfeit Indian arts and crafts.[50]

The election of President Bill Clinton to the White House in 1992 also marked the 500th anniversary of the arrival of Christopher Columbus to the Western Hemisphere. Like Nixon twenty years earlier, Clinton began a rash of land returns to tribes as a part of the "government to government" Indian policy. Addressing tribal leaders in Washington on April 29, 1994, President Clinton reaffirmed his commitment to helping American Indians and addressing their concerns. "For many of you, traditional religions and ceremonies are the essence of your culture and your existence," he said. "No agenda for religious freedom would be complete until traditional Native American religious practices have received the protections that they deserve. Legislation is needed to protect Native American religious practices threatened by federal action. The Native American Free Exercise of Religion Act is long overdue. My Administration will continue to work closely with you and Members of Congress to make sure the law is Constitutional and strong."[51]

In the following months, the Clinton administration took unforeseen action. In 1994 the entire island of Kaho'olawe was returned to Native Hawaiians by federal law. The Native Hawaiians had lobbied since 1978 to halt the U.S. Navy from the routine testing of bombs on the island. To the Hawaiians, over six hundred cultural and historical sites exist on Kaho'olawe. As a result, President George H. W. Bush had halted the practice of bombing in 1990.[52] In 1996 the Clinton administration returned a four-acre area in rural Siskiyou County, California, to the Karuk tribe after the Department of Justice had seized it from Bradley Throgmorton, a marijuana grower and fishing lodge owner on the Klamath River in northern California. The site is the historic center of a village named Katimin and considered a spiritual place to the Karuk. The tribe did not have the funds to purchase the land, which is being held in trust by the BIA.[53]

President Clinton's Executive Order 13007 of May 24, 1996, set out to protect tribal lands. The order intended "to give Native Americans access to sacred sites on federal lands and increase the protection of these places." As a result of this order, federal governmental agencies are required to "accommodate access to and ceremonial use of Indian sacred sites by Indian religious practitioners," to "avoid adversely affecting the physical integrity of such sacred sites," and to "promptly implement procedures." The order was believed to be a significant first step in the protection of Native sacred lands.[54]

American Indian artifacts, sacred places and burial sites continue to be exploited. While Indian repatriation experienced a rash of supportive legislation, the discovery of Kennewick Man on July 28, 1996, in Washington state caused great debate among Indians, whites, and all interested parties. At first thought to be an early Indian, Kennewick Man dates back as far as 9,300 years ago. However, it was later determined that he was about five feet eight inches tall and Caucasian. At present, the mystery of Kennewick Man remains unresolved, and this issue disrupted the Indian repatriation movement.[55] After a court ruling in favor of returning Kennewick to the Umatilla and an appeal was filed. At this date, Kennewick Man remains in the Burke Museum at the University of Washington and belongs to the U.S. Army Corps of Engineers since he was found on this agency's land.

As the century ended, it also marked the 175th anniversary of the BIA. Making a landmark in the history of U.S.-Indian relations, the assistant secretary of the Department of Interior, Kevin Gover (Pawnee), apologized publicly for the BIA under his supervision for the long history of poor relations. On September 8, 2000, in the Sidney Yates Auditorium of the Interior Building, Gover stated,

> And so today I stand before you as the leader of an institution that in the past has committed acts so terrible that they infect, diminish, and destroy the lives of Indian people decades later, generations later. These things occurred despite the efforts of many good people with good hearts who sought to prevent them. These wrongs must be acknowledged if the healing is to begin. I do not speak for the United States. That is the province of the nation's elected leaders, and I would not presume to speak on their behalf. I am empowered, however, to speak on behalf of this agency, the Bureau of Indian Affairs, and I am quite certain that the words that follow reflect the hearts of its 10,000 employees. . . . The Bureau of Indian Affairs was born in 1824 in a time of war on Indian people. May it live in the year 2000 and beyond as an instrument of their prosperity.[56]

The end of the twentieth century witnessed some reconciliation between tribes and the United States in their never-ending battle over Indian repatriation. Clinton's executive order had hardly been in effect several months when federal judge Alan Johnson ruled on December 6, 2001, that the local tribes had the legal right to use the Medicine Wheel site on

Medicine Mountain, Wyoming.[57] Although the site was not returned to the tribes, this was a noted landmark for Native ceremonies long ago.

Led by U.S. Senator Ben Nighthorse Campbell of Colorado (Northern Cheyenne), a bill was introduced pertaining to the Sand Creek massacre of 1864. Assistant Interior Secretary Gover's apology made a difference. On May 6, 2002, Congress voted to return the Sand Creek Massacre site, located in southeast Colorado near historic Fort Lyon, to the Cheyenne and Arapahoe tribes.[58] On May 14, 2002, Domtar Industries announced that it was returning Muwinwi Monihq, an ancient burial ground, to the Passamaquoddy tribe. Also known as Bear Island or Gordon Island in Big Lake, Maine, Domtar had acquired Georgia-Pacific Corporation, a pulp and paper mill company. Domtar and the Passamaquoddy held a special ceremony to return this twenty-five-acre island to the Native community.[59]

On May 23, 2004, the last legal struggle occurred over Rainbow Bridge located in Utah. Considered a national monument, the Navajo, Hopi, Kaibab Paiute, San Juan Southern Paiute, and White Mesa Ute tribes actually assisted the National Park Service in identifying and implementing culturally relevant practices for the management of visitors to the monument. Senior Circuit Judge Robert H. McWilliams entered the final ruling, citing the American Indian Religious Freedom Act that required the federal government "to protect and preserve for American Indians their inherent right to believe, express and exercise" their traditional beliefs.[60] Also in May, Eureka City returned a part of Indian island located near Humboldt Bay to the Wyiot First Nations people of the Table Bluff Reserve in Canada.[61]

In Nevada during August 2007, a federal appellate court upheld a decision to close Cave Rock at Lake Tahoe to mountain climbing and hiking. The court allowed the Washoe tribe to use Cave Rock in their ceremonies as they had traditionally. The popularity of the site had attracted tourists, mountain climbers, and hikers, who disregarded the wishes of the Washoe tribe to respect the sacred site.[62] One tribe obtained land that it once owned. On October 27, 2006, the Eastern Cherokee Tribe had purchased seventy-one acres in Macon Country in western North Carolina that held an ancient mound and Indian town site, including an unexcavated Indian mound, from a private owner.[63]

Collecting Indian artifacts illegally, disrespecting tribal beliefs, and protecting Native cultural rights are giant issues of consideration in this era of repatriation that is presently ongoing. Related to these concerns are mainstream disregard of Indian cultural rights, and the defacing of Native petroglyphs needs to be resolved. While these concerns continue to be addressed, the Smithsonian Institute completed the National Museum of the American Indian. The museum opened in Washington, DC, on September 21, 2004. It is a part of the Smithsonian Mall, displaying American Indian history and cultures from the entire Western Hemisphere and housing an estimated 80,000 artifacts of Native peoples in its collections. Rick West, a Cheyenne attorney, was the founding director of the museum, and in November 2007, Kevin Gover was named the new director. The National Museum of the American Indian continues to enjoy a national and international reputation as more people in the United States and the world become increasingly interested in Native peoples.

Sacred places and repatriation are two ongoing issues of conflict between Indians and other people who desecrate such important places and Native cultural artifacts and burial remains. This course of battles has continued for decades, and there is no resolution in sight to the satisfaction of all parties involved. All disputes end with resolutions found in federal-Indian law. Indian individuals, tribes, museums, universities, collectors, the federal government, and foreign governments are participants in this conflict of interests, and tribal leaders have become keen students of the law. To help protect Native sites, artifacts, and burial remains, more strong federal laws will need to be passed.

For Indian people, the circle remains incomplete. Their connection to sacred places has been abused and threatened. Their cultural rights have been disrespected. Countless tribal artifacts remain in the hands of collectors, museums, and universities. At least for the present, museums and universities are working together for the return of these items to tribal communities or to agreed places for preservation. At the same time, tribes are developing their own museums and archives at a rapid rate, with more than three hundred tribal museums established.

One of the important issues of this conflict of interests is the question of morality and human decency. Non-Indians in many cases have disrespected Indian rights by robbing graves and illegally excavating historic sites. People have robbed Indian graves and historic sites, as well as raided sacred sites in Indiana Jones fashion. Souvenir hunters, bounty hunters selling to collectors, amateur collectors, and thoughtless individuals have desecrated Indian historic places and graves and abused sacred sites. Why do they continue to do this? Why are not Indian sacred sites and cemeteries given the same respect as Arlington Cemetery and the Vatican in Rome? No one would think of digging up war heroes at Arlington or stealing religious pieces from the Vatican.

Figure 8.2. National Museum of the American Indian. Credit: Carol Highsmith (photographer), Library of Congress Prints and Photographs Division, Washington, DC.

In addition to stiffer laws, aggressive tribal leadership and changed attitudes will need to persist to stop grave robbing and the abuse of Indian sacred sites. Criminals who commit such crimes against Native people need to think about their own ancestors' graves being dug up and their own churches being desecrated. Until then, such desecration will continue with no end in sight. Through Indian eyes, this is injustice that needs to be corrected. Ironically, outsiders do not see their implication in the wrongs that have been committed against Indian people, or they choose to deny this dark side of the history of the American West. From a Native point of view, Indians are part of the modern West, and they are helping to develop it in the twenty-first century. They have found their voice in the mainstream by using the power of the law and economics. Resiliently strong, the Native communities are rebuilding their nations on the lands that mainstream Americans did not want. Adapting and reinventing themselves, the Native nations understand the power of federal Indian law, continuing to strengthen their tribal political economies to fit their people's needs, and remaining connected to the earth and their traditional pasts. In fact, they have learned to navigate within the cultural systems of both Indian and white; so it will be.

Resilience, Rebuilding Nations, and Problem Solved

It Does Matter

The human spirit is beautiful and stubborn at the same time. Resilient yet bending, the flexibility of American Indians is like river canes in the Muscogee Creek tradition that dwell by the rivers, weathering the most vicious storms but rising back toward the sky when all is done. Like canes, Indians have been able to respond and adjust to new situations, mostly harsh circumstances, and they succeed. This acquired flexibility called adaptation— essential for survival—enabled tribal leaders and their communities to exercise the powerful dual themes of resilience and rebuilding. After four hundred years of colonized suppression, the indigenous responded but not in the way that those in power thought. Certainly not over night, but within a century's stretch, the Native nations arose from the ashes of near ethnic cleansing and third-world neglect.

The twentieth century has been an erratic era of challenges, problems, and major adjustments for tribal communities and their governments throughout the West. Mainly problems and challenges plagued Indian Country as public impressions viewed Indians as the vanishing race in the late nineteenth century, as second-class citizens in the early decades of the twentieth century, dangerous militants in the 1960s, and nonexistent for the remaining decades until Indian gaming reminded forgetful Americans that there are indeed Indians in the United States.

On December 10, 2010, the last original Muscogee Creek allottee, Martha Berryhill, died. In the spring of 1993, I spoke at the rededication of the historic Creek Council House in Okmulgee, Oklahoma. As I made my presentation from the roof of the rear canopy of the Council House on that warm day, I remember seeing a half dozen original Creek allottees standing and sitting in lawn chairs under a shade tree. My dad, John Fixico, observed with admiration from where he sat in his own chair.

That vivid day is connected to my childhood memories of playing in the house of my grandfather Jonas Fixico and grandmother Lena Spencer Fixico on his allotment located north of the small town of Seminole, Oklahoma. My grandfather was Seminole, and my grandmother was Muscogee Creek. My grandfather is number 945 on the Dawes Rolls, and my great-grandfather Aharlock Fixico is 940. I never realized until many years later as a historian studying my people's history that my grandparents made huge cultural adjustments and personal sacrifices to farm the barren land that the Dawes Commission had assigned to my grandfather. My grandmother never attended school. That land, formerly a part of the Seminole reservation, is within the old boundaries of the present Seminole Nation. Like so many kinsmen, I danced as a child at the Gar Creek ceremonial ground, the last practicing Seminole stomp ground at present in the former Indian Territory. It is a truism that people change during their lives, but in another perspective they adapt and reinvent themselves as part of human evolution. In the case of Native people, they have done this and navigated within and between the cultural systems of two worlds—Indian and white—in a bicultural existence.

Attachment to the earth is what I learned as a young boy during the Green Corn ceremonies that I was a part of, and I can still hear the singing of those youthful times in my head on occasion. It was entrancing that I could nearly envision on the other side of the fire the silhouettes of my departed aunts and uncles when dancing during my adult summers at the Euchee Kellyville ground near Tulsa. The fire, the sacred ground, and the kinsmen in ceremonial togetherness celebrate the ancient past and present for they morph into one reality. Like on a disk in an ethereal reality where time is blurred, a spiritual oneness forges the elemental earth with the other central elements—fire, water, and wind.

Tremendous progress has occurred, if one will accept that the water gourd is half filled, and I truly believe that the Indian nations have accomplished much for themselves during the last hundred years and more. Another truistic observation is that perception is in the eyes of the beholder, and this can be sometimes misleading. In America, people believe rhetoric, not the truth, and convince themselves that the illusions of what they want to see are best. Commercialization has shrouded their reality. Through Indian eyes, life is a struggle of adapting and rebuilding and doing it again and again—hard work, something that my grandmother Fixico taught me as a young boy. In addition to working very hard no matter what kind of job you had, three other virtues that my grandmother taught me have guided my life: always respect others, always be clean, including looking as good as you can, and take care of family.

How the Native communities accomplish the rebuilding of their nations has been the central question of this study, especially after the indigenous population sank to its lowest ebb in the late nineteenth century. Imagine more than five million indigenous people when Columbus arrived to fewer than 238,000. The Indian nations accomplished this amazing feat of survival and progress in several ways.

First of all, Native people utilized their age-old quality of adaptability. After their removals to the West, the Indians adapted to reservations that became new homelands. They reestablished their connection with the earth in this manner—"moving fires"—even though living conditions and too often the terrain of the land were not desirable. Fires represented the heart of communities, and the people transported their ideologies and communal infrastructures during forced removals. By the end of treaty making in 1871, the federal government had created an estimated two hundred reservations, largely in the West. Intriguingly, the tribal communities embraced their new homelands and accepted their reservations, primarily because they had to.

The human spirit is also a remarkable continuum of hope that the indigenous of North America have exemplified. Over and over Indians have reestablished their homes and communities in new areas. This tenacious ability to readapt has served Indians impressively well. This ability is at the core of their identity and separates them from other people who are colonized.

A second key to Indian progress was the forced schooling of Native children in mission and boarding schools. Even Sitting Bull, who patriotically defended his people and tribal traditions, realized this was necessary, to learn the way of the white man's ability to read and write. In 1881 he learned to write his name in English instead of drawing a picture of a buffalo sitting, an epical act of cross-cultural borrowing. Becoming educated in the mainstream educational system unlocked much of the information that Native leaders and their peoples needed for survival and rebuilding their tribal nations. Although most became dependent upon the English language, education in Western-minded civilization enabled Native leaders to conduct their business more successfully after many decades of language barriers, mistrust, suspicion, and exploitation by white opportunists.

In the fall of 1969, I began my college education at Bacone Junior College, which started as a Christian boarding school with three students in 1880. Living on campus revealed that many students had come from far away. One of my roommates was Jonah Gorman, a Navajo math whiz from Arizona who loved calculus at a time that I thought I would never see that state—now I live there. I felt the homesickness of friends who were so far away from home as I learned that education was somehow important for the future. I did not realize at the time that it was a vital tool for later use. Nor did I think that I would ever one day be writing history books like this one. Some might call it fate; others would call it happenstance. My personal dream leaned toward science, without a definite plan. I graduated high school toward the end of the Vietnam War, and I recall that my physics teacher asked for everyone in our class who was going to college to raise their hand. I did not raise my hand because no one ever talked to me about going to college, except for an African American counselor who suggested that I should attend Southwestern Junior College in Weatherford. She said, "Indians learn best with their hands." Another boy, who I played baseball with and against, did not raise his hand. We were the only two who indicated by silence that we were not going to college. Interestingly, both of us attended nearby Bacone in the fall.

The government's final acceptance of the end of Indian land allotment enabled the introduction of a new policy of Indian reorganization, thus allowing the tribes to reorganize their communities and governments. John Collier's paternalistic approach offended many Native people who refused to believe that the Indian Reorganization Act of 1934 was a good thing for them. Although confused by the technical details of the law's provisions, the tribes utilized the act's assistance to their advantage to begin rebuilding their nations. The Indian New Deal represented a pivotal turning point, with tribes regaining external political control in U.S.-Indian relations. Although they internally continued to function as poor as they were during the Depression era, the tribes started to reestablish confidence in relations with Washington. My parents were born during the Depression; their families struggled and were poor, and I learned about poverty from an early age. Poor is growing up feeling cold and hungry, and being ashamed of the patched jeans that you wear. Fortunately for me, I went to a small country school outside of Shawnee, and a lot of boys wore patched blue jeans. I was glad when my two-year-younger brother Ron started school, which made two Indians at the school. I am sure that other Indians attended the school, but I was too shy to seek them out.

Although my family did not officially go on relocation, some of our relatives did. Relocation meant readjustment, adapting to a foreign city culture. We moved to Oklahoma City, and suddenly the rural countryside that I once saw as my entire playground to explore had walls of other people, not so friendly. I was a stranger in a city that was once a part of Indian Territory promised to and for only Indians. Relocation to cities tested the resilience of Native people who volunteered for the government program leading to new jobs and not so good housing in cities. With relocation at this time, the government introduced termination. As a doctoral student in history at the University of Oklahoma in the late 1970s, I wondered what worse federal Indian policy could there be than termination—the abolishing of Native peoples' tribal identities. There were few people that I could talk to who knew about termination, and *Termination and Relocation: Federal Indian Policy, 1945–1960* (1986) became my first book after heavily revising my doctoral dissertation after researching in libraries and archives in seventeen states.

Urbanization proved to be the test of the souls. Mixing it up on a daily basis in the urban crucible of working with and meeting all kinds of people became a part of modern Indian cultures. Like all human experiences embarking on a frontier, the first ones encountered various strange experiences; they were path breakers opening Pandora's box. They made it easier for the next generation, their children. They suffered the most, and many did not succeed, but resilience won over. The next generation of urban Indians launched an Indian middle class of fewer nonlaborers who worked inside at various jobs, including professional ones, earning their bread with their brain. The tools used by the Indian middle class were the same ones—education, proficient English, resource management, cultural navigation, and leadership—used to rebuild tribal governments and communities back home.

Historians should never underestimate timing in the shaping of history. Defining moments have launched mediocre individuals into historic leadership situations and caused predicted victories to collapse into shocking defeats. The score of years following the end of World War II prepared the stage for the rise of new leadership that Stan Steiner aptly named the "New Indians." Unsure of what they were doing, somewhat educated and politically intrepid, a generation of young warriors took the battle to Washington, especially during the summer of 1972 in their takeover of the Bureau of Indian Affairs building—the hegemonic institution that symbolized their sovereign imprisonment. The bureau controlled most of my early life—scholarship funding, dental care, health clinics, medicines, commodities, and waiting in line for them since we did not have a lot of money to buy these things. One might think about how these were free, but mostly you think about them as receiving welfare.

I lived these years, struggling as a college transfer student at the University of Oklahoma, a giant of a place through my Indian eyes. Intimidated by the university, my grades were good and not so good. I had to learn to think like a white college student. Memorizing facts like in high school was not enough at the university. Years later I realized that my Creek-Seminole worldview was different from mainstream logic, and more like that of my traditional elders. So many things happened in the late 1960s and 1970s that the only constant was constant change, that something big was going to happen, but no one knew when it was going to occur. As a child, I remember very well the night of the Cuban missile crisis, and this was the Cold War of living in fear. You just wanted to be safe. People protested the Vietnam War, and civil rights protests tore apart the country. I struggled gradewise to stay in college, waiting for the draft to come and get me, but the army never did after I survived three lotteries. I also believed that if I went, I would not return from Vietnam, for I knew that minorities were the first to die in combat.

The emergence of the American Indian Movement breathed new life of stubborn-kicking energy that rocked federal officials at levels of government from local to federal. The youthful driven energy forged Red Power and a reinvented identity for an entire generation that no one took lightly. Republicanized America of suburbs and conservative politicians frustrated relocated Indians abandoned in cities and created a backlash that altered the course of federal-Indian policy. This sociopolitical revolution was a turning point of resilience now accompanied by rebuilding while employing new Native thinking—as Einstein once wrote, "imagination is everything."

I could only imagine that more education was important and the key for me to achieve one of my life's ambitions—an indoor job. As a high school youth, I had always worked outside, in the summer's heat with hot roofing and the winter's cold at chilly gas stations. I envied the white boys working inside grocery stores sacking groceries, where they were clean and warm. A college education had to be the answer to a better life. But graduate school in history at the University of Oklahoma was no easy task. The graduate program there was a tough one, as anyone who graduated from there in those days would immediately agree. I was not a stellar student, but I possessed great determination. I became obsessed with earning a Ph.D.

I never realized that pure hard work could take someone like me so far. Grandma Fixico was right. I knew that I wanted to write books on modern Indian history that would help people now, especially Bureau of Indian Affairs officials and others at the federal level who made Indian policy that affected me, my family, relatives, and my four tribes—Shawnee, Sac and Fox, Muscogee Creek, and Seminole. Ironically, the Canadian government has summoned me four times thus far for my expertise on Native history.

My youth of growing up in the country and learning the urban ways of Oklahoma City would later convince me to write *The Urban Indian Experience in America* (2000), so that people would have some important insight into how Indians struggled and suffered painfully trying to live in cities. Ottawa called on me the first time because of this book. I also knew that Indians who are close to their tribal traditions thought differently from mainstream. From our various tribal worldviews, there are different tribal logics, and the Western paradigm of Western thinking compelled me to write *The American Indian Mind in a Linear World: American Indian Studies and Traditional Knowledge* (2003). I thought about how that was the same way that my traditional elders saw things. This book provides insight into Indian thinking about circularity and visual logic.

Life for Indians in modern America was hard. It was hard being Indian, and in retrospect, I wanted people to know that, which led to my writing *Daily Life of Native Americans in the Twentieth Century* (2006) and *American Indians in a Modern World* (2008), which are the same book but published under different titles by different presses. As an ethnohistorian and a policy historian, I have always wanted to write about the Bureau of Indian Affairs, since it has been always been a part of my life and history. This led to *Bureau of Indian Affairs* (2012), a dispassionate overview. The bureau is in virtually every part of Indian history, especially regarding natural resources, as I knew so well growing up in Oklahoma.

I have always contended that there is an Indian reality that combines the physical and metaphysical, according to tribal cultures. This combined reality is a real part of history that most historians do not understand, which convinced me to write *A Call for Change: The Medicine Way of American Indian History* (2013). This book, born out of frustration with mainstream academic historians writing "about" Indians, constructs an indigenous paradigm to offer a conceptual theory to write from a Native point of view. This view has also included the environment, the natural world, and how Indians are a part of it. Having now written and edited a dozen plus books, I research out of curiosity, and each volume is a mission that must be accomplished to offer something important to readers for a better understanding of American Indians. This is my personal goal.

For example, natural resources on tribal lands involving oil, gas, timber, coal, uranium, and water have been contested resources from the early 1970s to the present. One-third of the usable coal west of the Mississippi rests under tribal lands, and energy companies want it badly, as well as oil, as proven in the 1970s. I recall waiting in my car in long lines at gas stations to buy gasoline when the OPEC nations held an oil embargo during the Carter administration. People growled and swore as they inched their cars forward in a line, turning them off to save gas. This tense situation became a tedious process, with odd and even last numbers of our license plates determining which days of the week we could buy gas. These experiences compelled me to write *The Invasion of Indian Country in the Twentieth Century: American Capitalism and Tribal Natural Resources* (1998), now in its second edition (2012).

The coal was so heavily mined that the largest open mine, located in the Four Corners region, can be seen from outer space, according to astronauts. The power generation station at Page, Arizona, on the western edge of the Navajo Reservation produces colossal amounts of electricity. My wife, April, and I drove the long barren way to Page during the summer of 2010 to witness the daily towering plumes of smoke coming from the three stacks of the generation station that sent electricity through the power lines to Los Angeles and other parts of the Southwest, including our home in the Phoenix area. I have always thought it so ironic and wrong that even now not all of the Navajo homes in the Four Corners Area have electricity.

The acquiring of new values has enabled the Indian nations to take advantage of gaming to their betterment. This experiment introduced by the Florida Seminoles in the late 1970s launched tribal governments into the big business world of American capitalism, as Native leaders used an old French theory of political economy, born in 1615, that became internationalized, then modernized, and Indianized in what David Wilkins (Lumbee) and Dean Snow (Mohawk) have called tribal political economy. Modern political economy, normally used in discourse about third-world nation building, can be related to reservations with third-world conditions in the United States. Here all the chapters have been designed and demonstrated to argue that adaptation is the central theme while using the tools of education, navigating cultural systems, resource management, and applying imaginative leadership to use first resilience to survive and then imagination again to adapt in rebuilding nations for reasserting sovereign nationhood like it used to be—the Circle of Life.

The respect for sacred lands and fighting to protect them have come full circle in respecting the earth during the reservation era and allotment years. But there is one last resource that Native leaders have become cognizant of and learned to use—the power of federal Indian law. Learning the law and using it to one's advantage are the vanguard, along with the other essential tools that Native leaders today would put in their briefcases or type on their laptops and iPads. These are the ingredients, combined with resilience and rebuilding, that the Indian nations have used while remaining optimistic about the future. Overcoming pragmatic feelings hammered by inferiority created by a prejudiced mainstream, Indians are the underdog champions that have been seriously underestimated.

In conclusion, Native leaders and their communities discovered a political economy of their own making that dawned a new day of tribal sovereignty. Not new nations, but rebuilt ones, have begun to appear across the horizon of Indian Country. Equipped with the prescribed tools described earlier, tribal leaders of many exploited experiences of the past used their imaginative talents to advance Indian entrepreneurship that coincided with the market timing of the U.S. economy. Indians have learned to move forward and prayed to overcome bleak times, to believe and weave a dream of the old and new—the tenacity of the indigenous spirit. To all Indians, *it does matter.* The rest of society should look toward Indian Country and acknowledge the resilience of Native people and the rebuilding of their nations. The water gourd is half full.

Notes

Introduction

1. George P. Lee, *Silent Courage an Indian Story: The Autobiography of George P. Lee a Navajo* (Salt Lake City, UT: Deseret, 1987), xii.

2. R. Douglas Hurt, *The Big Empty: The Great Plains in the Twentieth Century* (Tucson: University of Arizona Press, 2011).

3. Vincent Crapanzano, *The Fifth World of Forester Bennett: Portrait of a Navajo* (Lincoln: University of Nebraska Press, 2003 [1972]), 25.

4. Leslie Silko, *Ceremony* (New York: New American Library, 1977), 47.

5. For wild west shows, see L. G. Moses, *Wild West Shows and the Images of American Indians 1883–1933* (Albuquerque: University of New Mexico Press, 1996) and Louis S. Warren, *Buffalo Bill's America* (New York: Random House, 2005).

6. Elwell S. Otis, *The Indian Question* (New York: Sheldon and Co., 1878).

7. George Manypenny, *Our Indian Wards* (Cincinnati: Robert Clarke and Co., 1880).

8. Helen Hunt Jackson, *A Century of Dishonor: A Sketch of the U.S. Government's Dealings with Some of the Indian Tribes* (Boston: Roberts Brothers, 1881).

9. Francis E. Leupp, *The Indian and His Problem* (New York: Scribner's Sons, 1910).

10. Edward B. Tylor, *Primitive Culture* (New York: J.P. Putnam's Sons, 1871).

11. Lewis Henry Morgan, *Ancient Society* (London: Macmillan, 1877).

12. Dee Brown, *Bury My Heart at Wounded Knee: An Indian History of the American West* (New York: Henry Holt, 1970).

13. Daniel Richter, *Facing East from Indian Country: A Native History of Early America* (Cambridge, MA: Harvard University Press, 2001).

14. Donald L. Fixico, *The American Indian Mind in a Linear World: American Indian Studies and Traditional Knowledge* (New York: Routledge, 2003).

15. Donald Parman, *Indians and the American West in the Twentieth Century* (Bloomington: Indiana University Press, 1994).

16. Peter Iverson, *"We Are Still Here": American Indians in the Twentieth Century* (Wheeling, IL: Harland Davidson, 1998).

17. James S. Olsen and Raymond Wilson, *Native Americans in the Twentieth Century* (Provo, UT: Brigham Young University Press, 1984).

18. Joel S. Migdal, *State in Society: Studying How States and Societies Transform and Constitute One Another* (Cambridge: Cambridge University Press, 2001).

19. David Chandler, *Empire in Denial: The Politics of State-building* (London: Pluto Press, 2006).

20. Dominik Zaum, *The Sovereignty Paradox: The Norms and Politics of International Statebuilding* (Oxford: Oxford University Press, 2007).

21. Nathan Hodge, *Armed Humanitarians: The Rise of Nation Builders* (New York: Bloomsbury, 2011).

22. David E. Wilkins, *American Indian Politics and the American Political System* (Lanham, MA: Rowman and Littlefield, 2007).

23. Dean Howard Smith, *Modern Tribal Development: Paths to Self-sufficiency and Cultural Integrity in Indian Country* (Walnut Creek, CA: AltaMira Press, 2000).

24. Gayatri Chakravorty Spivak, *Nationalism and the Imagination* (London: Seagull, 2010).

Chapter 1

1. "Treaty with the Creeks, 1832," March 24, 1832, in Charles J. Kappler, comp. and ed., *Indian Treaties 1778–1883* (New York: Interland, 1975), 341–343. The 1832 agreement was followed by the Treaty of Fort Gibson in 1833 to define the boundaries of their new homeland in the West. "Treaty with the Creeks, 1833," February 14, 1833, ibid., 388–391.

2. Brian W. Dippie, *The Vanishing American: White Attitudes and U.S. Indian Policy* (Lawrence: University Press of Kansas, 1982), 122–138.

3. Donald L. Fixico, "Introduction," in Donald L. Fixico, ed., *Treaties with American Indians: An Encyclopedia of Rights, Conflicts and Sovereignty* (Santa Barbara, CA: ABC-CLIO, 2007), vol. 1, xxi.

4. Felix Cohen, "Original Indian Title," *Minnesota Law Review*, vol. 32 (1947), 28–59. Political agreements of Uncas are in Alden T. Vaughan, *New England Frontier: Puritan and Indians 1620–1675* (Boston: Little, Brown, 1965), 154–167.

5. The legal basis for creating reservations involves sovereign and trust relations. Klaus Frantz, *Indian Reservations in the United States* (Chicago: University of Chicago Press, 1999), 45–50.

6. "[Sitting Bull Surrenders], July 20, 1881," *New York Post*, July 22, 1881, in Mark Diedrich, *Sitting Bull: The Collected Speeches* (Rochester, MN: Coyote, 1998), 139. Fort Buford in North Dakota was located at the confluence of the Yellowstone and Missouri rivers. The classic biography of Sitting Bull is Stanley Vestal, *Sitting Bull: Champion of the Sioux* (Norman: University of Oklahoma Press, 1957 [1932]). An updated biography is Robert M. Utley, *The Lance and the Shield: The Life and Times of Sitting Bull* (New York: Ballantine, 1993).

7. George W. Webb, *Chronological List of Engagements between the Regular Army of the United States and Various Tribes of Hostile Indians Which Occurred dur-*

ing the Years 1790–1895 (New York: AMS Press, 1976), 1–97. Diseases introduced to Indians are in Alfred W. Crosby, Jr., *The Columbia Exchange: Biological and Cultural Consequences of 1492* (Westport, CT: Greenwood Press, 1972), 122–164; Henry Dobyns, *Their Number Become Thinned: Native American Population Dynamics in Eastern North America* (Knoxville: University of Tennessee Press, 1983); David S. Jones, *Rationalizing Epidemics: Meanings and Uses of American Indian Mortality since 1600* (Cambridge, MA: Harvard University Press, 2004); and Roland Robertson, *Rotting Face: Smallpox and the American Indian* (Caldwell, ID: Caxton Press, 2001).

8. See Theodore Kroeber, *Ishi in Two Worlds: A Biography of the Last Wild Indian in North America* (Berkeley: University of California Press, 1961), 3. The killing of California Indians is in Albert L. Hurtado, *Indian Survival on the California Frontier* (New Haven, CT: Yale University Press, 1988), 125–149; and Benjamin Madley, "American Genocide: The California Indian Catastrophe, 1846–1873" (Ph.D. dissertation, Yale University, 2009).

9. Edward P. Thompson, "The Moral Economy of the English Crowd in the Eighteenth Century," *Past and Present*, vol. 50 (February 1971), 76–136. James C. Scott advanced the concept of moral economy in *The Moral Economy of the Peasant: Rebellion and Subsistence in Southeast Asia* (New Haven, CT: Yale University Press, 1976).

10. Hamlin Garland, *The Book of the American Indian* (New York: Harper and Brothers, 1923), 165; also in Stanley Vestal, "Sitting Bull's Maiden Speech," *The Frontier, Magazine of Northwest*, vol. 12 (March 1932), 269–71; and Diedrich, *Sitting Bull*, 63.

11. John Fahey, *The Flathead Indians* (Norman: University of Oklahoma Press, 1974), 148. Original source of quote is not cited by Fahey.

12. Virgil J. Vogel, *American Indian Medicine* (Norman: University of Oklahoma Press, 1970), 267–414. See also J. Donald Hughes, *American Indian Ecology* (El Paso: Texas Western Press, 1983), 49–77. The concept of Mother Earth is argued to exist in Sam D. Gill, *Mother Earth: An American Story* (Chicago: University of Chicago Press, 1987), 107–158.

13. Oliver Eastman (Sioux Wahpeton), interviewed by Joseph Cash, August 3, 1971, Sioux Falls, SD, tape 768, p. 15, USDIOHC.

14. The subaltern model of colonized people is in Gayatri Chakravorty Spivak, *Nationalism and the Imagination* (London: Seagull, 2010); other examples are in Richard Bessel and Claudia B. Haake, eds., *Removing Peoples: Forced Removal in the Modern World* (Oxford: Oxford University Press, 2009).

15. Roger W. Axford, ed., *Native Americans: 23 Indian Biographies* (Indiana, PA: A.G. Halldin, 1980), 27.

16. Thomas H. Leforge, *Memoirs of a White Crow Indian (Thomas H. LeForge) as Told by Thomas Marquis* (New York: Century, 1928), 175.

17. Ibid., 197.

18. Ibid., 116. Among the Nez Perce and other tribes, Indians often created a hybrid Christian religion by integrating Native cultures into Christianity. Bonnie Sue Lewis, *Creating Christian Indians: Native Clergy in the Presbyterian Church* (Norman: University of Oklahoma Press, 2003), 145–184.

19. Leforge, *Memoirs of a White Crow Indian*, 116.

20. Beverly Hungry Wolf, *The Ways of My Grandmother* (New York: Quill, 1982), 50.

21. Leforge, *Memoirs of a White Crow Indian*, 134–135.

22. Ibid., 134.

23. Ibid., 140–141. Concepts of power and the Sun Dance are interconnected. Thomas H. Lewis, *The Medicine Men: Oglala Sioux Ceremony and Healing* (Lincoln: University of Nebraska Press, 1990), 39–70.

24. Charles S. Brant, ed., *Jim Whitewolf: The Life of a Kiowa Apache Indian* (New York: Dover, 1969), 44–45.

25. A universal human-nature relationship existed on the plains, called a bioregion, according to Dan Flores, *The Natural West: Environmental History in the Great Plains and Rocky Mountains* (Norman: University of Oklahoma Press, 2001), 9–28, 89–106.

26. Daniel J. Gelo, *Indians of the Great Plains* (Boston: Pearson, 2012), 43–65; and David Dary, *Buffalo Book: The Full Saga of the American Animal* (Athens, OH: Swallow Press, 1989 [1974]), 52–68.

27. Richard White, *Railroaded: The Transcontinentals and the Making of Modern America* (New York: W.W. Norton, 2011), 59–83.

28. Old Lady Horse (Kiowa), "The Buffalo Go," in Peter Nabokov, ed., *Native American Testimony: A Chronicle of Indian-White Relations from Prophecy to the Present, 1492–1992* (New York: Penguin, 1992), 173–174.

29. In 2012 the Bureau of Indian Affairs reported a total of 326 federal reserved Indian and Alaska Native lands. Donald L. Fixico, *Bureau of Indian Affairs* (Westport, CT: Greenwood Press, 2012), xiii.

30. "An Act making Appropriations for the Current and Contingent Expenses of the Indian Department," March 3, 1871, 16 Stat. 566.

31. Carl Waldman, *Atlas of the North American Indian* (New York: Facts on File, 1985), 166.

32. Helen Hunt Jackson, *A Century of Dishonor: A Sketch of the U.S. Government's Dealings with Some of the Indian Tribes* (Boston: Roberts Brothers, 1881).

33. Quoted in Clark Wissler, *Red Man Reservations* (New York: Collier, 1971), 64.

34. Ibid., 65; "Sioux Act of 1889," March 2, 1889, 25 Stat. 888: "An act to divide a portion of the reservation of the Sioux Nation of Indians in Dakota into separate reservations and to secure the relinquishment of the Indian title to the remainder and for other purposes."

35. "Treaty with the Sioux—Brule, Oglala, Miniconjou, Yanktonai, Hunkpapa, Blackfeet, Cuthead, Two Kettle, Sana Arcs, and Santee and Arapaho" (Fort Laramie), April 29, 1868, in Charles J. Kappler, comp. and ed., *Indian Treaties 1778–1883* (New York: Interland, 1975), 998–1003.

36. William T. Hagan, *Indian Police and Judges: Experiment in Acculturation and Control* (New Haven, CT: Yale University Press, 1966), 25–50.

37. "Courts of Indian Offenses," August 27, 1892, House Executive Document, no. 1, 52d Cong., 2d sess., ser. 3088, pp. 28–31.

38. Ronan to Commissioner of Indian Affairs (CIA), June 12, 1889 (16035-89, NA), in Fahey, *Flathead Indians*, 245.

39. John Saul (Crow Creek), interviewed by Joseph Cash, June 6, 1968, Chamberlain, SD, tape 51, pp. 7–8, USDIOHC.

40. Michael Hittman, *Wovoka and the Ghost Dance*, ed.,. Don Lynch (Lincoln: University of Nebraska Press, 1997), 47–62.

41. James Creelman, *On the Great Highway: The Wanderings and Adventures of a special correspondent* (Boston: Lothrop, 1901), 298–303; also in Diedrich, *Sitting Bull*, 144.

42. Stanley Vestal, *New Sources of Indian History 1850–1891: The Ghost Dance, the Prairie Sioux, a Miscellany* (Norman: University of Oklahoma Press, 1934), 309–310; and Diedrich, *Sitting Bull*, 182.

43. Quoted in Donald J. Berthrong, *The Cheyenne and Arapaho Ordeal: Reservation and Agency Life in the Indian Territory, 1875–1907* (Norman: University of Oklahoma Press, 1976), 151.

44. Three Bears quoted originally in "Disposal of Surplus Lands of Blackfeet Indian Reservation, Montana," hearings before a subcommittee of the Committee on Indian Affairs of the House of Representatives on H.R. 14739, 64th Cong., 1st sess., July 12, 1916, reprinted in Hana Samek, *The Blackfeet Confederacy 1880–1920: A Comparative Study of Canadian and U.S. Indian Policy* (Albuquerque: University of New Mexico Press, 1987), 120.

45. "General Allotment Act" (Dawes Allotment Act), February 8, 1887, 24 Stat. 388.

46. "Agriculture on Indian Reservations," in *Twelfth Census of the United States, 1900* (Washington: U.S. Department of the Interior, 1900), vol. 5, 717–740, cited in Leonard A. Carlson, *Indians, Bureaucrats, and Land: The Dawes Act and the Decline of Indian Farming* (Westport, CT: Greenwood Press, 1981), 117–122.

47. Leonard A. Carlson, *Indians, Bureaucrats, and Land: The Dawes Act and the Decline of Indian Farming* (Westport, CT: Greenwood Press, 1981), 122–126.

48. "Readjustment of Indian Affairs," hearings on J.R. 7902 before the House of Representatives' Committee on Indian Affairs, 1934, pt. 9, 428–489, reprinted in Frederick Hoxie, *A Final Promise: The Campaign to Assimilate the Indians, 1880–1920* (Lincoln: University of Nebraska Press, 1984), 71; and D.S. Otis, *The Dawes Act and the Allotment of Indian Lands* (Norman: University of Oklahoma Press, 1973), 29.

49. Francis Paul Prucha, *The Great Father: The United States Government and the American Indian*, abr. ed. (Lincoln: University of Nebraska Press, 1986 [1984]), 222–223.

50. Wilcomb Washburn, *The Assault on Indian Tribalism: The General Allotment Law (Dawes Act) of 1887* (Philadelphia: J. B. Lippincott, 1975), 17.

51. Ibid., 20. While railroad companies benefited greatly from receiving tribal lands, this is not a part of the story of railroad history in Walter R. Borneman, *Rival Rails: The Race to Build America's Greatest Transcontinental Railroad* (New York: Random House, 2010), and even less so in Richard J. Orsi, *Sunset Limited: The Southern Pacific Railroad and the Development of the American West 1850–1930* (Berkeley: University of California Press, 2005).

52. Washburn, *Assault on Indian Tribalism*, 220–221.

53. Ibid., 21.

54. "General Allotment Act."

55. Ibid.

56. Nelson Act (Minnesota Chippewa Allotment Act), January 4, 1889, 25 Stat. 642.

57. "Act of 1891," 26 Stat. 794.

58. James S. Olson and Raymond Wilson, *Native Americans in the Twentieth Century* (Provo, UT: Brigham Young University Press, 1984), 69.

59. *Lone Wolf v. Hitchcock*, 187 U.S. 553, 23 S.Ct. 216, 47 L.Ed. 299; Blue Clark, *Lone Wolf v Hitchcock: Treaty Rights and Indian Law at the End of the Nineteenth Century* (Lincoln: University of Nebraska Press, 1994), 67–76.

60. Chitto Harjo, testimony of November 23, 1906, Elks Lodge, Tulsa, Oklahoma Territory, Western History Collections, University of Oklahoma, Norman.

61. Colonel Roy Hoffman's report on Chitto Harjo and the Snake Rebellion, August 11, 1909, Fred Barde Collection, Chitto Harjo file, box 11, Oklahoma Historical Society, Oklahoma City.

62. Ibid., and Daniel F. Littlefield, Jr., "The 'Crazy Snake Uprising' of 1909: A Red, Black, or White Affair?" *Arizona and the West*, vol. 20, no. 4 (Winter 1978), 309.

63. Angie Debo, *The Road to Disappearance: A History of the Creek Indians* (Norman: University of Oklahoma Press, 1941), 376–377.

64. "Creek, 14:398–99," in Theda Perdue, ed., *Nations Remembered: An Oral History of the Five Civilize Tribes, 1865–1907* (Westport, CT: Greenwood Press, 1980), 190-191.

65. Ibid., 194.

66. Angie Debo, *A History of the Indians of the United States* (Norman: University of Oklahoma Press, 1970), 308–309.

67. Theda Perdue, *The Cherokee* (New York: Chelsea House, 1989), 94.

68. Jesse O. McKee, *The Choctaw* (New York: Chelsea House, 1989), 83.

69. Angie Debo, *And Still the Waters Run: The Betrayal of the Five Civilized Tribes* (Princeton, NJ: Princeton University Press, 1973 [1968]).

70. "Alphabetical List of Creek Indians by Blood and Creek Freedmen," Western History Collections, University of Oklahoma. The young difficult life of Jackson Barnett and his troubled adult years are described in Benay Blend, "Jackson Barnett and the Oklahoma Indian Probate Court" (M.A. thesis, University of Texas, Arlington, 1978).

71. C.B. Glasscock, *Then Came Oil: The Story of the Last Frontier* (Indianapolis, IN: Bobbs-Merrill, 1938), 156.

72. Debo, *And Still the Waters Run*, 338.

73. Donald L. Fixico, *The Invasion of Indian Country: American Capitalism and Tribal Natural Resources*, 2nd ed. (Boulder: University Press of Colorado, 2012), 3–26. See also Tanis Thorne, *The World's Richest Indian: The Scandal over Jackson Barnett's Oil Fortune* (New York: Oxford University Press, 2005).

74. Leforge, *Memoirs of a White Crow Indian*, 338-339.

75. Thomas B. Marquis, *Wooden Leg: A Warrior Who Fought Custer* (Lincoln: University of Nebraska Press, 1965), 383–384.

76. "Citizenship for World War I Veterans," November 6, 1919, 41 Stat. 350.

Chapter 2

1. The practice of kidnapping indigenous children for boarding schools has occurred in other countries. See Margaret D. Jacobs, *White Mother to a Dark Race: Settler Colonialism, Maternalism, and the Removal of Indigenous Children in the American West and Australia, 1880–1940* (Lincoln: University of Nebraska Press, 2009), and Peter Read, *The Stolen Generations: The Removal of Aboriginal Children in New South Wales 1883 to 1969*, 2nd ed. (Sydney: New South Wales Department of Aboriginal Affairs, 1998).

2. See Kay Marie Porterfield and Emory Dean Keoke, *American Indian Contributions to the World* (New York: Checkmark, 2003), and Andrea Smith, "Soul Wound: The Legacy of Native American Schools," *Amnesty Magazine*, http://www.amnesty-usa.org/ammnestynow/soulwound.html, accessed February 19, 2008.

3. At this date, Indian boarding schools have become the most popular subject in American Indian history, with more than twenty-five books since Richard Henry Pratt's *Battlefield and Classroom: An Autobiography by Richard Henry Pratt*, ed. Robert M. Utley (New Haven, CT: Yale University Press, 2003 [1964]), and Charles A. Eastman's *From the Deep Woods to Civilization* (Boston: Little Brown, 1936 [1916]).

4. Allen Chuck Ross, "Brain Hemispheric Functions and the Native American," *Journal of American Indian Education*, vol. 21, no. 3 (May 1982), 2.

5. Donald L. Fixico, *The American Indian Mind in a Linear World: American Indian Studies and Traditional Knowledge* (New York: Routledge, 2003), 49–59.

6. Henri Lefebvre theorizes that geographic space is not dormant but is determined by mental space, social space, and physical space in *The Production of Space* (Oxford: Blackwell, 1991), 68–168.

7. Dan Flores, *The Natural West: Environmental History in the Great Plains and Rocky Mountains* (Norman: University of Oklahoma Press, 2001), 92.

8. Proceedings of the Lake Mohonk Conference of Friends of the Indian, 1885, in Annual Report of the Secretary of the Interior, 1885, 850, quoted in David Wallace Adams, *Education for Extinction: American Indians and the Boarding School Experience 1875–1928* (Lawrence: University Press of Kansas, 1995), 24.

9. Arrell M. Gibson, *Oklahoma: A History of Five Centuries* (Norman, OK: Harlow, 1965), 159–166.

10. From a boarding school, Bacone made the transition to junior college and then to full college. See John Williams and Howard L. Meredith, *Bacone Indian University: A History* (Oklahoma City: Western Heritage, 1980).

11. Ibid., 250; see also K. Tsianina Lomawaima, *They Called It Prairie Light: The Story of Chilocco Indian School* (Lincoln: University of Nebraska Press, 1994).

12. Adams, *Education for Extinction*, 28.

13. Funding for Indian education increased to $75,000 in 1880, $992,800 in 1885, $1,364,568 for 1890, and $2,060,695 for 1895, with the number of students being 4,651 for 1880, 8,143 for 1885, 12,232 for 1890, and 18,188 for 1895. Ibid. 27–28.

14. J. D. Miles to J. Q. Smith, January 1, 1876, and [January, 1876?], and Report, Commissioner of Indian Affairs, 1876, quoted in Donald J. Berthrong, *The Cheyenne and Arapaho Ordeal: Reservation and Agency Life in the Indian Territory, 1875–1907* (Norman: University of Oklahoma Press, 1976), 78–79.

15. David Shanahan to Commissioner of Indian Affairs, July 18, 23, 26, and August 1, 1873, quoted in John Fahey, *The Flathead Indians* (Norman: University of Oklahoma Press, 1974), 148, 177.

16. Pratt, *Battlefield and Classroom*.

17. Linda F. Witmer, *The Indian Industrial School Carlisle, Pennsylvania 1879–1918* (Carlisle, PA: Cumberland Country Historical Society, 1993), 1–3.

18. Adams, *Education for Extinction*, 52.

19. A history of the noted school is Witmer, *Indian Industrial School*.

20. Luther Standing Bear, *Land of the Spotted Eagle* (Lincoln: University of Nebraska Press, 1960), quoted in Luther Standing Bear, "Indian Education Should Not Destroy Indian Culture," in William Dudley, ed., *Native Americans: Opposing Viewpoints* (San Diego, CA: Greenhaven, 1998), 191–193.

21. Ted and Dorothy Lunderman (Brule Sioux), interviewed by Joseph Cash, July 27, 1971, Mission, SD, tape 744, p. 2, USDIOHC.

22. Ibid., p. 3.

23. George Dennison (Navajo), interviewed by S.I. Myers, October 15, 1975, Gallup, NM, no. 67, pt. 1, p. 1, NYTOHP.

24. Peter MacDonald, *The Last Warrior: Peter MacDonald and the Navajo Nation*, with Ted Schwarz (New York: Orbis, 1993), 27–29.

25. Lunderman interview, pp. 4–5.

26. Eastman, *From the Deep Woods to Civilization*, 21–23.

27. Francis La Flesche, *The Middle Five: Indian Schoolboys of the Omaha Tribe* (Lincoln: University of Nebraska Press, 1978 [1900]), xvii.

28. Lunderman interview, pp. 2–3.

29. Quoted in Frank B. Fiske, *Life and Death of Sitting Bull* (Fort Yates, ND: Pioneer-Arrow Print, 1933), 23–24; also in Mark Diedrich, ed., *Sitting Bull: The Collected Speeches* (Rochester, MN: Coyote, 1998), 168.

30. Helen Sekaquaptewa, *Me and Mine: The Life Story of Helen Sekaquaptewa* (Tucson: University of Arizona Press, 1969), 84; and Jacobs, *White Mother to a Dark Race*, 257.

31. Jacobs, *White Mother to a Dark Race*, 432.

32. Adrea Lawrence, *Lessons from an Indian Day School: Negotiating Colonization in Northern New Mexico, 1902–1907* (Lawrence: University Press of Kansas, 2011), 133–134.

33. Roger W. Axford, ed., *Native Americans: 23 Indian Biographies* (Indiana, PA: A.G. Halldin, 1980), 54.

34. Charles S. Brant, ed., *Jim Whitewolf: The Life of a Kiowa Apache Indian* (New York: Dover, 1969), 128. As of 2010, an estimated 300,000 Native people practiced the Peyote religion. See Thomas C. Maroukis, *The Peyote Road: Religious Freedom and the Native American Church* (Norman: University of Oklahoma Press, 2010).

35. Thomas B. Marquis, *Wooden Leg: A Warrior Who Fought Custer* (Lincoln: University of Nebraska Press, 1965), 364–365.

36. Brant, *Jim Whitewolf*, 135.

37. Ibid.

38. Quoted in Adams, *Education for Extinction*, 43.

39. Annual Report for the Commissioner of Indian Affairs, 1905, quoted in Adams, *Education for Extinction*, 57. A school at Riverside, California was opened in 1902 to replace the school at Perris, California, which was opened in 1893.

40. Lunderman interview, p. 5.

41. Axford, *Native Americans*, 72–73.

42. Ibid., 73.

43. Ibid., 92–93.

44. Ibid.

45. Ibid.

46. Pop Warner and Tewanima returned home together. After a month back at Carlisle Indian Industrial School, Tewanima decided to return to his Second Mesa and his Hopi people to tend his sheep and raise crops. In 1954 Bill Close, a newscaster and sportsreporter for KOOL-TV in Phoenix, accompanied Tewanima to New York City, where the Hopi athlete was named to the All-Time U.S. Olympic Track and Field Team. Ibid.

47. See Robert W. Wheeler, *Jim Thorpe: World's Greatest Athlete* (Norman: University of Oklahoma Press, 1975); Bill Crawford, *All American: The Rise and Fall of Jim*

Thorpe (Hoboken, NJ: Wiley and Sons, 2005); and Sally Jenkins, *The Real All Americans: The Team That Changed a Game, a People, a Nation* (New York: Doubleday, 2007).

48. Axford, *Native Americans*, 96.

49. Ibid.

50. Ibid.

51. Ibid., 97.

52. Ibid.

53. Ibid., 96–97. Thorpe's fame in sports caught the attention of film director Michael Curtez, who worked with Warner Brothers to produce a film about the world-famous athlete. Burt Lancaster played Jim Thorpe in the movie, Phyllis Thaxter played Thorpe's childhood sweetheart, and Charles Bickford was Pop Warner in *Jim Thorpe—All American* produced in 1951.

54. Ibid., 98.

55. Ibid.

56. Brant, *Jim Whitewolf*, 94–95.

57. Norman Guardipee, "Mending the Broken Circle," in E. K. Caldwell, ed., *Dreaming the Dawn: Conversations with Native Artists and Activists* (Lincoln: University of Nebraska Press, 1999), 25–26.

58. Ibid., 27.

Chapter 3

1. Francis Paul Prucha, *The Great Father: The United States Government and the American Indian*, abr. ad. (Lincoln: University of Nebraska Press, 1986 [1984]), 278.

2. Joel Pfister, *The Yale Indian: The Education of Henry Roe Cloud* (Durham, NC: Duke University Press, 2009), 137–146; and Lewis Meriam, et al., *The Problem of Indian Administration: A Report of a Survey Made at the Request of Honorable Hubert Work, Secretary of the Interior, and Submitted to Him, February 21, 1928* (Baltimore: Johns Hopkins Press, 1928), 346.

3. Oliver Eastman (Sioux Wahpeton), interviewed by Joseph Cash, August 3, 1971, Sioux Falls, SD, tape 768, p. 12, USDIOHC.

4. Lawrence C. Kelly, "Charles James Rhoads 1929-33," in Robert M. Kvasnicka and Herman Viola, eds., *The Commissioners of Indian Affairs, 1824–1977* (Lincoln: University of Nebraska Press, 1977), 263–272.

5. Ibid., 266–267.

6. Kenneth R. Philp, *John Collier's Crusade for Reform, 1920–1954* (Tucson: University of Arizona Press, 1977), 102.

7. Opposition to the Swing-John Bill stated by the Indian Rights Association and Mrs. Joseph Lyndon, April 10, 1930, microfilm, reel 14, John Collier Papers, Marquette University Library, Milwaukee, WI.

8. Leavitt Act, July 2, 1932, 47 Stat. 564.

9. Indian Irrigation Act, January 26, 1933, 47 Stat. 776.

10. Commissioner of Indian Affairs Charles Rhoads described Indian health, August 6, 1930, microfilm, reel 47, Collier Papers.

11. Report of the Commissioner of Indian Affairs, Charles Rhoads, June 30, 1932, microfiche, p. 3, ibid.

12. Ibid.

13. Arrell M. Gibson, *The American Indian: Prehistory to the Present* (Lexington, MA: D.C. Heath, 1980), 470–471.

14. This quote has been attributed to Franklin Roosevelt, but there is no known source according to the Franklin D. Roosevelt Presidential Library and Museum (Hyde Park, NY).

15. Philp, *John Collier's Crusade*, 113–117.

16. Ibid.

17. Graham D. Taylor, *The New Deal and American Indian Tribalism: The Administration of the Indian Reorganization Act, 1934–35* (Lincoln: University of Nebraska Press, 1980), 18.

18. Ibid.

19. Statement by Reverend Dr. Dirk Lay, March 31, 1933, microfilm, reel 5, Collier Papers.

20. Report of the Commissioner of Indian Affairs, John Collier, June 30, 1933, p. 111. Microfilm, reel 5, Collier Papers.

21. "Indian Timber Contracts Act," March 4, 1933, U.S. Statutes At Large, 47 pt. 1:1568-69. Other reform legislation during the early years of the 1930s included the Indian Arts and Crafts Board Act (August 27, 1935, 49 Stat. 891), the Johnson-O'Malley Act (April 16, 1934, 48 Stat. 596), the Oklahoma Indian Welfare Act (June 26, 1936, 49 Stat. 1967), and the Alaska Native Reorganization Act (May 1, 1936. U.S. Statutes At Large, 49, pt. 1:1250-51.

22. For information on the Indian Division of the Civilian Conservation Corps, see Donald L. Parman, "The Indian Civilian Conservation Corps," Ph.D. dissertation, University of Oklahoma, Norman, 1967.

23. Report of the Commissioner of Indian Affairs, John Collier, June 30, 1940, microfiche, p. 402, Collier Papers.

24. Taylor, *New Deal*, 77.

25. Joseph Cash and Herbert Hoover, eds., *To Be an Indian: An Oral History* (New York: Holt, Rinehart and Winston, 1971), 152.

26. Taylor, *New Deal*, 20.

27. Ibid.

28. Indian Reorganization Act, June 18, 1934, 48 Stat. 984.

29. Robert Morrison (Lakota), interviewed by Joseph Cash, Summer 1967, Sioux Falls, SD, tape 59, pp. 3–4, USDIOHC.

30. Richard LaRoche (Brule Sioux), interviewed by Gerald Wolff, August 25, 1971, Lower Brule, SD, tape 784, pp. 2–4, USDIOHC.

31. Dan Clark (Crow Creek), interviewed by Joseph Cash, Summer 1968, Chamberlain, SD, tape 51, pp. 1–4, USDIOHC.

32. John Saul (Crow Creek), interviewed by Joseph Cash, June 6, 1968, Chamberlain, SD, tape 51, pp. 1–4, USDIOHC.

33. "Speeches of a General Tribal Council Held July 20, 1929," in Paul C. Rosier, *Rebirth of the Blackfeet Nation, 1912–1954* (Lincoln: University of Nebraska Press, 2001), 57.

34. Report on talks made at a special meeting called by Mountainchief, October 1, 1933, in Senate Committee on Indian Affairs, *Survey of Conditions of the Indians in the United States*, cited in Rosier, *Rebirth of the Blackfeet Nation*, 72.

35. Minutes of the Plains Congress, March 4, 1934, cited in ibid., 83.

36. Cecil Provost, Yankton, interviewed by Joseph Cash, Summer 1968, Marty Mission, SD, tape 13, pp. 1–2, USDIOHC.

37. Taylor, *New Deal*, 140.

38. Ibid., 22–23.

39. Ibid., 24.

40. Jeffrey P. Shepherd, *We Are an Indian Nation: A History of the Hualapai People* (Tucson: University of Arizona Press, 2010), 109–135.

41. No Coat to Honorable Harold Ickes, February 20, 1937, quoted in Rosier, *Rebirth of the Blackfeet Nation*, 129.

42. Joe Brown to congressional subcommittee, 1944, ibid., 170.

43. Constitutional Convention Minutes, May 1, 1945, ibid., 202.

44. Tribal voting to receive IRA, "Results of Referendum Vote on Indian Reorganization Act Held October 27," October 27, 1936, microfilm, reel 17, Collier Papers.

45. Tribal voting to receive IRA, "Results of Referendum Vote on Indian Reorganization Act Held October 27," October 27, 1936, microfilm, reel 17, Collier Papers.

46. Ibid.

47. Peter MacDonald, *The Last Warrior: Peter MacDonald and the Navajo Nation*, with Ted Schwarz (New York: Orbis, 1993), 29. See also Martha Weisiger, *Dreaming of Sheep in Navajo Country* (Seattle: University of Washington Press, 1999).

48. Taylor, *New Deal*, 126–131.

49. William B. Benege, "Law and Order on Indian Reservations," *Federal Bar Journal*, vol. 20 (1960), 225–227. See also Vine Deloria, Jr., and Clifford Lytle, *The Nations Within: The Past and Future of American Indian Sovereignty* (New York: Pantheon, 1984).

50. Alfred Dubray, "Debate over IRA," in Peter Nabokov, ed., *Native American Testimony: A Chronicle of Indian-White Relations from Prophecy to the Present, 1492–1992* (New York: Penguin Books, 1991), 327–328.

51. Taylor, *New Deal*, 33.

52. "Indian Reorganization Act," June 18, 1934, 48 Stat. 984.

53. Rupert Costo, statement including Crow letter to Senator Burton Wheeler, in Nabakov, *Native American Testimony*, 326.

54. Ramon Roubideaux, Brule Lakota, in Cash and Hoover, *To Be an Indian*, 131–132.

55. Copy of a news article in the *Baltimore Sun*, June 30, 1933, microfilm, reel 17, Collier Papers.

56. Johnson-O'Malley Act, April 16, 1934, 48 Stat. 596.

57. Indian Arts and Crafts Board Act, August 27, 1935, 49 Stat. 891.

58. Ibid.

59. "Oklahoma and the Wheeler-Howard Act," *American Indian Life Bulletin*, no. 25, October 1934, p. 6, microfilm, reel 9, Collier Papers.

60. "Indian Reorganization Act," June 18, 1934, Stat. 984-88, also known as Wheeler-Howard Act.

61. "Oklahoma Indian Welfare Act," June 26, 1936, Stat. 1967-68.

62. The Oklahoma Indians levied continual criticism against the IRA until the Oklahoma Indian Welfare Act was passed in 1936. See K. Philp, *John Collier's Crusade*, 176–182.

63. Ibid.

64. L. Susan Work, *The Seminole Nation of Oklahoma: A Legal History* (Norman: University of Oklahoma Press, 2010), 121.

65. Rennard Strickland, *The Indians in Oklahoma* (Norman: University of Oklahoma Press, 1980), 73.

66. Report of the Commissioner of Indian Affairs, John Collier, June 30, 1937, microfiche, pp. 200, 234, Collier Papers.

67. Senate Hearing, April 26, 1936, John Collier Papers, reel 7, part 37.

68. Taylor, *New Deal*, 35.

69. For information about the Alaska Reorganization Act, refer to Thomas R. Berger, *Village Journey: The Report of the Alaska Native Review Commission* (New York: Hill and Wang, 1985), 132–142.

70. Philp, *John Collier's Crusade*, 309–327.

71. Olive Patricia Dickason, *Canada's First Nations: A History of Founding Peoples from Earliest Times* (Norman: University of Oklahoma Press, 1992), 382 and 395.

72. Taylor, *New Deal*, 141.

73. Report of the Commissioner of Indian Affairs, John Collier, June 30, 1938, microfiche, p. 229, Collier Papers.

74. Report of the Commissioner of Indian Affairs, John Collier, June 30, 1941, p. 424, ibid.

75. Taylor, *New Deal*, 67.

76. Ibid., 97.

77. David W. Daily, *Battle for the BIA: G.E.E. Lindquist and the Missionary Crusade against John Collier* (Tucson: University of Arizona Press, 2002), 60–100.

78. A copy of John Collier's resignation is in June 30, 1933, microfilm, reel 17, Collier Papers. Collier immediately organized the Institute of Ethnic Affairs in Washington, DC, to inform the public of social and economic problems facing Indians, and he wanted to monitor the treatment of American dependencies the United States acquired in World War II. The former commissioner also helped to organize the National Peace Conference, Catholic War Veterans, and United Nations of Philadelphia. In 1947 he published a book, *Indians of the Americas*. During the same year he accepted a visiting professorship in sociology and anthropology at City College of New York. After a divorce from his wife, Laura Thompson, in Mexico, he became a visiting professor at Knox College in Galesburg, Illinois, during 1955–1956. He retired to Taos, New Mexico, and lived at Talpa, three miles from Taos Pueblo, the people who originally influenced him to begin his long career in the Bureau of Indian Affairs. John Collier died on May 8, 1968, four days after his eighty-fourth birthday.

79. Rosier, *Rebirth of the Blackfeet Nation*, 101–169.

80. William J. Bauer, Jr., *We Were All like Migrant Workers Here: Work, Community, and Memory on California's Round Valley Reservation, 1850–1941* (Chapel Hill: University of North Carolina Press, 2009), 176–203.

Chapter 4

1. Barrett Tillman, *Heroes: U.S. Army Medal of Honor Recipients* (New York: Penguin, 2006), 95–166.

2. Donald L. Fixico, *Termination and Relocation: Federal Indian Policy, 1945–1960* (Albuquerque: University of New Mexico Press, 1986), 63–77.

3. The First Red Scare occurred 1917 to 1920 due to the rise of communism in the United States. Ellen Schrecker, *Many Are the Crimes: McCarthyism in America* (Boston: Little, Brown, 1998), 203–265.

4. Fixico, *Termination and Relocation*, 93.

5. House Concurrent Resolution 108, August 1, 1953, 67 Stat. B132.

6. Fixico, *Termination and Relocation*, 91–110; and Roberta Ulrich, *American Indian Nations from Termination to Restoration, 1953–2006* (Lincoln: University of Nebraska Press, 2010), 3–130.

7. William Willard, "Outing, Relocation, and Employment Assistance: The Impact of Federal Indian Population Dispersal Programs in the Bay Area," *Wicazo Sa Review*, vol. 12, no. 1 (Spring 1997), 29–46; and Donald L. Fixico, *The Urban Indian Experience in America* (Albuquerque: University of New Mexico Press, 2000), 9–24.

8. Wilma Mankiller and Michael Wallis, *Mankiller a Chief and Her People* (New York: St. Martin's Press, 1993), 69.

9. Ibid., 71.

10. Kimmis Henderick, "U.S. Helps Indians Move," *Christian Science Monitor*, March 6, 1956, 12.

11. Edith R. Mirrielees, "The Cloud of Mistrust," *Atlantic Monthly*, vol. 199 (February 1957), 55–59.

12. Russell Means, *Where White Men Fear to Tread: The Autobiography of Russell Means*, with Marvin J. Wolf (New York: St. Martin's Press, 1995), 68. While the relocation program was carried out during the Eisenhower administration, the idea for relocation occurred during the Truman years.

13. Kenneth R. Philp, "Stride toward Freedom: The Relocation of Indians to Cities, 1952–1960," *Western Historical Quarterly*, vol. 16 no. 1 (April 1985), 175–190.

14. Means, *Where White Men Fear to Tread*, 77.

15. Oliver Eastman (Sioux Wahpeton), interviewed by Joseph Cash, August 3, 1971, Sioux Falls, SD, tape 768, p. 13, USDIOHC.

16. Eugene Wilson (Nez Perce), interviewed by S.I. Myers, December 22, 1974, Phoenix, AZ, no. 4, pp. 15–16, NYTOHP.

17. Fixico, *Termination and Relocation*, 138.

18. Joseph C. Vasquez, interview by Floyd O'Neil, January 27, 1971, Los Angeles, CA, interview no. 1009, box 53, acc. no. 24, Doris Duke Indian Oral History Collection, Special Collections, Marriott Library, University of Utah, Salt Lake City.

19. La Verne Madigan, *American Indian Relocation Program* (New York: Association on American Indian Affairs, 1956), 17; James O. Palmer, "A Geographical Investigation of the Effects of the Bureau of Indian Affairs' Employment Assistance Program upon the Relocation of Oklahoma Indians, 1967–1971," Ph.D. dissertation, University of Oklahoma, Norman, 1975, 104; and U.S. Congress, Senate, discussion on the success of the Relocation Program, 85th Cong., 1st sess., March 14, 1957, *Congressional Record*, vol. 103, p. 3643.

20. Adult Indian Vocational Training Act, P.L. 959, August 3, 1956, 70 Stat. 986.

21. Howell Rains, "American Indians: Struggling for Power and Identity," *New York Times Magazine*, February 11, 1979, section 4, p. 28.

22. Ned Blackhawk, "I Can Carry On from Here: The Relocation of American Indians to Los Angeles," *Wicazo Sa Review*, vol. 11, no. 2 (Fall 1995), 21.

23. Eastman interview, p. 14.

24. Ibid.

25. Richard Woods and Arthur M. Harkins, "An Examination of the 1968–1969 Urban Indian Hearings Held by the National Council on Indian Opportunity. Part V: Multiple Problems of Adaptation," Training Center for Community Programs, in coordination with the Office of Community Programs, Center for Urban and Region Affairs (Minneapolis: University of Minnesota, October 1971), 28.

26. Nicholas G. Rosenthal, *Reimagining Indian Country: Native American Migration and Identity in Twentieth-Century Los Angeles* (Chapel Hill: University of North Carolina Press, 2012), 3.

27. Roger W. Axford, ed., *Native Americans: 23 Indian Biographies* (Indiana, PA: A.G. Halldin, 1980), 37.

28. Allan Parachini, "Chicago's Indian Ghetto Where Hopes Slowly Die," *Chicago Sun-Times*, May 2, 1976, box 35, folder Indian News Clippings 5, Theodore Marrs Papers, Gerald R. Ford Presidential Library, Ann Arbor, MI.

29. Minutes of First Meeting of the Task Force on Racially-Isolated Urban Indians, December 12 and 13, 1969, box 114, folder Urban Indians 4 of 4, White House Central Files, Leonard Garment Papers, Richard Nixon Materials Project, College Park, MD.

30. Judith Anne Antell, "American Indian Women Activists," Ph.D. dissertation, Department of Ethnic Studies, University of California, Berkeley, 1990, 24.

31. Means, *Where White Men Fear to Tread*, 82.

31. Ibid.

32. Mankiller and Wallis, *Mankiller*, 103.

33. In his study, Bailey obtained his information from the Senior Workers Action Program of Oklahoma County, Nutrition Program for the Elderly, Area Development Education Placement and Training Program, Head Start, Youth Development Program, and Oklahoma City Housing Authority. See Bill Sampson, "Urban Indians 'Forgotten'," *Tulsa Tribune*, September 22, 1976, box 4, folder, news clippings (3), Brad Patterson Papers, Gerald R. Ford Presidential Library, Ann Arbor, MI.

34. Daniel M. Cobb, *Native Activism in Cold War America: The Struggle for Sovereignty* (Lawrence: University Press of Kansas, 2008), 181.

35. Fixico, *Urban Indian Experience*, 135–160.

36. Association on American Indian Affairs, "Senate Probes Child Welfare Crises," *Indian Family Defense*, no. 2 (Summer 1974), 1.

37. Ibid., 3–6.

38. Ibid.

39. Ibid.

40. "Navajos Need New Values," *Gallup Independent*, January 30, 1976, box 35, folder Indian News Clippings 3, Theodore Marrs Papers.

41. Josephine Robertson, "Pat Locke—Liaison between Two Cultures," *Christian Science Monitor*, February 2, 1976.

42. "Report on Urban and Rural Non-reservation Indians, Task Force Eight: Urban and Rural, Non-reservation Indian," in *Final Report to the American Indian Policy Review Commission* (Washington, DC: U.S. Government Printing Office, 1976), 11.

Chapter 5

1. Thomas W. Cowger, *The National Congress of American Indians: The Founding Years* (Lincoln: University of Nebraska Press, 1999), 30.

2. "Declaration of Indian Purpose: The Voice of the American Indian," American Indian Chicago Conference, University of Chicago, June 13–20, 1961, p. 5, copy in the author's collection.

3. Daniel M. Cobb, *Native Activism in Cold War America: The Struggle for Sovereignty* (Lawrence: University Press of Kansas, 2008), 30–79; and Paul C. Rosier, *Serving Their Country: American Indian Politics and Patriotism in the Twentieth Century* (Cambridge, MA: Harvard University Press, 2009), 214–220.

4. Bradley G. Shreve, *Red Power Rising: The National Indian Youth Council and the Origins of Native Activism* (Norman: University of Oklahoma Press, 2011), 3–5. See also Sherry L. Smith, *Hippies, Indians, and the Fight for Red Power* (New York: Oxford University Press, 2012).

5. Stan Steiner, *The New Indians* (New York: Harper and Row, 1968).

6. Dick Gregory, quoted in Charles Wilkinson, *Messages from Frank's Landing: A Story of Salmon, Treaties, and the Indian Way* (Seattle: University of Washington Press, 2000), 40.

7. Ibid., 49–50.

8. Ibid., 56.

9. Dennis Banks, *Ojibwa Warrior: Dennis Banks and the Rise of the American Indian Movement*, with Richard Erodes (Norman: University of Oklahoma Press, 2004), 59.

10. Marion Hall, *American Indians of Minneapolis—an Update* (Minneapolis: League of Women's Voters of Minneapolis, 1984), 4.

11. Ibid., 5.

12. Floyd Taylor (Hunkpapa), interviewed by Joseph Cash, August 9, 1968, Fort Thompson, SD, tape 50, p. 4, USDIOHC.

13. "The Forgotten American," Special Message to Congress, March 6, 1968, *Public Papers of the Presidents of the United States: Lyndon B. Johnson, 1968–69* (Ann Arbor, MI: University of Michigan Library, 2005), vol. 1: 336–337, 343–344.

14. For information on American Indians who served in Vietnam, see Tom Holm, *Strong Hearts Wounded Souls: Native American Veterans of the Vietnam War* (Austin: University of Texas Press, 1996).

15. Michael Miller and Laura Waterman Wittstock, *American Indian Alcoholism in St. Paul: A Needs Assessment Conducted Jointly by the Community Planning Organization and the Juel Fairbanks Aftercare Residence* (Minneapolis: Center for Urban and Regional Affairs, University of Minnesota and the Community Planning Organization, 1982), 6–7.

16. "Report on Urban and Rural Non-reservation Indians, Task Force Eight: Urban and Rural Non-reservation Indians," in *Final Report to the American Indian Policy Review Commission* (Washington, D.C.: Government Printing Office, 1976).

17. "Laymen Urge Donations Go to Negroes, Indians," *Minneapolis Star*, March 21, 1968, 21B.

18. Joseph Westermeyer, "Chippewa and Majority Alcoholism in the Twin Cities: A Comparison," *Journal of Nervous and Mental Disease*, vol. 155 (November 1972), 325.

19. Maurice L. Sievers, "Cigarette and Alcohol Usage by Southwestern American Indians," *American Journal of Public Health*, vol. 58, no. 5 (January 1968), 75.

20. Hall, *American Indians of Minneapolis*, 17.

21. John H. Hamer, "Acculturation Stress and the Functions of Alcohol among the Forest Potawatomi," *Quarterly Journal of Studies on Alcohol*, vol. 26, no. 2 (June 1965), 289.

22. Gerald Vizenor, "American Indians and Drunkenness," *Journal of Ethnic Studies*, vol. 11, no. 4 (Winter 1984), 84.

23. Proposal submitted by All Indian Pueblo Council (letter from Robert Robertson, director of National Council on Indian Opportunity, to Brad Patterson), April 28, 1972, in Nixon White House Central Files, Bureau of Indian Affairs box 100, folder Indian Alcoholism, Leonard Garment Papers, Richard Nixon Presidential Materials Project, College Park, MD.

24. Letter from Herb Powless, director of AIM, to Brad Patterson, assistant to U.S. president, October 26, 1972, ibid.

25. Deseret News (California City, CA), November 1, 1985, in Indian Affairs Collection, box 11, Ronald Reagan Presidential Library, Simi Valley, CA.

26. John Hurst, "Indians, Poverty, Alcohol, Cops—the Combination Doesn't Mix," *San Francisco Examiner*, July 16, 1969, 16.

27. Ibid.

28. Richard G. Woods and Arthur M. Harkins, "An Examination of the 1968–1969 Urban Indian Hearings Held by the National Council on Indian Opportunity. Part V: Multiple Problems of Adaptation," Training Center for Community Programs, in coordination with the Office of Community Programs, Center for Urban and Regional Affairs (Minneapolis: University of Minnesota, October 1971), 37.

29. E. Alan Morinis, "'Getting Straight': Behavior Patterns in a Skid Row Indian Community," *Urban Anthropology*, vol. 11, no. 2 (Summer 1982), 209.

30. Ibid.

31. See Gary Clayton Anderson, *Little Crow: Spokesman for the Sioux* (St. Paul: Minnesota Historical Society Press, 1986).

32. Abe Altrowitz, "Ft. Snelling Coming to Life Again," *Minneapolis Star*, April 13, 1968, 5A.

33. Banks, *Ojibwa Warrior*, 62–65.

34. Dorothy Lewis, "Red School House Has Mad Impact," *St. Paul Pioneer Press*, February 29, 1976, Box 35, Folder Indian News Clippings (4), Theodore Marrs Papers, Gerald Ford Presidential Library, Ann Arbor, MI.

35. After their releases they stayed in contact and then seemed to lose track of each other. Eventually George Mitchell, another Ojibwa, would join them. The three would become cofounders of AIM. Ibid.

36. Banks, *Ojibwa Warrior*, 39.

37. Andrew Barlow, "The Student Movement of the 1960s and the Politics of Race," *Journal of Ethnic Studies* vol. 19, no. 3 (Fall 1991), 7.

38. Beatrice Medicine, "Red Power: Real or Potential?," in *Indian Voices: The First Convocation of American Indian Scholars* (San Francisco: Indian Historian Press, 1970), 300, 324.

39. Russell Means, *Where White Men Fear to Tread: The Autobiography of Russell Means*, with Marvin J. Wolf (New York: St. Martin's Press, 1995), 72.

40. Banks, *Ojibwa Warrior*, 39.

41. Ibid., 62.

42. Vernon Bellecourt (Ojibwa) interview, ca. 1969, in Peter Nabokov, ed., *Native American Testimony: A Chronicle of Indian-White Relations from Prophecy to the Present, 1492–1992* (New York: Penguin, 1992), 375.

43. Banks, *Ojibwa Warrior*, 62.

44. Means, *Where White Men Fear to Tread*, 46.

45. Ibid., 150.

46. Ibid., 152.

47. Dino Butler, "Embracing Respect for All Life," in E. K. Caldwell, ed., *Dreaming the Dawn: Conversations with Native Artists and Activists* (Lincoln: University of Nebraska Press, 1999), 115–116.

48. "Treaty with the Sioux—Brule, Oglala, Miniconjou, Yanktonai, Hunkpapa, Blackfeet, Cuthead, Two Kettle, Sana Arcs, and Santee and Arapaho" (Fort Laramie), April 29, 1868, in Charles J. Kappler, comp. and ed., *Indian Treaties 1778–1883* (New York: Interland, 1975), 998–1003.

49. Adam Fortunate Eagle, *Alcatraz! Alcatraz! The Indian Occupation of 1969–1971* (Berkeley: Heyday, 1992), 71–74.

50. Adam Fortunate Eagle, *Heart of the Rock: The Indian Invasion of Alcatraz* (Norman: University of Oklahoma Press, 2002), 101.

51. Fortunate Eagle, *Alcatraz!*, 118–120.

52. Ibid., 133–136.

53. Troy R. Johnson, *The Occupation of Alcatraz Island: Indian Self-Determination and the Rise of Indian Activism* (Urbana: University of Illinois Press, 1996), 231.

54. Jay C. Fikes, *Reuben Snake, Your Humble Servant Indian Visionary and Activist* (Santa Fe, NM: Clear Light, 1996), 113–115.

55. Banks, *Ojibwa Warrior*, 64.

56. Means, *Where White Men Fear to Tread*, 155.

57. Ibid., 167–171.

58. Paul Chaat Smith and Robert Warrior, *Like a Hurricane: The Indian Movement from Alcatraz to Wounded Knee* (New York: New Press, 1996), 112–117.

59. State Attorney Office, Albuquerque to acting FBI director, memorandum, March 17, 1973, FBI files of AIM and Wounded Knee, reel 2, file 100-462483, vol. 5, microfilm, University of Minnesota Library, Minnesota, MI.

60. Bradley H. Patterson, Jr., to Assistant Secretary William Buffam, International Organization Affairs, Department of State, memorandum, June 27, 1974, box 8, folder American Indian Movement, Norman E. Ross Papers, Gerald Ford Presidential Library, Ann Arbor, MI.

61. Banks, *Ojibwa Warrior*, 150–156.

62. James G. Abourezk, *Advise and Dissent: Memoirs of South Dakota and the U.S. Senate* (Chicago: Lawrence Hill, 1989), 206.

63. Ibid., 209–210.

64. Banks, *Ojibwa Warrior*, 171.

65. Ibid., 209.

66. "Sioux in S.D. End Occupation of Plant," *Denver Post*, March 20, 1975; and "Indians Seize Plant in South Dakota," *Rocky Mountains News* (Denver, CO), March 18, 1975.

67. Cathy Wilson (Nez Perce), interviewed by S. I. Myers, December 30, 1974, Tempe, AZ, no. 3, p. 26, NYTOHP.

68. Janice Nacke (Shoshone-Navajo), interviewed by S. I. Myers, October 30, 1975, Pocatello, ID, no. 96, p. 14, NYTOHP.

69. Rosalie Wax, "The Warrior Dropout," in John R. Howard, ed., *Awakening Minorities: American Indians, Mexican Americans, Puerto Ricans* (New Brunswick, NJ: Transaction, 1970), 40-46.

70. Butler, "Embracing Respect," 115–116.

71. Melvin McKenzie (Navajo), interviewed by S. I. Myers, October 20, 1975, Tsaile, AZ, no. 75, p. 13, NYTOHP.

72. Marcus Sekayouma (Hopi), interviewed by S. I. Myers, December 16, 1975, Sacaton, AZ, no. 122, pt. 1, p. 27, NYTOHP.

73. Smith and Warrior, *Like a Hurricane*, 278.

Chapter 6

1. Perry Cody and Collin Perry, *Iron Eyes: My Life as a Hollywood Indian* (New York: Books Sales, 1984), 11.

2. Thomas Marquis, ed., *Wooden Leg: A Warrior Who Fought Custer* (Lincoln: University of Nebraska Press, 1965), 374.

3. "Blackfeet Tribal Council Proceedings," February 24, 1927, in Paul C. Rosier, *Rebirth of the Blackfeet Nation, 1912–1954* (Lincoln: University of Nebraska Press, 2001), 50.

4. William E. Coffer, *Sipapu: The Story of the Indians of Arizona and New Mexico* (New York: Van Nostrand Reinhold, 1982), 79. For more information on the Hopi and their culture, see Edward P. Dozier, *The Hopi-Tewa of Arizona* (Berkeley: University of California Press, 1954), and Dozier, *The Pueblo Indians of North America* (New York: Holt, Rinehart and Winston, 1970).

5. Vincent Crapanzano, *The Fifth World of Forester Bennett: Portrait of a Navajo* (Lincoln: University of Nebraska Press, 2003 [1972]), 45.

6. Leslie Silko, *Ceremony* (New York: New American Library, 1977), 70.

7. Dan Katchongva (Hopi), interview, "He Will Use Any Means to Get What He Wants," in Peter Nabokov, ed., *Native American Testimony: A Chronicle of Indian-White Relations from Prophecy to the Present, 1491–1992* (New York: Penguin, 1992), 6–7.

8. Indian Self-Determination and Education Assistance Act, P.L. 93-68, January 4, 1975, 88 Stat. 2203.

9. Joane Nagel, "The Politics of American Indian Economic Development: The Reservation/Urban Nexus," with Carol Ward and Timothy Knapp, in Matthew Snipp, ed., *Public Policy Impacts on American Indian Economic Development* (Albuquerque: Native American Studies Institute for Native American Development, 1988), 40.

10. Oliver Eastman (Sioux Wahpeton), interviewed by Joseph Cash, August 3, 1971, Sioux Falls, SD, tape 768, p. 3, USDIOHC.

11. Philip Reno, *Mother Earth, Father Sky, and Economic Development: Navajo Resources and Their Use* (Albuquerque: University of New Mexico Press, 1981), 133.

12. Jim Pierce, Council of Energy Resource Tribes chief administrative officer, report in *CERT First Decade Report for 1985*. In author's collection.

13. Peter MacDonald, *The Last Warrior: Peter MacDonald and the Navajo Nation*, with Ted Schwarz (New York: Orbis, 1993), 228.

14. Marjane Ambler, *Breaking the Iron Bonds: Indian Control of Energy Development* (Lawrence: University Press of Kansas, 1990), 106, 107, 110.

15. "Energy Conservation and Production Revenue Act of 1976: Report to Accompany H.R. 6860," U.S. Senate Committee on Finance, 94th Congress, 2nd sess., Senate Rep. no. 94-1181.

16. Surface Mining Control and Reclamation Act, P.L. 95-87, August 3, 1977, 91 Stat. 445.

17. Natural Gas Policy Act, P.L. 95-621, November 8, 1978, 92 Stat. 3350.

18. National Energy Conservation Policy Act, P.L. 95-619, November 9, 1978, 92 Stat. 3206.

19. Federal Oil and Gas Royalty Management Act, P.L. 97-451, January 12, 1982, 96 Stat. 2457.

20. Indian Mineral Development Act, P.L. 97-382, December 22, 1982, 96 Stat. 1938.

21. "Indians Want a Bigger Share of Their Wealth," *Business Week*, May 3, 1976, 101; and "A Crow Indian Threat to Western Strip Mines," *Business Week*, October 13, 1975, 37.

22. "A Crow Indian Threat"; and "The Black Hills Alliance," *Akwesasne Notes*, vol. 2, no. 2 (May 1979).

23. Annie Wauneka (Navajo), interviewed by S.I. Myers, October 19, 1975, Klagetoh, AZ, no. 74, pp. 13–14, NYTOHP.

24. Luci Tapahonso, *Blue Horses Rush In: Poems and Stories* (Tucson: University of Arizona Press, 1997), 15.

25. Mary Shepardson, "The Gender Status of Navajo Women," in Laura F. Klein and Lillian A. Ackerman, eds., *Women and Power in Native North America* (Norman: University of Oklahoma Press, 1995), 160. For information on Navajo religion, see Gladys A. Reichard, *Navaho Religion: A Study of Symbolism* (Princeton, NJ: Princeton University Press, 1974 [1950]).

26. Shepardson, "Gender Status of Navajo Women," 172.

27. George P. Lee, *Silent Courage an Indian Story: The Autobiography of George P. Lee a Navajo* (Salt Lake City, UT: Deseret, 1987), 29.

28. "White Shell Woman: Beloved of the Navajo," in Scott Peterson, *Native American Prophecies* (St. Paul: Paragon House, 1990), 132.

29. See John R. Swanton, "The Social History and Usages of the Creek Confederacy," in *Forth-Second Annual Report of the Bureau of American Ethnology* (Washington, DC: U.S. Government Printing Office, 1928), 33–156.

30. Coffer, *Sipapu*, 126–127.

31. Luci Tapahonso, *Saanii Dahataal: The Women Are Singing* (Tucson: University of Arizona Press, 1993), 19.

32. Coffer, *Sipapu*, 70–73.

33. Harold Courlander, *The Fourth World of the Hopis: The Epic Story of the Hopi Indians as Preserved in Their Legends and Traditions* (Albuquerque: University of New Mexico Press, 1971), 9.

34. Ibid.

35. Ibid., 10–11.

36. Crapanzano, *Fifth World of Forester Bennett*, 34–35.

37. Silko, *Ceremony*, 236.

38. Indian Civil Rights Act, P.L. 99-570, October 27, 1986, 100 Stat. 3207.

39. Indian Housing Act, P.L. 100-358, June 29, 1988, 102 Stat. 676.

40. Indian Law Enforcement Reform Act, P.L. 101-379, August 18, 1990, 104 Stat. 473.

41. Indian Environmental Regulatory Enhancement Act, P.L. 101-408, October 4, 1990, 104 Stat. 883.

42. National Indian Forest Resources Management Act, P.L. 101-630, November 28, 1990, 104 Stat. 4532.

43. "Energy Policy Act," P.L. 109-58, July 29, 2005, 119 Stat. 594.

44. Lee, *Silent Courage*, 47.

45. Thomas Banyacya Sr., testimony, in *Poison Fire, Sacred Earth (Testimonies, Lectures, Conclusions), the World Uranium Hearing*, Salzburg, 1992, pp. 32–36, available at http://www.ratical.org/radiation/WorldUraniumHearing/ThomasBanyacya.html, accessed August 1, 2007.

46. "White Shell Woman," 128.

47. Peterson Zah, "Foreword," in Adriel Heisey and Kenji Kawano, eds., *In the Fifth World: Portrait of the Navajo Nation* (Tucson, AZ: Rio Nuevo, 2001), 2.

48. Cambridge Energy Research Associates. "Gasoline and the American People 2007," http://seekerblog.com/2007/01/23/gasoline-and-the-american-people-2007/, accessed April 19, 2013.

49. See Severt Young Bear and R.D. Theisz, *Standing in the Light: A Lakota Way of Seeing* (Lincoln: University of Nebraska Press, 1994), and Donald L. Fixico, *The American Indian Mind in a Linear World: American Indian Studies and Traditional Knowledge* (New York: Routledge, 2003).

Chapter 7

1. For the origin of moral economy, see Edward P. Thompson, "The Moral Economy of the English Crowd in the Eighteenth Century," *Past and Present*, no. 50 (February 1971), 76–136; and James C. Scott, *The Moral Economy of the Peasant: Subsistence and Rebellion in Southeast Asia* (New Haven, CT: Yale University Press, 1979).

2. See David E. Wilkins, *American Indian Politics and the American Political System* (Lanham, MA: Rowman and Littlefield, 2007), 163–192; and Dean Howard Smith, *Modern Tribal Development: Paths to Self-Sufficiency and Cultural Integrity in Indian Country* (Walnut Creek, CA: AltaMira Press, 2000), 45–76.

3. Wayne King, "Trump, in a Federal Lawsuit, Seeks to Block Indian Casinos," *New York Times*, May 4, 1993.

4. Each player rolled one marble underhanded to land in the proper hole, or to knock another player's marble out of the way. A player had two chances to knock each of the opposing team's marbles away from a hole, and after a player was hit twice, he was considered "dead." A Cherokee National Holiday Marble Tournament is held each year during Labor Day weekend in the Cherokee Nation, and marble fields are in Adair, Cherokee, Delaware, and Mayes County in Oklahoma. "Marbles Is an Old

and Complex Game," *News from Indian Country* (Hayward, WI), vol. 10, no. 23 (Mid-December 1996), 11B.

5. Deanne Stillman, *Mustang: The Sage of the Wild Horse in the American West* (New York: Houghton Mifflin, 2008), 63.

6. Stewart Culin, *Games of the North American Indians*, in "Twenty-Fourth Annual Report of the Bureau of American Ethnology to the Smithsonian Institution, 1902-1903," (New York: Dover Publications, 1975), 31–43.

7. Kim Isaac Eisler, *Revenge of the Pequots: How a Small Native American Tribe Created the World's Most Profitable Casino* (New York: Simon and Schuster, 2001), 91.

8. Ibid., 92.

9. See Jessica Cattelino, *High Stakes: Florida Seminole Gaming and Sovereignty* (Durham, NC: Duke University Press, 2008).

10. James W. Covington, *The Seminoles of Florida* (Gainesville: University Press of Florida, 1993), 253.

11. Ibid., 254.

12. "Puyallups OK Casino Plan—U.S. Approval Is Pending," *Seattle Press-Intelligencer,* March 11, 1979, accession no. 3560-5, box 83, folder 8, Henry Jackson Papers, Archives Division, Allen Library, University of Washington, Seattle.

13. "Tacoma Mayor Opposes Casinos," *Seattle Times,* March 14, 1979, ibid.

14. Cecil Andrus to Henry Jackson, March 30, 1979, folder 9, ibid.

15. Covington, *Seminoles of Florida,* 254–255.

16. Barbara Oeffner, *Champion of the Everglades: A Biography of Seminole Chief James Billie* (Palm Beach, FL: Cape Cod Writers, 1995), 103.

17. *Seminole Tribe of Florida v. Butterworth,* 658 F.2d 310 (1981), 246.

18. Robert Clinton, Nell Jessup Newton, and Monroe Price, *American Indian Law: Cases and Materials,* 3rd ed. (Charlottesville, VA: Michie, 1991), 621.

19. Indian Tribal Governmental Tax Status Act, P.L. 97-473, January 14, 1983, 97 Stat. 2607.

20. Ambrose I. Lane, Sr., *Return of the Buffalo: The Story Behind America's Indian Gaming Explosion* (Westport, CT: Bergin and Garvey, 1995), 126–127.

21. Ibid.

22. Criminal and Civil Jurisdiction Act, P.L. 280, August 15,1953, 67 Stat. 588.

23. *California v. Cabazon Band of Mission Indians et al.,* 480 U.S. 202 (1987), 205, 215, 247.

24. Ibid.

25. Eisler, *Revenge of the Pequots,* 55–56.

26. Ibid., 105.

27. Ibid., 107, 133.

28. Ibid., 110.

29. W. Dale Mason, *Indian Gaming: Tribal Sovereignty and American Politics* (Norman: University of Oklahoma Press, 2000), 61.

30. Ibid.

31. Ibid., 62.

32. Ibid., 63–64; "National Indian Gaming Commission Report to Congress," December 31, 1991, White House Office of Records Management, Subject File "Indians," box 3, folder 296253-301061, George Bush Presidential Library, College Station, TX.

33. Indian Gaming Regulatory Act, P.L. 100-497, October 17, 1988, 102 Stat. 2467.

34. Ibid.

35. Tom Meager, "Opponents Bet They Can Defeat Casino," *Lawrence Journal World* (Lawrence, KS), August 14, 2000, 2B.

36. "Reservations Bucking States, Taking Gamble with Gambling," *Vicksburg (MS) Sunday Post*, December 29, 1991, D3.

37. Statement by Paul L. Maloney, senior counsel for the Policy Criminal Division, before the Select Committee on Indian Affairs, U.S. Senate, March 18, 1992, quoted in Franke Wilmer, "Indian Gaming: Players and Stakes," *Wicazo Sa Review* vol. 12, no. 1 (Spring 1997), 96.

38. Paul C. Rosier, *Native American Issues* (Westport, CT: Greenwood Press, 2003), 121.

39. Sandra Chereb, "Campbell Warns about Greenbacks," *News from Indian Country: The Nations Native Journal*, vol. 10, no. 23 (Mid-December 1996), 6A.

40. Testimony of the author who attended the "Gila River Indian Community 2012 Inauguration: A New Generation for the People," January 7, 2012.

41. Roberto A. Jackson, "Agreement Will Bring Outlets to Wild Horse Pass," *Gila River Indian News*, vol. 15, no. 2 (February 2012), 8.

42. Principle Chief George Tiger, Inaugural Address, "Muscogee (Creek) Nation Inaugural Ceremonies," January 7, 2012, in author's personal collection.

43. Post-1960s Creek progress is in Donald L. Fixico, "The Muscogee Creeks: A Nativistic People," in Arrell M. Gibson, ed., *Between Two Worlds, the Survival of Twentieth Century Indians* (Oklahoma City: Oklahoma Historical Society, 1986), 30–43.

44. "Compulsive Gambling Council to Make Pitch," *South Bend Tribune*, November 25, 1996, B7.

45. "Experts: Be Strict Regulating Casinos," *South Bend Tribune*, November 26, 1996, B5.

46. Carolin Vesely, "Poplar's Prairie of Dreams," in *Montana's Indians: Gambling on Gaming* (Billings: University of Montana, ca. 1993), 30–31.

47. Ibid.

48. Covington, *Seminoles of Florida*, 255.

49. "Cherokee Nation Adopts Act; Ready for Class III Gaming," *Cherokee Advocate* (Tahlequah, OK), vol. 20, no. 1 (January 1996).

50. Mark Leibovich, "Abramoff, from Prison to a Pizzeria Job," *New York Times*, June 23, 2010; Jean Marbella, "Jack Abramoff's New Job: Selling Pizza, Not Influence," *Baltimore Sun*, June 22, 2010.

51. National Indian Gaming Commission, "List and Location of Tribal Gaming Operations," http://www.nigc.gov/Reading_Room/List_and_Location_of_Tribal_Gaming_Operations.aspx, accessed June 10, 2011.

Chapter 8

1. Robert E. Bieder, "The Representations of Indian Bodies in Nineteenth-Century American Anthropology," *American Indian Quarterly*, vol. 20, no. 2 (Spring 1996), 169.

2. Ibid., 174.

3. Roger C. Echo-Hawk and Walter R. Echo-Hawk, *Battlefields and Burial Grounds: The Indian Struggle to Protect Ancestral Graves in the United States* (Minneapolis: Lerner, 1994), 26.

4. Ibid., 26–30.

5. Ibid.

6. Thomas H. Leforge, *Memoirs of a White Crow Indian (Thomas H. LeForge) as Told by Thomas Marquis* (New York: Century, 1928), 88.

7. Antiquities Act, P.L. 59-209, June 8, 1906, 34 Stat. 225.

8. Jeanne Rogers, *Standing Witness: Devil's Tower National Monument: A History* (Washington, DC: National Park Service, 2007), 1–9.

9. Thomas B. Marquis, *Wooden Leg: A Warrior Who Fought Custer* (Lincoln: University of Nebraska Press, 1965), 54–55.

10. Leforge, *Memoirs of a White Crow Indian*, 88.

11. Marquis, *Wooden Leg*, 54.

12. Alfonso Ortiz, *The Tewa World: Space, Time, Being and Becoming in a Pueblo Society* (Chicago: University of Chicago Press, 1969), 13–28.

13. Ibid.

14. Somewhat similar is Homi Bhabba's Third Space of cultural hybridity. Bhabha, *The Location of Culture* (New York: Routledge, 1994), 53–56.

15. Charles H. Coe, *Red Patriots: The Story of the Seminoles* (Gainesville: University Press of Florida, 1974), originally published 1898, 110–111.

16. Ibid., 113.

17. Jeffrey Kluger, "The Legal Battle: Archaeology: Who Should Own the Bones?" *Time Magazine*, March 5, 2006, 2.

18. Norman Guardipee, "Mending the Broken Circle," in E. K. Caldwell, ed., *Dreaming the Dawn: Conversations with Native Artists and Activists* (Lincoln: University of Nebraska Press, 1999), 28.

19. James Mencarelli and Steven Severin, *Protest 3: Red, Black, Brown Experience in America* (Grand Rapids, MI: William B. Eerdmans, 1975), 150–151.

20. David E. Jones, *Sanapia: Comanche Medicine Woman* (Prospect Heights, IL: Waveland Press, 1974 [1972]), 15–34.

21. Black Elk (1933), quoted in Norbert S. Hill, Jr., ed., *Words of Power: Voices from Indian America* (Golden, CO: Fulcrum, 1994), xi.

22. John Neihardt, *Black Elk Speaks: Being the Life Story of a Holy Man of the Oglala Sioux* (Lincoln: University of Nebraska Press, 1961), 36.

23. Indian Boundary Markers Act, P.L. 86-634, July 12, 1960, 74 Stat. 469.

24. National Historic Preservation Act, P.L. 89-665, October 15, 1966, 80 Stat. 915 amended as P.L. 102-575, October 30, 1992, 16 U.S.C. 470a(d) "Establish Program and Regulations to Assist Indian Tribes.".

25. Donald L. Fixico, *Bureau of Indian Affairs* (Westport, CT: Greenwood Press, 2012), 137–138.

26. Quoted in Duane Champagne, ed., *The Native North American Almanac: A Reference Work on Native North Americans in the United States and Canada* (Detroit, MI: Gales Research, 1994), 573.

27. John Reyna, governor of Taos Indian Pueblo, letter to President Richard Nixon, August 14, 1971, box IN-2, folder 10/1/71–12/31/71, White House Central Files, Richard Nixon Presidential Materials Project, College Park, MD.

28. Leo W. Vocu, NCAI executive director, to President Richard Nixon, letter, September 28, 1971, IN-Indian Affairs, box 6, folder General IN 10/1/71–12/21/71, ibid.

29. James White, president of Determination of Rights and Unity for Menominee Shareholders, to all members of the Senate and House Committees on Interior and Insular Affairs, Memorandum, November 24, 1971, part 2, series 3, box 10, folder 12, Sam Steiger Papers, Special Collections, Northern Arizona University Library, Flagstaff.

30. Roberta Ulrich, *American Indian Nations from Termination to Restoration* (Lincoln: University of Nebraska Press, 2010), 247.

31. John Bordridge, Jr., president of the Central Council of Tlingit and Haida Indians of Alaska, to Congressman Sam Steiger, January 6, 1972, part 2, series 3, box 18, folder 31, Steiger Papers.

32. "Yakima" was later changed back to its original spelling of Yakama. "Annual Message to the Congress on the State of the Union," January 30, 1974, in *Public Papers of the Presidents of the United States: Richard Nixon 1974* (Washington, DC: U.S. Government Printing Office, 1975), 75.

33. "Statement Supporting Legislation to Enlarge the Havasupai Indian Reservation," May 3, 1974, in ibid., 410.

34. Beverly Crum (Shoshone), interviewed by S.I. Myers, October 29, 1975, Salt Lake City, UT, no. 92, p. 7, NYTOHP.

35. Donald L. Fixico, *The American Indian Mind in a Linear World: American Indian Studies and Traditional Knowledge* (New York: Routledge, 2003), 3, 11.

36. Ed McGaa, *Native Wisdom: Perceptions of the Natural Way* (Minneapolis: Four Directions, 1995), 29.

37. In his usage of culture, Alfonso Ortiz agreed with Clifford Geertz's emphasis of symbols having meanings that provided an order of culture for people. Clifford Geertz, *The Interpretation of Cultures* (New York: Basic, 1973), 33–86.

38. Archaeological Resources Protection Act, P.L. 96-95, October 31, 1979, 93 Stat. 721.

39. American Indian Religious Freedom Act, P.L. 95-341, August 11, 1978, 92 Stat. 46.

40. Archeological Resources Protection Act, P.L. 96-95, October 31, 1979, 93 Stat. 721.

41. Statement by Lakota Chief Matthew King, ca, 1970, in Harvey Arden, compiler and editor, *Noble Red Man: Lakota Wisdomkeeper* (Hillsboro, OR: Beyond Words Publishing, Inc., 1994), 47.

42. Champagne, *Native North American Almanac*, 573.

43. In the same year of the actions by the Smithsonian, New York State agreed to return twelve wampum belts, some of which had been in the state's possession since the late 1800s, to the Onondaga Nation, which had actively sought their return since the 1950s. Ibid.

44. National Museum of the American Indian Act, 101 P.L. 101-185, November 28, 1989, 103 Stat. 1336.

45. Indian Environmental Regulatory Enhancement Act, P.L. 101-408, October 4, 1990, 104 Stat. 883.

46. Native American Languages Act, P.L. 101-477. October 30, 1990, 104 Stat. 1153.

47. Anthropologist Frank Cushing worked among the Zuni communities. For information on the Zuni, see Cushing, *Zuni Folk Tales* (Tucson: University of Arizona Press, 1986); Cushing, *The Mythic World of the Zuni* (Albuquerque: University of New Mexico Press, 1988); and Cushing, *Zuni Fetishes* (Flagstaff, AZ: K.C. Publications, 1966).

48. T. J. Ferguson, "The Repatriation of AHAYA: DA Zuni War Gods; An Interview with the Zuni Tribal Council on April 25, 1990," *Museum Anthropology*, vol. 14, no. 2 (May 1990), 7–14; "Zuni God Repatriated," Zuni Tribal Council Press Release, *Museum Anthropology*, vol. 15, no. 3 (August 1991), 28.

49. Native American Graves Protection and Repatriation Act, P.L. 101-601, November 16, 1990, 104 Stat. 3048.

50. Indian Arts and Crafts Act, P.L. 101-644, November 29, 1990, 104 Stat. 4662.

51. "President William Jefferson Clinton Tribal Leaders Event," April 29, 1994, Carol Rosco subject file, box 15, folder 5, William Clinton Presidential Library, Little Rock, AR.

52. Sacred Land Film Project, "Mauna Kea, Kaho'olawe, Hawaii," http://www.sacredland.org/endangered_sites_pages/mauna/kea.html, accessed February 8, 2008.

53. Lisa Jones, "Four-Acres Return to Karuk Tribe," *High Country News*, March 4, 1996, http://www.hcn.org/servlets/hcn.Article?article_id=1679, accessed February 8, 2008.

54. Executive Order 13007, "Executive Orders Disposition Tables: William J. Clinton—1996," National Archives, http://www.archives.gov/federal-register/executive-orders/1996.html. See also Executive Order 13007, *American Indian History Online*, http://www.fofweb.com.ezproxy1.lib.asu.edu/activelink2.asp?ItimID=WE43&iPin=ind5802&SingleRecord=True, accessed February 19, 2008.

55. See Kathleen A. Fine-Dare, *Grave Injustice: The American Indian Repatriation Movement and NAGPRA* (Lincoln: University of Nebraska Press, 2002), and David Hurst Thomas, *Skull Wars: Kennewick Man: Archaeology and the Battle for Native American Identity* (New York: Basic Books, 2000).

56. "Remarks of Kevin Gover, Assistant Secretary-Indian Affairs, Department of the Interior at the Ceremony Acknowledging the 175th Anniversary of the Establishing of the Bureau of Indian Affairs" (National Apology for the Bureau of Indian Affairs), September 8, 2000, Clinton Administration History Project, box 13, folder 2, William Clinton Presidential Library, Little Rock, AR.

57. Judge Johnson ruled in favor of a historic preservation plan that protects the Bighorn Medicine Wheel and Medicine Mountain in Wyoming—though not returned, the site is allowed to be used for traditional cultural activities by Indian tribes. Sacred Land Film Project, "Medicine Wheel, Wyoming," http://www.sacredland.org/historical_sites_pp./medicine_wheel.html, accessed February 8, 2008.

58. "Sand Creek Massacre National Historic Site Study Act," P.L. 105-243, October 6, 1998, 112 Stat. 1579.

59. Indian Burial and Sacred Grounds Watch, "Domtar Gives Island to Passamaquoddies—Returned Land Includes Tribal Burial Ground," May 14, 2002, http://www.ibsgwatch.imagedjinn.com/learn/2002514ny.htm, accessed February 8, 2008.

60. Rainbow Bridge, Utah, is partially protected as a national monument, but tourism stills overrides return to tribes "Rainbow Bridge, Utah," http://www.sacredland.org/endangered_sites_pp./rainbow_bridge.html, accessed February 8, 2008.

61. "Indian Island," *North Coast Journal*, July 1, 2004, http://www.northcoastjournal.com/070104/cover0701.html, accessed February 8, 2008.

62. Matthew S. Makley and Michael J. Makley, *Cave Rock: Climbers, Courts, and a Washoe Indian Sacred Place* (Reno: University of Nevada Press, 2010), 49–57, 76–79.

63. Colin McCandless, "Ancient Mound and Town Site Return to the Cherokee." Franklin Press, October 27, 2006. http://www.thefranklinpress.com/articles//2006/10/31/news/04news.txt. accessed April 19, 2013.

Bibliography

Abbreviations

NYTOHP: New York Times Oral History Program, Listening to Indians, Labriola National American Indian Data Center, Carl Hayden Library, Arizona State University, Tempe.
USDIOHC: University of South Dakota Indian Oral History Collection, microfiche, Labriola National American Indian Data Center, Carl Hayden Library, Arizona State University, Tempe.

Primary Sources

Reports, Papers, and Testimonies

"Alphabetical List of Creek Indians by Blood and Creek Freedmen." Western History Collections. University of Oklahoma, Norman.
"Annual Message to the Congress on the State of the Union." January 30, 1974. *Public Papers of the Presidents of the United States: Richard Nixon 1974.* Washington, DC. U.S. Government Printing Office. 1975. 56–77.
Brad Patterson Papers. Gerald R. Ford Presidential Library. Ann Arbor, MI.
Carol Rosco Subject File. William Clinton Presidential Library. Little Rock, AR.
Clinton Administration History Project. William Clinton Presidential Library. Little Rock, AR.
"Courts of Indian Offenses." August 27, 1892. House Executive Document, no. 1, 52d Cong., 2d sess., ser. 3088, pp. 28–31.
"Energy Conservation and Production Revenue Act of 1976: Report to Accompany H.R. 6860." U.S. Senate Committee on Finance, 94th Congress, 2d sess., Senate rep. 94-1181.

FBI Files of AIM and Wounded Knee. Reel 2, file 100-462483, vol. 5, microfilm. University of Minnesota Library. Minneapolis, MN.

"The Forgotten American." Special Message to Congress, March 6, 1968. In *Public Papers of the Presidents of the United States: Lyndon B. Johnson, 1968–69.* Ann Arbor, MI. University of Michigan Library. 2005. Vol. 1: 336–37, 343–344.

Fred Harris Papers. Carl Albert Congressional Research and Studies Center, Congressional Archives. University of Oklahoma, Norman.

Harjo, Chitto. Testimony of November 23, 1906, Elks Lodge, Tulsa, Oklahoma Territory. Western History Collections. University of Oklahoma, Norman.

Henry Jackson Papers. Archives Division, Allen Library. University of Washington, Seattle.

Hoffman, Roy. Report on Chitto Harjo and Snake Rebellion, August 11, 1909. Fred Barde Collection, Chitto Harjo file, box 11. Oklahoma Historical Society. Oklahoma City.

Indian Affairs Collection. Ronald Reagan Presidential Library. Simi Valley, CA.

Indian Rights Association Papers. Microfilm. Marquette University Library. Milwaukee, WI.

John Collier Papers. Microfilm and microfiche. Marquette University Library. Milwaukee, WI.

Leonard Garment Papers. Richard Nixon Presidential Materials Project. College Park, MD.

Meriam, Lewis, et al. *The Problem of Indian Administration: A Report of a Survey Made at the Request of Honorable Hubert Work, Secretary of the Interior, and Submitted to Him, February 21, 1928.* Baltimore. Johns Hopkins Press. 1928.

Miller, Michael, and Laura Waterman Wittstock. *American Indian Alcoholism in St. Paul: A Needs Assessment Conducted Jointly by the Community Planning Organization and the Juel Fairbanks Aftercare Residence.* Minneapolis. Center for Urban and Regional Affairs, University of Minnesota and the Community Planning Organization. 1982.

"National Indian Gaming Commission Report to Congress." December 31, 1991. White House Office of Records Management, subject file "Indians," box 3, folder 296253-301061. George Bush Presidential Library. College Station, TX.

Norman E. Ross Papers. Gerald Ford Presidential Library. Ann Arbor, MI.

Pierce, Jim, Council of Energy Resource Tribes chief administrative officer. Report in *CERT First Decade Report for 1985.* Author's collection.

"Report on Urban and Rural Non-reservation Indians, Task Force Eight: Urban and Rural, Non-reservation Indian." In *Final Report to the American Indian Policy Review Commission.* Washington, DC. U.S. Government Printing Office. 1976.

Richard Nixon Presidential Materials Project. White House Central Files. College Park, MD.

Sam Steiger Papers. Special Collections, Northern Arizona University Library. Flagstaff, AZ.

"Statement Supporting Legislation to Enlarge the Havasupai Indian Reservation." May 3, 1974. In *Public Papers of the President of the United States: Richard Nixon 1974.* Washington, DC. U.S. Government Printing Office. 1975. 410–411.

Swanton, John R. "The Social History and Usages of the Creek Confederacy." In *Forth-Second Annual Report of the Bureau of American Ethnology.* Washington, DC. U.S. Government Printing Office. 1928: 133–156.

Theodore Marrs Papers. Gerald R. Ford Presidential Library. Ann Arbor, MI.

Tiger, George, Principle Chief. Inaugural Address. "Muscogee (Creek) Nation Inaugural Ceremonies." January 7, 2012. Special Issue, *Dreamcatcher Magazine*, 2012, pp. 20–21. Author's personal collection.

"Treaty with the Creeks, 1832." March 24, 1832. In Charles J. Kappler, comp. and ed. *Indian Treaties 1778–1883*. New York. Interland. 1975.

"Treaty with the Creeks, 1833." February 14, 1833. In Charles J. Kappler, comp. and ed. *Indian Treaties 1778–1883*. New York. Interland. 1975. 388–391.

"Treaty with the Sioux—Brule, Oglala, Miniconjou, Yanktonai, Hunkpapa, Blackfeet, Cuthead, Two Kettle, Sana Arcs, and Santee and Arapaho" (Fort Laramie). April 29, 1868. In Charles J. Kappler, comp. and ed. *Indian Treaties 1778–1883*. New York. Interland. 1975. 998–1003.

U.S. Congress, Senate, discussion on the success of the Relocation Program. 85th Cong., 1st sess., March 14, 1957. *Congressional Record* 103: 3643.

Vesely, Caroline. "Poplar's Prairie of Dreams." In *Montana's Indians Gambling on Gaming*. Billings. University of Montana. Ca. 1993. 30–31.

Woods, Richard, and Arthur M. Harkins, "An Examination of the 1968–1969 Urban Indian Hearings Held by the National Council on Indian Opportunity. Part V: Multiple Problems of Adaptation." Training Center for Community Programs, in coordination with the Office of Community Programs, Center for Urban and Region Affairs. Minneapolis. University of Minnesota. October 1971. 28.

Acts and Resolutions

"An Act Making Appropriations for the Current and Contingent Expenses of the Indian Department," March 3, 1871, 16 Stat. 566.

Adult Indian Vocational Training Act, P.L. 959, August 3, 1956, 70 Stat. 986.

Alaska Native Reorganization Act, May 1, 1936 U.S. Statutes At Large, 49, pt. 1:1250–51.

American Indian Religious Freedom Act, P.L. 95-341, August 11, 1978, 92 Stat. 46.

Antiquities Act, P.L. 59-209, June 8, 1906, 34 Stat. 225.

Archaeological Resources Protection Act, P.L. 96-95, October 31, 1979, 93 Stat. 721.

"Citizenship for World War I Veterans," November 6, 1919, 41 Stat. 350.

Criminal and Civil Jurisdiction Act, P.L. 280, August 15, 1953, 67 Stat. 588.

Energy Policy Act, P.L. 109-58, July 29, 2005, 119 Stat. 594.

Federal Oil and Gas Royalty Management Act, P.L. 97-451, January 12, 1982, 96 Stat. 2457.

General Allotment Act (Dawes Allotment Act), February 8, 1887, 24 Stat. 388.

"General Allotment Amendment," February 28, 1891, 26 Stat. 794.

House Concurrent Resolution 108, August 1, 1953, 67 Stat. B132.

Indian Arts and Crafts Act, P.L. 101-644, November 29, 1990, 104 Stat. 4662.

Indian Arts and Crafts Board Act, August 27, 1935, 49 Stat. 891.

Indian Boundary Markers Act, P.L. 86-634, July 12, 1960, 74 Stat. 469.

Indian Civil Rights Act, P.L. 99-570, October 27, 1986, 100 Stat. 3207.

Indian Environmental Regulatory Enhancement Act, P.L. 101-408, October 4, 1990, 104 Stat. 883.

Indian Gaming Regulatory Act, P.L. 100-497, October 17, 1988, 102 Stat. 2467.

Indian Housing Act, P.L. 100-358, June 29, 1988, 102 Stat. 676.

Indian Irrigation Act, January 26, 1933, 47 Stat. 776.
Indian Law Enforcement Reform Act, P.L. 101-379, August 18, 1990, 104 Stat. 473.
Indian Mineral Development Act, P.L. 97-382, December 22, 1982, 96 Stat. 1938.
Indian Reorganization Act, June 18, 1934, 48 Stat. 984.
Indian Self-Determination and Education Assistance Act, P.L. 93-68, January 4, 1975, 88 Stat. 2203.
Indian Timber Contracts Act, March 4, 1933, U.S. Statutes At Large, 47 pt. 1:1568–69.
Indian Tribal Governmental Tax Status Act, P.L. 97-473, January 14, 1983, 97 Stat. 2607.
Johnson-O'Malley Act, April 16, 1934, 48 Stat. 596.
Leavitt Act, July 2, 1932, 47 Stat. 564.
National Energy Conservation Policy Act, P.L. 95-619, November 9, 1978, 92 Stat. 3206.
National Historic Preservation Act, P.L. 89-665, October 15, 1966, 80 Stat. 915. Amendment, P.L. 102-575, October 30, 1992, 16 U.S.C. 470a(d) "Establish Program and Regulations to Assist Indian Tribes."
National Indian Forest Resources Management Act, P.L. 101-630, November 28, 1990, 104 Stat. 4532.
National Museum of the American Indian Act, P.L. 101-185, November 28, 1989, 103 Stat. 1336.
Native American Graves Protection and Repatriation Act, P.L. 101-601, November 16, 1990, 104 Stat. 3048.
Native American Languages Act, P.L. 101-477, October 30, 1990, 104 Stat. 1153.
Natural Gas Policy Act, P.L. 95-621, November 8, 1978, 92 Stat. 3350.
Nelson Act, January 4, 1889, 25 Stat. 642.
Oklahoma Indian Welfare Act, June 26, 1936, 49 Stat. 1967.
Sand Creek Massacre National Historic Site Study Act, P.L. 105-243, October 6, 1998, 112 Stat. 1579.
Sioux Act of 1889, March 2, 1889, 25 Stat. 888.
Surface Mining Control and Reclamation Act, P.L. 95-87, August 3, 1977, 91 Stat. 445.
Wheeler-Howard Act, June 18, 1934, 48 Stat. 984.

Court Decisions

California v. Cabazon Band of Mission Indians et al., 480 U.S. 202 (1987) 202.
Lone Wolf v. Hitchcock, 187 U.S. 553, 23 S.Ct. 216, 47 L.Ed. 299.
Seminole Tribe of Florida v. Butterworth, 658 F.2d 310 (1981) 246.

Books

Abourezk, James G. *Advise and Dissent: Memoirs of South Dakota and the U.S. Senate.* Chicago: Lawrence Hill, 1989.
Adams, David Wallace. *Education for Extinction: American Indians and the Boarding School Experience 1875–1928.* Lawrence: University Press of Kansas, 1995.
Alvord, Lori Arviso, and Elizabeth Cohen Van Pelt. *The Scalpel and the Silver Bear.* New York: Bantam, 1999.

Ambler, Marjane. *Breaking the Iron Bonds: Indian Control of Energy Development.* Lawrence: University Press of Kansas, 1990.

Anderson, Gary Clayton. *Little Crow: Spokesman for the Sioux.* St. Paul: Minnesota Historical Society, 1986.

Arden, Harvey. compiler and editor, *Noble Red Man: Lakota Wisdomkeeper.* Hillsboro, Oregon: Beyond Words Publishing, Inc., 1994.

Axford, Roger W., ed. *Native Americans: 23 Indian Biographies.* Indiana, PA: A. G. Halldin, 1980.

Banks, Dennis. *Ojibwa Warrior: Dennis Banks and the Rise of the American Indian Movement.* With Richard Erodes. Norman: University of Oklahoma Press, 2004.

Bauer, William J., Jr. *We Were All like Migrant Workers Here: Work, Community, and Memory on California's Round Valley Reservation, 1850–1941.* Chapel Hill: University of North Carolina Press, 2009.

Berger, Thomas R. *Village Journey: The Report of the Alaska Native Review Commission.* New York: Hill and Wang, 1985.

Berthrong, Donald J. *The Cheyenne and Arapaho Ordeal: Reservation and Agency Life in the Indian Territory, 1875–1907.* Norman: University of Oklahoma Press, 1976.

Bessel, Richard, and Claudia B. Haake, eds. *Removing Peoples: Forced Removal in the Modern World.* Oxford: Oxford University Press, 2009.

Bhabha, Homi. *The Location of Culture.* New York: Routledge, 1994.

Borneman, Walter R. *Rival Rails: The Race to Build America's Greatest Transcontinental Railroad.* New York: Random House, 2010.

Brant, Charles S., ed. *Jim Whitewolf: The Life of a Kiowa Apache Indian.* New York: Dover, 1969.

Brown, Dee. *Bury My Heart at Wounded Knee: An Indian History of the American West.* New York: Henry Holt, 1970.

Brown, Joseph Epes, ed. *The Sacred Pipe: Black Elk's Account of the Seven Rites of the Oglala Sioux.* New York: Penguin, 1971 [1953].

Carlson, Leonard A. *Indians, Bureaucrats, and Land: The Dawes Act and the Decline of Indian Farming.* Westport, CT: Greenwood Press, 1981.

Cash, Joseph, and Herbert Hoover, eds. *To Be an Indian: An Oral History.* New York: Holt, Rinehart and Winston, 1971.

Cattelino, Jessica. *High Stakes: Florida Seminole Gaming and Sovereignty.* Durham, NC: Duke University Press, 2008.

Champagne, Duane, ed. *The Native North American Almanac: A Reference Work on Native North Americans in the United States and Canada.* Detroit, MI: Gales Research, 1994.

Chandler, David. *Empire in Denial: The Politics of State-building.* London: Pluto Press, 2006.

Clark, Blue. *Lone Wolf v Hitchcock: Treaty Rights and Indian Law at the End of the Nineteenth Century.* Lincoln: University of Nebraska Press, 1994.

Clinton, Robert, Nell Jessup Newton, and Monroe Price. *American Indian Law: Cases and Materials.* 3rd ed. Charlottesville, VA: Michie, 1991.

Cobb, Daniel M. *Native Activism in Cold War America: The Struggle for Sovereignty.* Lawrence: University Press of Kansas, 2008.

Cody, Perry, and Collin Perry. *Iron Eyes: My Life as a Hollywood Indian.* New York: Books Sales, 1984.

Coe, Charles H. *Red Patriots: The Story of the Seminoles.* Gainesville: University Press of Florida, 1974.

Coffer, William E. *Sipapu: The Story of the Indians of Arizona and New Mexico.* New York: Van Nostrand Reinhold, 1982.

Collier, John. *Indians of the Americas: The Long Hope.* New York: New American Library, 1947.

Courlander, Harold. *The Fourth World of the Hopis: The Epic Story of the Hopi Indians as Preserved in Their Legends and Traditions.* Albuquerque: University of New Mexico Press, 1971.

Covington, James W. *The Seminoles of Florida.* Gainesville: University Press of Florida, 1993.

Cowger, Thomas W. *The National Congress of American Indians: The Founding Years.* Lincoln: University of Nebraska Press, 1999.

Crapanzano, Vincent. *The Fifth World of Forester Bennett: Portrait of a Navajo.* Lincoln: University of Nebraska Press, 2003 [1972].

Crawford, Bill. *All American: The Rise and Fall of Jim Thorpe.* Hoboken, NJ: Wiley and Sons, 2005.

Creelman, James. *On the Great Highway: The Wanderings and Adventures of a Special Correspondent.* Boston: Lothrop, 1901.

Crosby, Alfred W., Jr. *The Columbia Exchange: Biological and Cultural Consequences of 1492.* Westport, CT: Greenwood Press, 1972.

Cushing, Frank. *Zuni Fetishes.* Flagstaff, AZ: K. C. Publications, 1966.

Cushing, Frank. *Zuni Folk Tales.* Tucson: University of Arizona Press, 1986.

Cushing, Frank. *The Mythic World of the Zuni.* Albuquerque: University of New Mexico Press, 1988.

Daily, David W. *Battle for the BIA: G.E.E. Lindquist and the Missionary Crusade against John Collier.* Tucson: University of Arizona Press, 2002.

Dary, David. *Buffalo Book: The Full Saga of the American Animal.* Athens, OH: Swallow Press, 1989 [1974].

Debo, Angie. *The Road to Disappearance: A History of the Creek Indians.* Norman: University of Oklahoma Press, 1941.

Debo, Angie. *A History of the Indians of the United States.* Norman: University of Oklahoma Press, 1970.

Debo, Angie. *And Still the Waters Run: The Betrayal of the Five Civilized Tribes.* Princeton, NJ: Princeton University Press, 1973 [1968].

Deloria, Vine, Jr., and Clifford Lytle. *The Nations Within: The Past and Future of American Indian Sovereignty.* New York: Pantheon, 1984.

Diedrich, Mark, ed. *Sitting Bull: The Collected Speeches.* Rochester, MN: Coyote, 1998.

Dippie, Brian W. *The Vanishing American: White Attitudes and U.S. Indian Policy.* Lawrence: University Press of Kansas, 1982.

Dobyns, Henry. *Their Number Become Thinned: Native American Population Dynamics in Eastern North America.* Knoxville: University of Tennessee Press, 1983.

Dozier, Edward P. *The Hopi-Tewa of Arizona.* Berkeley: University of California Press, 1954.

Dozier, Edward P. *The Pueblo Indians of North America.* New York: Holt, Rinehart and Winston, 1970.

Dudley, William, ed. *Native Americans: Opposing Viewpoints.* San Diego: Greenhaven Press, 1998.

Eastman, Charles A. *From the Deep Woods to Civilization: Chapter in the Autobiography of an Indian*. Lincoln: University of Nebraska Press, 1936 [1916].

Echo-Hawk, Roger C., and Walter R. Echo-Hawk. *Battlefields and Burial Grounds: The Indian Struggle to Protect Ancestral Graves in the United States*. Minneapolis: Lerner, 1994.

Eisler, Kim Isaac. *Revenge of the Pequots: How a Small Native American Tribe Created the World's Most Profitable Casino*. New York: Simon and Schuster, 2001.

Fahey, John. *The Flathead Indians*. Norman: University of Oklahoma Press, 1974.

Fikes, Jay C. *Reuben Snake, Your Humble Servant Indian Visionary and Activist*. Santa Fe, NM: Clear Light, 1996.

Fine-Dare, Kathleen A. *Grave Injustice: The American Indian Repatriation Movement and NAGPRA*. Lincoln: University of Nebraska Press, 2002.

Fiske, Frank B. *Life and Death of Sitting Bull*. Fort Yates, ND: Pioneer-Arrow Print, 1933.

Fixico, Donald L. *Termination and Relocation: Federal Indian Policy, 1945–1960*. Albuquerque: University of New Mexico Press, 1986.

Fixico, Donald L. *The Urban Indian Experience in America*. Albuquerque: University of New Mexico Press, 2000.

Fixico, Donald L. *The American Indian Mind in a Linear World: American Indian Studies and Traditional Knowledge*. New York: Routledge, 2003.

Fixico, Donald L. *Bureau of Indian Affairs*. Westport, CT: Greenwood Press, 2012.

Fixico, Donald L. *The Invasion of Indian Country: American Capitalism and Tribal Natural Resources*. 2nd ed. Boulder: University Press of Colorado, 2012.

Flores, Dan. *The Natural West: Environmental History in the Great Plains and Rocky Mountains*. Norman: University of Oklahoma Press, 2001.

Fortune Eagle, Adam. *Alcatraz! Alcatraz! The Indian Occupation of 1969–1971*. Berkeley: Heyday, 1992.

Fortunate Eagle, Adam. *Heart of the Rock: The Indian Invasion of Alcatraz*. Norman: University of Oklahoma Press, 2002.

Frantz, Klaus. *Indian Reservations in the United States*. Chicago: University of Chicago Press, 1999.

Garland, Hamlin. *The Book of the American Indian*. New York: Harper and Brothers, 1923.

Geertz, Clifford. *The Interpretation of Cultures*. New York: Basic, 1973.

Gelo, Daniel J. *Indians of the Great Plains*. Boston: Pearson, 2012.

Gibson, Arrell M. *Oklahoma: A History of Five Centuries*. Norman: Harlow, 1965.

Gill, Sam D. *Mother Earth: An American Story*. Chicago: University of Chicago Press, 1987.

Glasscock, C.B. *Then Came Oil: The Story of the Last Frontier*. Indianapolis, IN: Bobbs-Merrill, 1938.

Hagan, William T. *Indian Police and Judges: Experiment in Acculturation and Control*. New Haven, CT: Yale University Press, 1966.

Hall, Marion. *American Indians of Minneapolis—an Update*. Minneapolis: League of Women's Voters of Minneapolis, 1984.

Hatch, Thom. *Black Kettle: The Cheyenne Chief Who Sought Peace but Found War*. Hoboken, NJ: John Wiley and Sons, 2004.

Hill, Norbert S., Jr., ed. *Words of Power: Voices from Indian America*. Golden, CO: Fulcrum, 1994.

Hittman, Michael. *Wovoka and the Ghost Dance.* Edited by Don Lynch. Lincoln: University of Nebraska Press, 1997.

Hodge, Nathan. *Armed Humanitarians: The Rise of Nation Builders.* New York: Bloomsbury, 2011.

Holm, Tom. *Strong Hearts Wounded Souls: Native American Veterans of the Vietnam War.* Austin: University of Texas Press, 1996.

Hoxie, Frederick. *A Final Promise: The Campaign to Assimilate the Indians, 1880–1920.* Lincoln: University of Nebraska Press, 1984.

Hughes, J. Donald. *American Indian Ecology.* El Paso: Texas Western Press, 1983.

Hungry Wolf, Beverly. *The Ways of My Grandmothers.* New York: Quill, 1982.

Hurt, R. Douglas. *The Big Empty: The Great Plains in the Twentieth Century.* Tucson: University of Arizona Press, 2011.

Hurtado, Albert L. *Indian Survival on the California Frontier.* New Haven, CT: Yale University Press, 1988.

Iverson, Peter. *"We Are Still Here": American Indians in the Twentieth Century.* Wheeling, IL: Harland Davidson, 1998.

Jackson, Helen Hunt. *A Century of Dishonor: A Sketch of the U.S. Government's Dealings with Some of the Indian Tribes.* Boston: Roberts Brothers, 1881.

Jacobs, Margaret D. *White Mother to a Dark Race: Settler Colonialism, Maternalism, and the Removal of Indigenous Children in the American West and Australia, 1880–1940.* Lincoln: University of Nebraska Press, 2009.

Jenkins, Sally. *The Real All Americans: The Team That Changed a Game, a People, a Nation.* New York: Doubleday, 2007.

Johnson, Troy R. *The Occupation of Alcatraz Island: Indian Self-Determination and the Rise of Indian Activism.* Urbana: University of Illinois Press, 1996.

Jones, David E. *Sanapia: Comanche Medicine Woman.* Prospect Heights, IL: Waveland Press, 1974 [1972].

Jones, David S. *Rationalizing Epidemics: Meanings and Uses of American Indian Mortality since 1600.* Cambridge, MA: Harvard University Press, 2004.

Kroeber, Theodore. *Ishi in Two Worlds: A Biography of the Last Wild Indian in North America.* Berkeley: University of California Press, 1961.

Lane, Ambrose I., Sr. *Return of the Buffalo: The Story Behind America's Indian Gaming Explosion.* Westport, CT: Bergin and Garvey, 1995.

Lawrence, Adrea. *Lessons from an Indian Day School: Negotiating Colonization in Northern New Mexico, 1902–1907.* Lawrence: University Press of Kansas, 2011.

La Flesche, Francis. *The Middle Five: Indian Schoolboys of the Omaha Tribe.* Lincoln: University of Nebraska Press, 1978 [1900].

Lee, George P. *Silent Courage an Indian Story: The Autobiography of George P. Lee a Navajo.* Salt Lake City, UT: Deseret, 1987.

Lefebvre, Henri. *The Production of Space.* Oxford: Blackwell, 1991.

Leforge, Thomas H. *Memoirs of a White Crow Indian (Thomas H. LeForge) as Told by Thomas Marquis.* New York: Century, 1928.

Leupp, Francis E. *The Indian and His Problem.* New York: Scribner's Sons, 1910.

Lewis, Bonnie Sue. *Creating Christian Indians: Native Clergy in the Presbyterian Church.* Norman: University of Oklahoma Press, 2003.

Lewis, Thomas H. *The Medicine Men: Oglala Sioux Ceremony and Healing.* Lincoln: University of Nebraska Press, 1990.

Lomawaima, K. Tsianina. *They Called It Prairie Light: The Story of Chilocco Indian School.* Lincoln: University of Nebraska Press, 1994.

MacDonald, Peter. *The Last Warrior: Peter MacDonald and the Navajo Nation.* With Ted Schwarz. New York: Orbis, 1993.

Madigan, La Verne. *American Indian Relocation Program.* New York: Association on American Indian Affairs, 1956.

Makley, Matthew S., and Michael J. Makley. *Cave Rock: Climbers, Courts, and A Washoe Indian Sacred Place.* Reno: University of Nevada Press, 2010.

Mankiller, Wilma, and Michael Wallis, *Mankiller a Chief and Her People.* New York: St. Martin's Press, 1993.

Manypenny, George. *Our Indian Wards.* Cincinnati: Robert Clarke, 1880.

Maroukis, Thomas C. *The Peyote Road: Religious Freedom and the Native American Church.* Norman: University of Oklahoma Press, 2010.

Marquis, Thomas B. *Wooden Leg: A Warrior Who Fought Custer.* Lincoln: University of Nebraska Press, 1965.

Mason, W. Dale. *Indian Gaming: Tribal Sovereignty and American Politics.* Norman: University of Oklahoma Press, 2000.

McGaa, Ed. *Native Wisdom: Perceptions of the Natural Way.* Minneapolis: Four Directions, 1995.

McKee, Jesse O. *The Choctaw.* New York: Chelsea House, 1989.

Means, Russell, *Where White Men Fear to Tread: The Autobiography of Russell Means.* With Marvin J. Wolf. New York: St. Martin's Press, 1995.

Mencarelli, James, and Steven Severin. *Protest 3: Red, Black, Brown Experience in America.* Grand Rapids, MI: William B. Eerdmans, 1975.

Migdal, Joel S. *State in Society: Studying How States and Societies Transform and Constitute One Another.* Cambridge: Cambridge University Press, 2001.

Morgan, Lewis Henry. *Ancient Society.* London: Macmillan, 1877.

Moses, L.G. *Wild West Shows and the Images of American Indians 1883–1933.* Albuquerque: University of New Mexico Press, 1996.

Nabokov, Peter, ed. *Native American Testimony: A Chronicle of Indian-White Relations from Prophecy to the Present, 1492–1992.* New York: Penguin, 1992.

Neihardt, John. *Black Elk Speaks: Being the Life Story of a Holy Man of the Oglala Sioux.* Lincoln: University of Nebraska Press, 1961.

Oeffner, Barbara. *Champion of the Everglades: A Biography of Seminole Chief James Billie.* Palm Beach, FL: Cape Cod Writers, 1995.

Olson, James S., and Raymond Wilson. *Native Americans in the Twentieth Century.* Provo, UT: Brigham Young University Press, 1984.

Orsi, Richard J. *Sunset Limited: The Southern Pacific Railroad and the Development of the American West 1850–1930.* Berkeley: University of California Press, 2005.

Ortiz, Alfonso. *The Tewa World: Space, Time, Being and Becoming in a Pueblo Society.* Chicago: University of Chicago Press, 1969.

Otis, D.S. *The Dawes Act and the Allotment of Indian Lands.* Norman: University of Oklahoma Press, 1973.

Otis, Elwell S. *The Indian Question.* New York: Sheldon, 1878.

Parman, Donald. *Indians and the American West in the Twentieth Century.* Bloomington: Indiana University Press, 1994.

Perdue, Theda. *The Cherokee.* New York: Chelsea House, 1989.

Pfister, Joel. *The Yale Indian: The Education of Henry Roe Cloud*. Durham, NC: Duke University Press, 2009.

Philp, Kenneth R. *John Collier's Crusade for Reform, 1920–1954*. Tucson: University of Arizona Press, 1977.

Porterfield, Kay Marie, and Emory Dean Keoke. *American Indian Contributions to the World*. New York: Checkmark, 2003.

Powers-Beck, Jeffrey. *The American Indian Integration of Baseball*. Lincoln: University of Nebraska Press, 2004.

Pratt, Richard Henry. *Battlefield and Classroom: An Autobiography by Richard Henry Pratt*. Edited by Robert M. Utley. Norman: University of Oklahoma Press, 2003 [1964].

Prucha, Francis Paul. *The Great Father: The United States Government and the American Indian*, abr. ed. Lincoln: University of Nebraska Press, 1986 [1984].

Read, Peter. *The Stolen Generations: The Removal of Aboriginal Children in New South Wales 1883 to 1969*. 2nd ed. Sydney: New South Wales Department of Aboriginal Affairs, 1998.

Reichard, Gladys A. *Navaho Religion: A Study of Symbolism*. Princeton, NJ: Princeton University Press, 1974 [1950].

Reno, Philip. *Mother Earth, Father Sky, and Economic Development: Navajo Resources and Their Use*. Albuquerque: University of New Mexico Press, 1981.

Richter, Daniel. *Facing East from Indian Country: A Native History of Early America*. Cambridge, MA: Harvard University Press, 2001.

Robertson, Roland. *Rotting Face: Smallpox and the American Indian*. Caldwell, ID: Caxton Press, 2001.

Rogers, Jeanne. *Standing Witness: Devil's Tower National Monument: A History*. Washington, DC: National Park Service, 2007.

Rosenthal, Nicholas G. *Reimagining Indian Country: Native American Migration and Identity in Twentieth-Century Los Angeles*. Chapel Hill: University of North Carolina Press, 2012.

Rosier, Paul C. *Rebirth of the Blackfeet Nation, 1912–1954*. Lincoln: University of Nebraska Press, 2001.

Rosier, Paul C. *Native American Issues*. Westport, CT: Greenwood Press, 2003.

Samek, Hana. *The Blackfeet Confederacy 1880–1920: A Comparative Study of Canadian and U.S. Indian Policy*. Albuquerque: University of New Mexico Press, 1987.

Schrecker, Ellen. *Many Are the Crimes: McCarthyism in America*. Boston: Little, Brown, 1998.

Scott, James C. *The Moral Economy of the Peasant: Rebellion and Subsistence in Southeast Asia*. New Haven, CT: Yale University Press, 1976.

Sekaquaptewa, Helen. *Me and Mine: The Life Story of Helen Sekaquaptewa*. Tucson: University of Arizona Press, 1969.

Shepherd, Jeffrey P. *We Are an Indian Nation: A History of the Hualapai People*. Tucson: University of Arizona Press, 2010.

Shreve, Bradley G. *Red Power Rising: The National Indian Youth Council and the Origins of Native Activism*. Norman: University of Oklahoma Press, 2011.

Silko, Leslie. *Ceremony*. New York: New American Library, 1977.

Smith, Dean Howard. *Modern Tribal Development: Paths to Self-Sufficiency and Cultural Integrity in Indian Country*. Walnut Creek, CA: AltaMira Press, 2000.

Smith, Paul Chaat, and Robert Warrior. *Like a Hurricane: The Indian Movement from Alcatraz to Wounded Knee*. New York: New Press, 1996.

Smith, Sherry L. *Hippies, Indians, and the Fight for Red Power*. New York: Oxford University Press, 2012.

Spivak, Gayatri Chakravorty. *Nationalism and the Imagination*. London: Seagull, 2010.

Steiner, Stan. *The New Indians*. New York: Harper and Row, 1968.

Stillman, Deanne. *Mustang: The Sage of the Wild Horse in the American West*. New York: Houghton Mifflin, 2008.

Strickland, Rennard. *The Indians in Oklahoma*. Norman: University of Oklahoma Press, 1980.

Tapahonso, Luci. *Saanii Dahataal: The Women Are Singing*. Tucson: University of Arizona Press, 1993.

Tapahonso, Luci. *Blue Horses Rush In: Poems and Stories*. Tucson: University of Arizona Press, 1997.

Taylor, Graham D. *The New Deal and American Indian Tribalism: The Administration of the Indian Reorganization Act, 1934–35*. Lincoln: University of Nebraska Press, 1980.

Thomas, David Hurst. *Skull Wars: Kennewick Man: Archaeology and the Battle for Native American Identity*. New York: Basic, 2000.

Thorne, Tanis. *The World's Richest Indian: The Scandal over Jackson Barnett's Oil Fortune*. New York: Oxford University Press, 2005.

Tillman, Barrett. *Heroes: U.S. Army Medal of Honor Recipients*. New York: Penguin, 2006.

Tylor, Edward B. *Primitive Culture*. New York: J. P. Putnam's Sons, 1871.

Ulrich, Roberta. *American Indian Nations from Termination to Restoration, 1953–2006*. Lincoln: University of Nebraska Press, 2010.

Utley, Robert M. *The Lance and the Shield: The Life and Times of Sitting Bull*. New York: Ballantine, 1993.

Vaughan, Alden T. *New England Frontier: Puritan and Indians 1620–1675*. Boston: Little, Brown, 1965.

Vestal, Stanley. *New Sources of Indian History 1850–1891: The Ghost Dance, the Prairie Sioux, a Miscellany*. Norman: University of Oklahoma Press, 1934.

Vestal, Stanley. *Sitting Bull: Champion of the Sioux*. Norman: University of Oklahoma Press, 1957 [1932].

Vogel, Virgil J. *American Indian Medicine*. Norman: University of Oklahoma Press, 1970.

Waldman, Carl. *Atlas of the North American Indian*. New York: Facts on File, 1985.

Warren, Louis S. *Buffalo Bill's America*. New York: Random House, 2005.

Washburn, Wilcomb. *The Assault on Indian Tribalism: The General Allotment Law (Dawes Act) of 1887*. Philadelphia: J. B. Lippincott, 1975.

Webb, George W. *Chronological List of Engagements between the Regular Army of the United States and Various Tribes of Hostile Indians Which Occurred during the Years 1790–1895*. New York: AMS Press, 1976.

Weisiger, Martha. *Dreaming of Sheep in Navajo Country*. Seattle: University of Washington Press, 1999.

Wheeler, Robert W. *Jim Thorpe: World's Greatest Athlete*. Norman: University of Oklahoma Press, 1975.

White, Richard. *Railroaded: The Transcontinentals and the Making of Modern America.* New York: W. W. Norton, 2011.

Wilkins, David E. *American Indian Politics and the American Political System.* Lanham, MA: Rowman and Littlefield, 2007.

Wilkinson, Charles. *Messages from Frank's Landing: A Story of Salmon, Treaties, and the Indian Way.* Seattle: University of Washington Press, 2000.

Williams, John, and Howard L. Meredith. *Bacone Indian University: A History.* Oklahoma City: Western Heritage, 1980.

Wissler, Clark. *Red Man Reservations.* New York: Collier, 1971.

Witmer, Linda F. *The Indian Industrial School Carlisle, Pennsylvania 1879–1918.* Carlisle, PA: Cumberland Country Historical Society, 1993.

Work, L. Susan. *The Seminole Nation of Oklahoma: A Legal History.* Norman: University of Oklahoma Press, 2010.

Young Bear, Severt, and R.D. Theisz. *Standing in the Light: A Lakota Way of Seeing.* Lincoln: University of Nebraska Press, 1994.

Zaum, Dominik. *The Sovereignty Paradox: The Norms and Politics of International Statebuilding.* Oxford: Oxford University Press, 2007.

Articles and Book Chapters

Association on American Indian Affairs. "Senate Probes Child Welfare Crisis." *Indian Family Defense,* no. 2 (Summer 1974): 1–6.

Barlow, Andrew. "The Student Movement of the 1960s and the Politics of Race." *Journal of Ethnic Studies* 19, no. 3 (Fall 1991): 1–22.

Beider, Robert E. "The Representations of Indian Bodies in Nineteenth-Century American Anthropology." *American Indian Quarterly* 20, no. 2 (Spring 1996): 165–179.

Benege, William B. "Law and Order on Indian Reservations." *Federal Bar Journal* 20 (1960): 225–227.

Blackhawk, Ned. "I Can Carry on from Here: The Relocation of American Indians to Los Angeles." *Wicazo Sa Review* 11, no. 2 (Fall 1995): 16–30.

Butler, Dino. "Embracing Respect for All Life." In *Dreaming the Dawn: Conversations with Native Artists and Activists,* ed. E. K. Caldwell, 115–116. Lincoln: University of Nebraska Press, 1999.

Cohen, Felix. "Original Indian Title." *Minnesota Law Review* 32 (December 1947): 28–59.

"Creek, 14:398–99." In *Nations Remembered: An Oral History of the Five Civilize Tribes, 1865–1907,* ed. Theda Perdue, 190–191, 194. Westport, CT: Greenwood Press, 1980.

"A Crow Indian Threat to Western Strip Mines." *Business Week,* October 13, 1975, 37.

Dubray, Alfred. "Debate over IRA." In Nabokov, *Native American Testimony,* 327–328.

Ferguson, T. J. "The Repatriation of AHAYA: DA Zuni War Gods; An Interview with the Zuni Tribal Council on April 25, 1990." *Museum Anthropology* 14, no. 2 (May 1990): 7–14.

Fixico, Donald L. "The Muscogee Creeks: A Nativistic People." In *Between Two Worlds, the Survival of Twentieth Century Indians,* ed. Arrell M. Gibson, 30–43. Oklahoma City: Oklahoma Historical Society, 1986.

Fixico, Donald L. "Introduction." In *Treaties with American Indians: An Encyclopedia of Rights, Conflicts and Sovereignty*, vol. 1, ed. Donald L. Fixico, xxi. Santa Barbara, CA. ABC-CLIO, 2007.

Guardipee, Norman. "Mending the Broken Circle." In *Dreaming the Dawn: Conversations with Native Artists and Activists*, ed. E. K. Caldwell, 25–26. Lincoln: University of Nebraska Press, 1999.

Hamer, John H. "Acculturation Stress and the Functions of Alcohol among the Forest Potawatomi." *Quarterly Journal of Studies on Alcohol* 26, no. 2 (June 1965): 285–302.

"Indians Want a Bigger Share of Their Wealth." *Business Week*, May 3, 1976, 101.

Kelly, Lawrence C. "Charles James Rhoads 1929–33." In *The Commissioners of Indian Affairs, 1824–1977*, ed. Robert M. Kvasnicka and Herman Viola. Lincoln: University of Nebraska Press, 1977.

Kluger, Jeffrey. "The Legal Battle: Archaeology: Who Should Own the Bones?" *Time Magazine*, March 5, 2006, 1–2.

Littlefield, Daniel F., Jr. "The 'Crazy Snake Uprising' of 1909: A Red, Black, or White Affair?" *Arizona and the West* 20, no. 4 (Winter 1978): 307–324.

Luther Standing Bear. "Indian Education Should Not Destroy Indian Culture." In *Native Americans: Opposing Viewpoints*, ed. William Dudley, 191–193. San Diego, CA: Greenhaven, 1998.

Medicine, Beatrice. "Red Power: Real or Potential?" In *Indian Voices: The First Convocation of American Indian Scholars*, 297–307. San Francisco: Indian Historian Press, 1970.

Mirrielees, Edith R. "The Cloud of Mistrust." *Atlantic Monthly* 199 (February 1957): 55–59.

Morinis, Alan E. "'Getting Straight': Behavior Patterns in a Skid Row Indian Community." *Urban Anthropology* 11, no. 2 (Summer 1982): 193–212.

Nagel, Joane, "The Politics of American Indian Economic Development: The Reservation/Urban Nexus." With Carol Ward and Timothy Knapp. In *Public Policy Impacts on American Indian Economic Development*, ed. Matthew Snipp, 39–76. Albuquerque, NM: Native American Studies Institute on Native American Development, 1988.

Old Lady Horse (Kiowa). "The Buffalo Go." In Nabokov, *Native American Testimony*, 173–174.

Philp, Kenneth R. "Stride toward Freedom: The Relocation of Indians to Cities, 1952–1960." *Western Historical Quarterly* 16, no. 1 (April 1985): 175–190.

Ross, Allen Chuck. "A Brain Hemispheric Functions and the Native American." *Journal of American Indian Education* 21, no. 3 (May 1982): 2–5.

Seivers, Maurice L. "Cigarette and Alcohol Usage by Southwestern American Indians." *American Journal of Public Health* 58, no. 5 (January 1968): 71–82.

Shepardson, Mary. "The Gender Status of Navajo Women." In *Women and Power in Native North America*, ed. Laura F. Klein and Lillian A. Ackerman, 159–176. Norman: University of Oklahoma Press, 1995.

"Speeches of a General Tribal Council Held July 20, 1929." In *Rebirth of the Blackfeet Nation, 1912–1954*, by Paul C. Rosier, 57. Lincoln: University of Nebraska Press, 2001.

Thompson, Edward P. "The Moral Economy of the English Crowd in the Eighteenth Century." *Past and Present*, no. 50 (February 1971): 76–136.

Vestal, Stanley. "Sitting Bull's Maiden Speech." *The Frontier, Magazine of Northwest* 12 (March 1932): 269–271.

Vizenor, Gerald. "American Indians and Drunkenness." *Journal of Ethnic Studies* 11, no. 4 (Winter 1984): 83–87.

Wax, Rosalie. "The Warrior Dropout." In *Awakening Minorities: American Indians, Mexican Americans, Puerto Ricans*, ed. John R. Howard, 40–46. New Brunswick, NJ: Transaction, 1970.

Westermeyer, Joseph. "Chippewa and Majority Alcoholism in the Twin Cities: A Comparison." *Journal of Nervous and Mental Disease* 155 (November 1972): 322–327.

"White Shell Woman: Beloved of the Navajo." In *Native American Prophecies*, ed. Scott Peterson, 127–158. St. Paul, MN: Paragon House, 1990.

Willard, William. "Outing, Relocation, and Employment Assistance: The Impact of Federal Indian Population Dispersal Programs in the Bay Area." *Wicazo Sa Review* 12, no. 1 (Spring 1997): 29–46.

Wilmer, Franke. "Indian Gaming: Players and Stakes." *Wicazo Sa Review* 12, no. 1 (Spring 1997): 89–114.

Zah, Peterson. "Foreword." In *In the Fifth World: Portrait of the Navajo Nation*, ed. Adriel Heisey and Kenji Kawano, 1–2. Tucson, AZ: Rio Nuevo, 2001.

Dissertations and Theses

Antell, Judith Anne. "American Indian Women Activists." Ph.D. dissertation, Department of Ethnic Studies, University of California, Berkeley, 1990.

Blend, Benay. "Jackson Barnett and the Oklahoma Indian Probate Court." M.A. thesis, University of Texas, Arlington, 1978.

Madley, Benjamin. "American Genocide: The California Indian Catastrophe, 1846–1873." Ph.D. dissertation, Yale University, 2009.

Palmer, James O. "A Geographical Investigation of the Effects of the Bureau of Indian Affairs' Employment Assistance Program upon the Relocation of Oklahoma Indians, 1967–1971." Ph.D. dissertation, University of Oklahoma, Norman, 1975.

Parman, Donald L. "The Indian Civilian Conservation Corps." Ph.D. dissertation, University of Oklahoma, Norman, 1967.

Newspapers, Newsletters, and Press Releases

Altrowitz, Abe, "Ft. Snelling Coming to Life Again." *Minneapolis Star*, April 13, 1968, 5A.

"The Black Hills Alliance." *Akwesasne Notes*, vol. 2, no. 2 (May 1979).

Chereb, Sandra. "Campbell Warns about Greenbacks." *News from Indian Country: The Nations Native Journal*, vol. 10, no. 23 (Mid-December 1996), 6A.

"Cherokee Nation Adopts Act; Ready for Class III Gaming." *Cherokee Advocate* (Tahlequah, OK), vol. 20, no. 1 (January 1996).

"Compulsive Gambling Council to Make Pitch." *South Bend Tribune*, November 25, 1996, B7.

"Experts: Be Strict Regulating Casinos." *South Bend Tribune*, November 26, 1996, B5.

Henderick, Kimmis. "U.S. Helps Indians Move." *Christian Science Monitor*, March 6, 1956, 12.

Hurst, John. "Indians, Poverty, Alcohol, Cops—the Combination Doesn't Mix." *San Francisco Examiner*, July 16, 1969, 16.

King, Wayne. "Trump, in a Federal Lawsuit, Seeks to Block Indian Casinos." *New York Times*, May 4, 1993.

"Indians Seize Plant in South Dakota." *Rocky Mountains News* (Denver, CO), March 18, 1975.

Jackson, Roberto A. "Agreement Will Bring Outlets to Wild Horse Pass." *Gila River Indian News*, vol. 15, no. 2 (February 2012).

"Laymen Urge Donations Go to Negroes, Indians." *Minneapolis Star*, March 21, 1968, 21B.

Leibovich, Mark. "Abramhoff, from Prison to a Pizzeria Job." *New York Times*, June 23, 2010.

Marbella, Jean. "Jack Abramoff's New Job: Selling Pizza, Not Influence." *Baltimore Sun*, June 22, 2010

"Marbles Is an Old and Complex Game." *News from Indian Country* (Hayward, WI), vol. 10, no. 23 (Mid-December 1996), 11B.

Meager, Tom. "Opponents Bet They Can Defeat Casino." *Lawrence Journal World*, August 14, 2000, 2B.

Rains, Howell. "American Indians: Struggling for Power and Identity." *New York Times Magazine*, February 11, 1979, section 4, p. 28.

"Reservations Bucking States, Taking Gamble with Gambling." *Vicksburg (MS) Sunday Post*, December 29, 1991, D3.

Robertson, Josephine. "Pat Locke—Liaison between Two Cultures." *Christian Science Monitor*, February 2, 1976.

"Sioux in S.D. End Occupation of Plant." *Denver Post*, March 20, 1975.

"Zuni God Repatriated." Zuni Tribal Council Press Release. *Museum Anthropology*, vol. 15, no. 3 (August 1991), 28.

Oral Histories and Interviews

Bellecourt, Vernon (Ojibwa). Interview, ca. 1969. In Nabokov, *Native American Testimony*. 372–375.

Clark, Dan (Crow Creek). Interviewed by Joseph Cash, Summer 1968, Chamberlain, SD. Tape 51, pp. 1–4, USDIOHC.

Crum, Beverly (Shoshone). Interviewed by S.I. Myers, October 29, 1975, Salt Lake City, UT. No. 92, p. 7, NYTOHP.

Dennison, George (Navajo). Interviewed by S.I. Myers, October 15, 1975, Gallup, NM. No. 67, pt. 1, p. 1, NYTOHP.

Eastman, Oliver (Sioux Wahpeton). Interviewed by Joseph Cash, August 3, 1971, Sioux Falls, SD. Tape 768, p. 15, USDIOHC.

Katchongva, Dan (Hopi). Interview, "He Will Use Any Means to Get What He Wants." In Nabokov, *Native American Testimony*, 6–7.

LaRoche, Richard (Brule Sioux). Interviewed by Gerald Wolff, August 25, 1971, Lower Brule, SD. Tape 784, pp. 1–5, USDIOHC.

Lunderman, Ted, and Dorothy Lunderman (Brule Sioux). Interviewed by Joseph Cash, July 27, 1971, Mission, SD. Tape 744, USDIOHC. 1–4.

McKenzie, Melvin (Navajo). Interviewed by S.I. Myers, October 20, 1975, Tsaile, AZ. No. 75, p. 13, NYTOHP.

Morrison, Robert (Lakota). Interviewed by Joseph Cash, Summer 1967, Sioux Falls, SD. Tape 59, pp. 3–4, USDIOHC.

Nacke, Janice (Shoshone-Navajo). Interviewed by S.I. Myers, October 30, 1975, Pocatello, ID. No. 96, p. 14, NYTOHP.

Provost, Cecil (Yankton). Interviewed by Joseph Cash, Summer 1968, Marty Mission, SD. Tape 13, pp. 1–2, USDIOHC.

Saul, John (Crow Creek). Interviewed by Joseph Cash, June 6, 1968, Chamberlain, SD. Tape 51, pp. 7–8, USDIOHC.

Sekayouma, Marcus (Hopi). Interviewed by S.I. Myers, December 16, 1975, Sacaton, AZ. No. 122, pt. 1, p. 27, NYTOHP.

Taylor, Floyd (Hunkpapa). Interviewed by Joseph Cash, August 9, 1968, Fort Thompson, SD. Tape 50, p. 4, USDIOHC.

Vasquez, Joseph C. Interview by Floyd O'Neil, January 27, 1971, Los Angeles, CA. Doris Duke Indian Oral History Collection, interview no. 1009, box 53, acc. no. 24. Special Collections, Marriott Library, University of Utah, Salt Lake City.

Wauneka, Annie (Navajo). Interviewed by S.I. Myers, October 19, 1975, Klagetoh, AZ. No. 74, pp. 13–14, NYTOHP.

Wilson, Cathy (Nez Perce). Interviewed by S.I. Myers, December 30, 1974, Tempe, AZ. No. 3, p. 26, NYTOHP.

Wilson, Eugene (Nez Perce). Interviewed by S.I. Myers, December 22, 1974, Phoenix, AZ. No. 4, pp. 15–16, NYTOHP.

Online Sources

Banyacya, Thomas, Sr. Testimony. In *Poison Fire, Sacred Earth: Testimonies, Lectures, Conclusions, the World Uranium Hearing, Salzburg, 1992.* 32–36. Available at http://www.ratical.org/radiation/WorldUraniumHearing/ThomasBanyacya.html, accessed August 1, 2007.

Cambridge Energy Research Associates. "Gasoline and the American People 2007," http://seekerblog.com/2007/01/23/gasoline-and-the-american-people-2007/, accessed April 19, 2013.—Selected Media Coverage." December 31, 2006. http://www.cera.com/aspx/cda/public1/news/pressCoverage/pressCoverageDetails.aspx?CID=8533, accessed February 17, 2008.

Executive Order 13007. "Executive Orders Disposition Tables: William J. Clinton—1996." National Archives. http://www.archives.gov/federal-register/executive-orders/1996.html.

Indian Burial and Sacred Grounds Watch. "Domtar Gives Island to Passamaquoddies—Returned Land Includes Tribal Burial Ground." May 14, 2002. http://www.ibsgwatch.imagedjinn.com/learn/2002514ny.htm, accessed February 8, 2008.

"Indian Island." *North Coast Journal,* July 1, 2004. http://www.northcoastjournal.com/070104/cover0701.html, accessed February 8, 2008.

Jones, Lisa. "Four-Acres Return to Karuk Tribe." *High Country News,* March 4, 1996. http://www.hcn.org/servlets/hcn.Article?article_id=1679, accessed February 8, 2008.

McCandless, Colin. "Ancient Mound and Town Site Return to the Cherokee." Franklin Press, October 27, 2006.http://www.thefranklinpress.com/articles//2006/10/31/news/04news.txt. accessed April 19, 2013.

National Indian Gaming Commission. "List and Location of Tribal Gaming Operations." http://www.nigc.gov/Reading_Room/List_and_Location_of_Tribal_Gaming_Operations.aspx, accessed June 10, 2011.

Sacred Land Film Project. "Kaho'olawe, Hawaii." 1994. http://www.sacredland.org/endangered_sites_pp./mauna_kea.html, accessed February 8, 2008.

Sacred Land Film Project, "Medicine Wheel, Wyoming." http://www.sacredland.org/historical_sites_pp./medicine_wheel.html, accessed February 8, 2008.

Sacred Land Film Project. "Rainbow Bridge, Utah." http://www.sacredland.org/endangered_sites_pages/rainbow_bridge.html, accessed February 8, 2008.

Smith, Andrea. "Soul Wound: The Legacy of Native American Schools." *Amnesty Magazine.* http://www.amnestyusa.org/amnestynow/soulwound.html, accessed February 19, 2008.

Index

Page numbers in italic indicate illustrations.

About the Author

Donald L. Fixico is Distinguished Foundation Professor of History in the School of Historical, Philosophical and Religious Studies, as well as faculty affiliate in American Indian studies and faculty affiliate in the School of Public Affairs at Arizona State University. He is the author and editor of a dozen books, and he has worked on twenty documentaries about American Indians. His books relating to this one are *Termination and Relocation: Federal Indian Policy, 19445–1960* (1986), *The Invasion of Indian Country in the Twentieth Century: Tribal Natural Resources and American Capitalism* (1998), *The Urban Indian Experience in America* (2000), *The American Indian Mind in a Linear World: American Indian Studies and Traditional Knowledge* (2003), *Daily Life of Native Americans in the Twentieth Century* (2006), *American Indians in a Modern World* (2008), and *Bureau of Indian Affairs* (2012).

He was born and grew up in Oklahoma in the Muscogee Creek and Seminole traditions. He is also Shawnee and Sac and Fox and completed his undergraduate and graduate work at the University of Oklahoma. After completing the Ph.D., he took postdoctoral fellowship at UCLA and another one the following year at the Newberry Library. He has been on the faculty at four universities and been a visiting professor at six universities, including living and teaching abroad at the University of Nottingham in England and at the Frie University in Berlin, Germany.

Before coming to Arizona State University, he was the founding director of the Center for Indigenous Studies at the University of Kansas and the founding editor of the *Indigenous Nations Studies Journal*. At Kansas, he was the Thomas Bowlus Distinguished Professor of History. He also held the John Rhodes Chair of American Public Policy in the Barrett Honors College at Arizona State University.